First Steps in SAP® S/4HANA Finance

Janet Salmon
Claus Wild

Thank you for purchasing this book from Espresso Tutorials!

Like a cup of espresso coffee, Espresso Tutorials SAP books are concise and effective. We know that your time is valuable and we deliver information in a succinct and straightforward manner. It only takes our readers a short amount of time to consume SAP concepts. Our books are well recognized in the industry for leveraging tutorial-style instruction and videos to show you step by step how to successfully work with SAP.

Check out our YouTube channel to watch our videos at
https://www.youtube.com/user/EspressoTutorials.

If you are interested in SAP Finance and Controlling, join us at
http://www.fico-forum.com/forum2/
to get your SAP questions answered and contribute to discussions.

Related titles from Espresso Tutorials:

▶ Bert Vanstechelman: The SAP® HANA Deployment Guide
  http://5171.espresso-tutorials.com

▶ Dominique Alfermann, Stefan Hartmann, Benedikt Engel:
  SAP® HANA Advanced Modeling
  http://5110.espresso-tutorials.com

Janet Salmon, Claus Wild
First Steps in SAP® S/4HANA Finance

ISBN: 978-1-5407-6217-7

Editor: Tracey Duffy

Cover Design: Philip Esch

Cover Photo: fotolia #16757910 © Stefan Richter

Interior Design: Johann-Christian Hanke

All rights reserved.

1st Edition 2016, Gleichen

© 2016 by Espresso Tutorials GmbH

URL: *www.espresso-tutorials.com*

Feedback
We greatly appreciate any kind of feedback you have concerning this book. Please mail us at *info@espresso-tutorials.com*.

Table of Contents

Introduction

If you work in finance, you might think that discussions about databases are best left to your colleagues in IT. In this book, however, we show you how a new database technology changes the way your financial data is stored and thus allows SAP to completely re-architect its solution. We explain how the High-Performance Analytic Appliance (HANA) differs from a conventional database. We explain concepts such as the universal journal, which combines data from multiple application components, and Central Finance, which allows you to merge accounting documents from multiple source systems. We discuss how the various applications are being rebuilt to take advantage of the new database, explaining what changes, but also what stays the same, so that you have the skills to help your organization improve the efficiency of its finance function.

We have added a few icons to highlight important information. These include:

	**Tips**
	Tips highlight information that provides more details about the subject being described and/or additional background information.

	**Attention**
	Attention notices highlight information that you should be aware of when you go through the examples in this book on your own.

Finally, a note concerning the copyright: all screenshots printed in this book are the copyright of SAP SE. All rights are reserved by SAP SE.

Copyright pertains to all SAP images in this publication. For simplification, we will not mention this specifically underneath every screenshot.

1 SAP S/4HANA Finance—the next big thing

SAP S/4HANA Finance is being marketed as the next big thing in terms of software architecture. In this chapter, we look briefly at how the technology has evolved from the mainframes of the 1980s, to the client/server architecture of the 1990s, to web services in the Internet era, and finally, to the revolution of in-memory computing that we are experiencing today. We explain what is special about SAP HANA and why it enables SAP to firstly re-architect its financial applications to store data, thus making this data easier to consume in reporting, and secondly, to present this data more intuitively to provide instant insight into the state of the business. Finally, we introduce the three pillars of SAP S/4HANA Finance.

1.1 A little history

As a product name, SAP S/4HANA Finance gives an indication of SAP's aspirations for its latest product. The company was founded back in 1972 and its first products, R/1 and R/2, were ERP systems designed for the *mainframes* that most large companies ran in the 1970s and 1980s. The "R" in the product names stood for *real time*, the idea being that financial transactions could be captured in real time using online terminals rather than relying on batch processes to update the journals periodically. Back in the early 1990s, SAP trainers and consultants would patiently explain to customers what it meant to capture materials movements as they happened, along with the related journal entries, rather than waiting for a batch process to load the data to the finance system nightly or at period close.

In the summer of 1992, SAP introduced a new product, SAP R/3, designed to maintain the concept of real time but to work with the then revolutionary *client/server architecture*. The UNIX servers were significantly cheaper than the mainframe equivalent and it was possible to link multiple servers whenever more processing power was required. The client/server architecture comprised three layers: the database layer, the application layer, and the presentation layer. Without going into too much detail, this architecture meant that the customer could choose the *database* he preferred (and there was a regular flow of announcements as new databases were certified), the *application layer* contained the code for the various software modules (Materials Management, Production Planning, Financial Accounting, and so on), and the *presentation layer* provided a graphical user interface. Let's not forget that in the days before smartphones and consumer websites, the graphical user interface delivered with SAP R/3 was more attractive and easier to use than many of the mainframe interfaces that accounting clerks were using at the time.

This three-tier architecture is still the heart of many SAP applications today. When the R/3 product was renamed SAP ERP in 2004, the key technology change was the underlying SAP NetWeaver stack which allowed the use of *web services*. This meant that the ERP system could communicate with other applications such as Customer Relationship Management and Supplier Relationship Management using standard protocols. It also allowed significant changes to the user interface because new web applications could be built and delivered in the Enterprise Portal, such as those in Manager Self-Service or Employee Self-Service. The ERP world focused ever more strongly on transactional processing, capturing the sales orders, invoices, purchase orders, and goods movements at the heart of a company's operations.

Sometime in the late 1990s, many companies also started to work with dedicated *management information systems* — data warehouses and data marts that were designed to make the vast quantities of data being captured in the company's various operations easy to query and report on. SAP's Business Information Warehouse (BW) offered online analytical processing (OLAP), as did many other products on the market. The result was that each night, huge quantities of data would be loaded from SAP ERP, SAP CRM, and other systems into the data warehouse and transformed for reporting purposes.

At its simplest, this meant putting the data associated with an invoice or an order into a *star schema* to allow *multidimensional reporting* on the customers served and the products sold in the relevant regions. In many cases, it also involved significant *data cleansing* to solve underlying master data issues as well as transformation into a group chart of accounts, a group profit center structure, and so on. Multi-national companies needed a data warehouse to handle the volumes of data generated in their operations but the nightly load was at odds with the "R" in real time. These organizations were paying a high price for the flexibility of their management information systems in terms of the timeliness of their data.

More to the point, if you were to ask most financial analysts how they actually worked in those days, the answer would be neither SAP ERP nor in a data warehouse directly, but in a *spreadsheet*. This was the era of Microsoft Excel, with the operations of vast companies being run from "spreadmarts".

In 2011, Hasso Plattner, one of the founders of SAP, published his book, *In-Memory Data Management*. This book described the architecture of SAP HANA and envisioned a management meeting of the future: instead of the participants arriving with a set of laboriously compiled briefing books—which tried to anticipate every question that might be asked and by their very nature, were out of date by the time the managers entered the meeting room—the managers would have instant access to real-time business information and could spend the meeting simulating the effect of various assumptions on their bottom line before agreeing on the actions to follow. Essentially, SAP S/4HANA Finance is the realization of the vision illustrated in Figure 1.1. SAP CFO Luka Mucic really does use the SAP Digital Boardroom to guide his fellow executives through the key KPIs for the organization and discuss scenarios for the future.

Of course, this vision does not apply only to the time the board members are in the meeting room; they need the same information in real time on every device they use. We will look at how SAP Fiori is helping them to access this information while they are on the move. And this real-time information is required not only by the board members but also by every manager in the organization.

1.1 Information in Real Time – Anything, Anytime, Anywhere

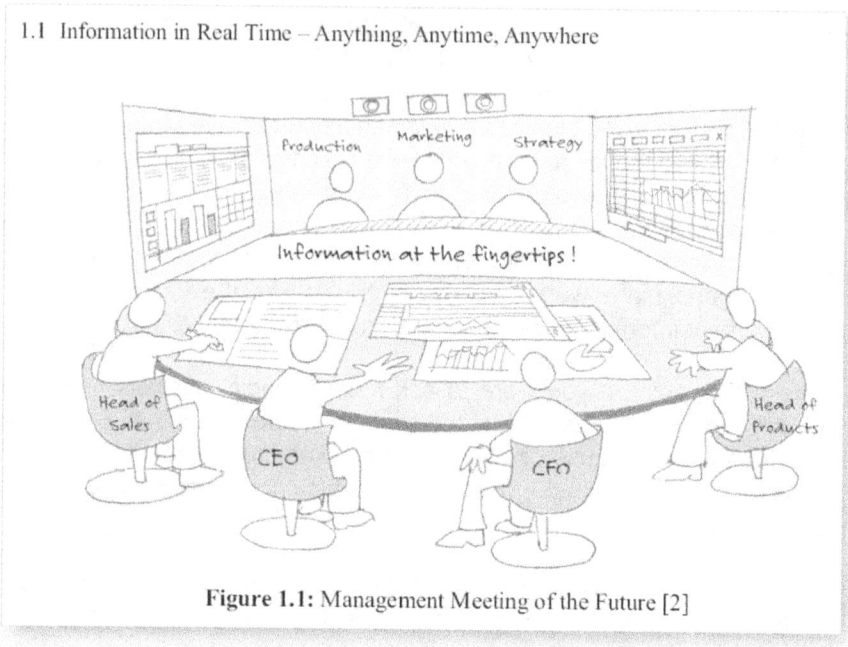

Figure 1.1: Management Meeting of the Future [2]

Figure 1.1. Hasso Plattner's vision of a management meeting of the future

As this vision becomes reality, we are seeing the re-architected system becoming the *digital core* and organizations connecting cloud services to this digital core using HANA Cloud Integration. But first, let us focus on how SAP HANA allows SAP to re-architect the Financial Accounting, Asset Accounting, Controlling, and Inventory Accounting applications to be ready for the digital age.

1.2 SAP HANA

SAP HANA evolved from Hasso Plattner's work with his students at the Hasso Plattner Institute (http://hpi.de/en.html) in Potsdam, Germany. From a technical point of view, the radical changes are that all data is kept in main memory rather than on a hard disk and that massive parallel processing is possible. Both of these changes significantly accelerate data processing.

1.2.1 From row stores to column stores

For a financial analyst, the key difference between an SAP HANA database and a traditional database is the shift from a *row store* to a *column store*. Because this switch is critical to understanding how SAP S/4HANA Finance works, let us spend a moment thinking through a simple example. Imagine that we want to calculate the total revenue for Germany in a particular period by aggregating the figures in the relevant invoices.

▶ In a row store, each invoice line is stored as a row in the database. This row contains the amount in the invoice together with the data used to select the relevant invoices for reporting, such as the accounting period, the fiscal year, the company code, and the account. To determine the rows containing the German company code, the system has to read **every line** in the database and then aggregate the amounts for the relevant lines. Because there are typically millions of invoice lines on the database, if aggregating revenue by company code is a common query, there will probably be an *index*—an additional table to support selection by company code. In some cases, the query may still be too slow and the chances are that the developer will have added a totals table to pre-aggregate the data by accounting period and fiscal year.

▶ In a column store, the data is organized in columns. If you are querying the document number, then the number of lines to be queried will be the same in both the column store and the row store. However, if you are selecting the revenue lines by company code, then the **column** for the company code will only contain one entry per company code and even a major multi-national organization probably will not have more than a few hundred company codes in that column. Instead of querying millions of lines, the system can select the German company from a couple of hundred lines. The result is available in seconds with no need to create an additional index table. The period selection works in the same way, aggregating the relevant figures for the selected periods on the fly with no need to create an additional totals table.

Now imagine that the data record includes not only the period, the year, the company code, and the account, but all fifty characteristics that can currently be included in an operating concern for Profitability Analysis (CO-PA). A typical operating concern contains reporting characteristics such as product, product group, customer, customer group, region, sales office, and so on. Multidimensional reporting in Profitability Analysis was already available in R/2; what is new is that you can now change a single setting in your existing profitability drill-down reports (READ UPON EACH NAVIGATION STEP) to ensure that instead of reading *pre-aggregated* data, the system executes a new *select statement* each time you navigate to a new view of the report data. This means that when you have finished looking at the revenue for Germany and decide to look at the revenue for France, this triggers a new select statement on the invoice data in real time. If you drill down from there to the sales office in Paris, this triggers another select statement. If you then pull in the product categories that are selling well in the Paris office, the system begins another select statement. These fast select statements are what make Hasso Plattner's vison for the future possible today. This is technically what happens as Luka Mucic navigates through the SAP Digital Boardroom. However, if you choose to continue to use the drill-down reports (transaction KE30) that have been available since the 1990s, you do not need to retrain your entire user community and can move ahead with the new technology at your own speed. This stability is key to the idea of offering *innovation without disruption*. You can continue to use all the CO-PA reports your organization has built up over the years and simply change one parameter to benefit from the new architecture.

What does change is that you no longer need to maintain summarization levels in Profitability Analysis. Assessment cycles that previously relied on pre-aggregated data to determine the drivers for the allocation can aggregate such data on the fly. You no longer need to load profitability data to a data warehouse and instead, you can work with virtual InfoProviders to achieve a BW look without a data warehouse or build data marts to prepare this data for the briefing books.

1.2.2 From updates to inserts

Another key element to understand about SAP HANA is that it is much faster to *insert* a single record than to *update* (or change) a totals table (or several totals tables). If a single business transaction, such as an invoice or a goods movement, can be captured as one document in Financials, the system simply needs to issue a document number and record the relevant information in the document. This is what we mean by an insert.

Every time an update is required to store totals by period and cost center, profit center, and so on, the system has to **lock** that record to perform the update and this can significantly slow down period-end processes, such as huge allocations or top-down distributions. With each application in Financials having its own line item and totals table, one simple invoice could be triggering updates to the totals in Cost Center Accounting, Profit Center Accounting, and Accounts Payable.

This situation becomes even more critical when we are posting goods movements, where the same material may be required in multiple production orders or where the same material is going from a retail distribution center to several stores on different trucks. In an extreme case, these locks on the various tables can stop a production line if several production orders try to record their usage of a common part or the trucks at a retail center because the goods issues for each store lock each other out. If you can get rid of the locks, you can record more goods movements on the same system and the whole dynamics of your system sizing changes dramatically. This is essentially what is happening as SAP re-architects its solution for SAP HANA.

1.2.3 The move to SAP HANA

Although the last two sections sound radical, it is important to understand that you can make the move to SAP HANA in a series of small steps.

- ▶ You may already have heard of the *CO-PA accelerator* or the *side-car approach* introduced in 2011. All that this meant was that the transactional data for Profitability Analysis (table CE1 for costing-based Profitability Analysis or table COEP for account-based Profitability Analysis) was moved to a separate SAP HANA database and updated in near real time whenever a new invoice or cost posting was added to the ERP database (the *primary database* in this context). Drill-down reporting for Profitability Analysis was then redirected to read from the SAP HANA database (the *secondary database*) rather than the ERP database. Similar accelerators are available for General Ledger Accounting (new and classic), Special Ledger, Profit Center Accounting, Cost Center Accounting, Order and Project Accounting, Asset Accounting, Investment Management, and the Material Ledger. The charm of this approach was that it posed no risk. If the SAP HANA database was unavailable for any reason, then the report would simply select from the main database. The response might be slower, but the report would still return a result.

► *SAP Business Suite powered by HANA* was introduced in 2012 and goes one stage further, replacing the standard database with an SAP HANA database. At first glance, not much has changed. You will still find the familiar menus for Financial Accounting, Controlling, Materials Management, Production Planning, and so on, but you benefit from all the accelerations due to the faster select statements detailed above. You will also find a handful of new transactions in the menu, such as KSB1N for faster cost center line item reporting, KOB1N for faster order line item reporting, CJ13N for faster project line item reporting, and drill-down reporting for the material ledger using transaction KKML0.

To find out more about these approaches, refer to *SAP HANA for ERP Financials* (Espresso Tutorials 2011).

1.3   SAP applications

SAP S/4HANA Finance is more than just a database change. Over recent years, SAP has been rewriting its financial applications because the programming paradigms that prevailed back in the 1990s no longer apply and the software architecture can be simplified. To help you understand what is happening, we will look at some examples of the major changes under way.

1.3.1 Index and totals tables

Index tables were originally used to improve selection, as we saw when we looked at the selection of revenues by company code. By comparison, *totals tables* pre-aggregate the financial data into period blocks to make it easy to select the total cost center costs for the relevant fiscal period either for reporting or for use in a process such as allocations or settlement.

▶ As a first step, let us take a look at the index tables in Financial Accounting.
In the past, when you selected a list of open items for a supplier, the application would have used index table BSIK to find the relevant items. To select those supplier items that had been cleared, the application would have used index table BSAK. For a list of open items for a customer, it would have been index table BSID, and for those customer items that had been cleared, index table BSAD. There were index tables BSIS and BSAS for G/L accounts (or index tables FAGLBSIS and FAGLBSAS for new G/L) and index table BSIM for materials. With SAP HANA, these index tables have become superfluous because the selection can work directly on the primary tables for the open items or the accounts. That is already seven tables fewer to keep synchronized when you are building an application and seven fewer tables occupying space on the database.

▶ When we looked at navigation within a profitability report, we said that we were selecting with each navigation step rather than reading from pre-aggregated data. Almost all standard reports read from such pre-aggregated tables or totals tables. Customer data is updated to KNC1 and KNC3, supplier data to LFC1 and LFC3, data in Classic General Ledger Accounting to GLT1 and GLT3, data in new General Ledger Accounting to FAGLFLEXT, and in Controlling, to COSP and COSS. In the past, the challenge here was two-fold: on the one hand, you had aggregated data that had to be kept synchronized with the supporting line item data. The result of aggregating the general ledger line items by company code and business area should always be the **same** as the total stored in the totals table for the period of aggregation. As we discussed in Section 1.2.2, you might have experienced **locking** problems when trying to perform huge data loads or large allocations at period close. To write a new line item, the system simply issues a new document number and creates a record, but to update the totals table, the system has to lock the totals table for cost center XYZ in the relevant period and then release it again once the new line item has been included in the totals for the period. If you have a lot of data records trying to update a small number of totals tables because you only have a small number of profit centers, this can cause significant problems.

▶ This locking of the aggregate tables was particularly problematic in Inventory Management, where there are many tables storing inventory values by plant, storage location, and so on and for the various stock types. The impact of changing this data structure can be significant, sometimes making postings faster by a factor of up to ten.

If SAP were to rebuild its applications from scratch, then the fact that the index tables and the totals tables are no longer needed would be of minor academic interest. In practice, however, hundreds of programs read from these totals tables and not all of them were built by SAP. In Controlling, around 180 standard programs read from tables COSP and COSS in the course of the period close. This is because it was easier to select the cost center data to be allocated during the period-end close from a table that has already pre-aggregated this data rather than aggregating on the fly.

The technical trick has been to provide *compatibility views* for all the tables that have been removed. Figure 1.2 shows the compatibility view for the general ledger totals (the former table GLT0). This has exactly the same structure as the old totals table and ensures that any program— either an SAP program or a program from a partner or customer—that previously read from this table works as before but aggregates the data on the fly from the underlying line item table rather than reading the totals table. In some cases, this on-the-fly aggregation might not be fast enough and SAP is gradually rewriting the programs for allocations, settlement, and so on to read directly from the line items. However, this simple technical trick means that you can make the move to SAP HANA at your own pace. Note also table GLT0_BCK in Figure 1.2: this is used during migration as a back-up to store the contents of the original totals tables to make sure that no data is missing in the line item table. New journal entries created after migration is complete will not be added to this table.

Dictionary: Display View

DDL SQL View	GLT0	Active
Short Description	Generates fr.DDL Srce GLT0_DDL	

Attributes	Table/Join Conditions	View Fld	Selection Conditions	Maint.Status

View field	Table	Field	Key	Data elem.	M...	DTyp	Length	Short description
RCLNT	GLT0_BCK	RCLNT		MANDT		CLNT	3	Client
RLDNR	GLT0_BCK	RLDNR		RLDNR		CHAR	2	Ledger
RRCTY	GLT0_BCK	RRCTY		RRCTY		CHAR	1	Record Type
RVERS	GLT0_BCK	RVERS		RVERS		CHAR	3	Version
BUKRS	GLT0_BCK	BUKRS		BUKRS		CHAR	4	Company Code
RYEAR	GLT0_BCK	RYEAR		GJAHR		NUMC	4	Fiscal Year
RACCT	GLT0_BCK	RACCT		RACCT		CHAR	10	Account Number
RBUSA	GLT0_BCK	RBUSA		GSBER		CHAR	4	Business Area
RTCUR	GLT0_BCK	RTCUR		RTCUR		CUKY	5	Currency Key
DRCRK	GLT0_BCK	DRCRK		SHKZG		CHAR	1	Debit/Credit Indicator
RPMAX	GLT0_BCK	RPMAX		RPMAX		NUMC	3	Period
TSLVT	GLT0_BCK	TSLVT		TSLVT		CURR	15	Balance carried forward in transaction currency
TSL01	GLT0_BCK	TSL01		TSLXX		CURR	15	Total transactions of the period in transaction currency
TSL02	GLT0_BCK	TSL02		TSLXX		CURR	15	Total transactions of the period in transaction currency
TSL03	GLT0_BCK	TSL03		TSLXX		CURR	15	Total transactions of the period in transaction currency

Figure 1.2: Compatibility view for table GLT0

1.3.2 Universal journal

The *universal journal* is probably the most fundamental change with SAP S/4HANA Finance: it alters the way the transactional data is stored. Instead of using separate tables for General Ledger Accounting, Asset Accounting, Controlling and the Material Ledger, the transactional data for these applications is stored in the universal journal, which, from a technical perspective, is a single table, ACDOCA. This means that there is no longer any need to reconcile the data in the separate applications and it is easy to build reports that cross the old component boundaries because all the reporting dimensions are contained in a single data string. To understand what this means, let us think through a simple business example. If an asset is acquired, the value of the asset was stored in Asset Accounting, the vendor and payment details were stored in Accounts Payable, and if the asset was assigned to a cost center so that the asset costs could be depreciated later, then the asset acquisition was also recorded in Cost Center Accounting. The operational part of these applications remains largely unchanged—there is a purchase order for the asset with an account assignment to the cost center. The asset is delivered and the supplier sends his invoice which you pay having performed a three-way match. What does change is that a **single table** provides details of the asset, the vendor, the G/L account, and the assigned cost center, meaning that you can report on that business transaction in ways that were not possible before. Essentially, you can see relationships that were inherent in the business process (the asset, the vendor, the cost center) but were lost in the past because the business transaction was chopped up for storage in the Asset Accounting, Accounts Payable, and Cost Center Accounting modules.

Figure 1.3 shows the key fields in the new line item table for the universal journal. We will return to this table to look at the various reporting dimensions for Accounting and Controlling in Chapter 2, but note for now that the table contains more than 370 fields (this varies depending on the industries active, the use of coding block extensions, and the number of columns generated for the fields in CO-PA) and that the posting item now allows **six digits**, whereas previously, you could only post 999 items in a single document. Other fields, such as COMPANY CODE, FISCAL YEAR, and RECORD TYPE will look completely familiar. One myth is that table ACDOCA is the only table in SAP S/4HANA Finance. This is not true: table BSEG still exists and captures all FI line items, including open and cleared payment line items and line items arriving from Materials Management, Payroll, and so on. What has changed is that you can now radically summarize the BSEG line items (remove material line items from an invoice, cost center line items from a payroll posting, and so on) but pass the detail on to table ACDOCA. This means, for example, that the huge POS (point-of-sales) documents that are created in an IS-Retail system can be summarized for update in table BSEG but can include the quantities and values per store and article in table ACDOCA; or that backflush updates with huge bills of materials in an engineering system can be summarized to remove the material components in table BSEG but can include the quantities and values for each component in table ACDOCA.

Dictionary: Display Table

← → ⚙ ⠿ 📋 🖋 ⚡ ⤓ ⤒ ☰ ▯ ⬚ ▦ Technical Settings Indexes... Append Structure...

Transparent Table	ACDOCA		Active	
Short Description	Universal Journal Entry Line Items			

Attributes	Delivery and Maintenance	Fields	Entry help/check	Currency/Quantity Fields

⎀ ▦ ▦ ▦   ⌄ ⏷ ▦ ▣   ▣ Srch Help   Predefined Type   1 / 372

Field	Key	Ini...	Data element	Data Type	Length	Deci...	Short Description	Group
RCLNT	✓	✓	MANDT	CLNT	3		0 Client	
RLDNR	✓	✓	FINS_LEDGER	CHAR	2		0 Ledger in General Ledger Accounting	
RBUKRS	✓	✓	BUKRS	CHAR	4		0 Company Code	
GJAHR	✓	✓	GJAHR	NUMC	4		0 Fiscal Year	
BELNR	✓	✓	BELNR_D	CHAR	10		0 Accounting Document Number	
DOCLN	✓	✓	DOCLN6	CHAR	6		0 Six-Character Posting Item for Ledger	
RYEAR			GJAHR_POS	NUMC	4		0 General Ledger Fiscal Year	
RRCTY		✓	RRCTY	CHAR	1		0 Record Type	
.INCLUDE		✓	ACDOC_SI_00	STRU	0		0 Universal Journal Entry: Transaction, Currencies, Units	TRANSACTION_CURR_UNIT

Figure 1.3: Line items in the universal journal

1.4   SAP Fiori

These architectural changes might be interesting to the system administrator, but if we return to Hasso Plattner's vision of the management
meeting of the future, it becomes clear that the user interface plays just
as important a role as the data structures that support the reporting
tasks. With the briefing book consigned to history, new user interfaces
have to be intuitive enough for everyone from the CFO to a line manager
to use and to make it easy for an accounts payable clerk to work efficiently with only minimal training.

To get a sense of what has changed, let us take a look at how Accounts
Receivable will look going forward. Figure 1.4 shows a sample starting
page for an ACCOUNTS RECEIVABLE MANAGER. We accessed the tiles via a
URL that can be called from a desktop, a tablet device, or a smartphone.
This URL shows only those applications assigned to the user's role (no
searching in a menu for the relevant transactions) and the figures shown
in the tiles are color-coded to make it clear immediately what is positive
and negative. From there, the manager can intuitively drill down to the
details, with no training in how to set up report variants. We are worlds
away from the classic SAP GUI transactions for customer line item analysis and, in this example, we can immediately see that there is cause for
concern in that the overdue receivables are way too high and there are a
worrying number of outstanding promises to pay, while the other key
performance indicators are currently green.

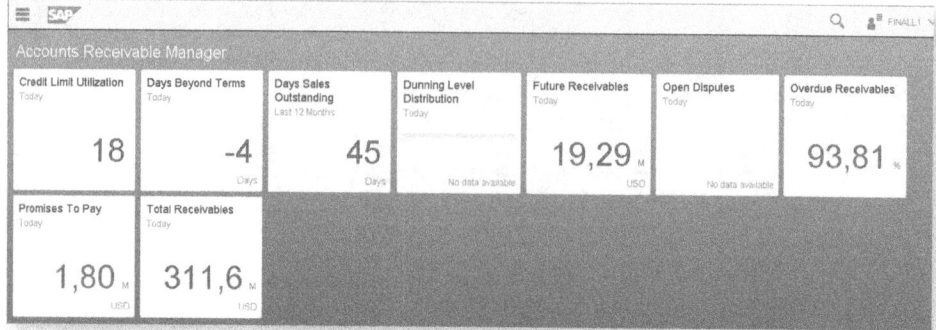

Figure 1.4: SAP Fiori launchpad for an Accounts Receivable Manager

To find out more about the overdue receivables, click on the OVERDUE RECEIVABLES tile in Figure 1.4. Figure 1.5 shows details of the overdue receivables grouped by due date. Each column represents the sum of the open items for each band of due dates. Along the top of the application, you will notice that you can select by ACCOUNTING CLERK, COMPANY CODE, CUSTOMER, CUSTOMER COUNTRY, and CUSTOMER REGION to understand exactly where the problems lie. Technically, each of these selection options is provided by a *view*. To return to the launchpad and switch to a different analysis, choose the HOME icon at the far left of the screen.

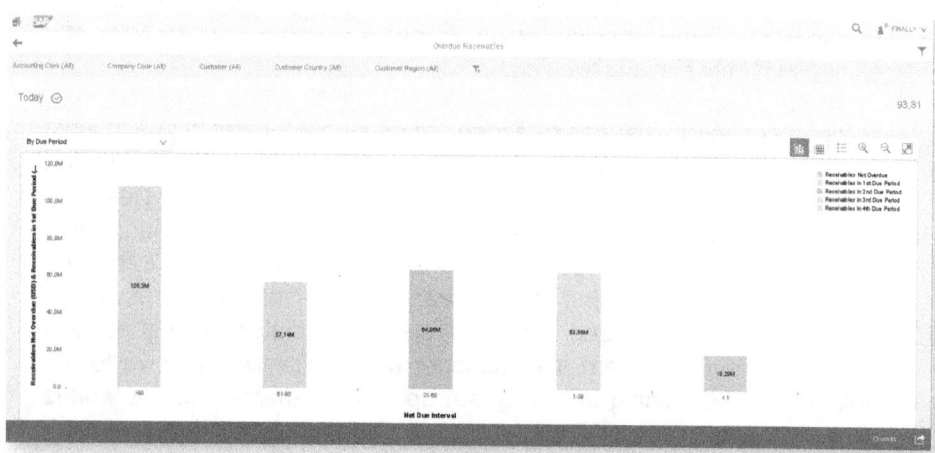

Figure 1.5: SAP Smart Business application showing outstanding receivables by due date

From this view, we can drill down to see the receivables by customer and due date bucket, as shown in Figure 1.6.

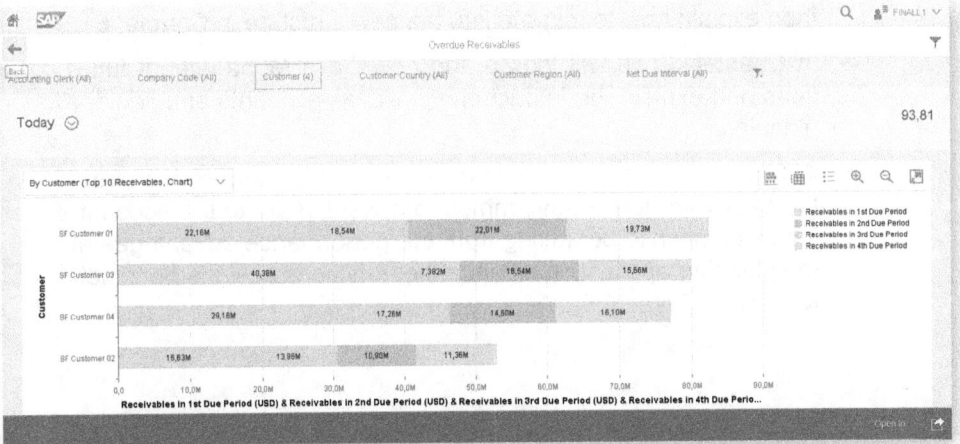

Figure 1.6: Smart Business application showing receivables by customer, together with aging

Clearly, we are scratching the surface of accounts receivables management but these views already give an idea of how easy the system is to use. What we cannot show in a book format is that these applications read the data in real time. There is no data mart or data warehouse behind the amounts shown in Figure 1.5 and Figure 1.6. If a new open item is created for one of these customers, it is instantly visible to the Accounts Receivable Manager without any interim steps, providing instant insight in a user interface that makes sense to any business person. We will come back to how to work with these roles and business catalogs when we look at SAP Fiori in more detail in Chapter 8.

1.5 The three pillars of SAP S/4HANA Finance

As the name implies, SAP S/4HANA Finance uses the SAP HANA database and offers new functions for SAP Accounting, SAP Cash Management, and SAP Business Planning and Consolidation. Figure 1.7 shows the three pillars of SAP S/4HANA Finance. Note that they all require the use of SAP HANA as a platform. In the chapters that follow we will look at each of the pillars in turn:

▶ In Chapter 2, we will look at SAP Accounting and explain the impact of the architectural changes on General Ledger Accounting, Controlling, Asset Accounting, and Inventory Accounting. We will then explain how to migrate into the new structure in Chapter 6.

▶ In Chapter 3, we will look at the new Cash Management functions and explain the impact on your bank accounts and liquidity planning.

▶ In Chapter 5, we will look at how planning is moving back from the data warehouse environment of recent years to the accounting system while benefiting from the performance advantages of the planning application kit and other functions designed originally for SAP BW.

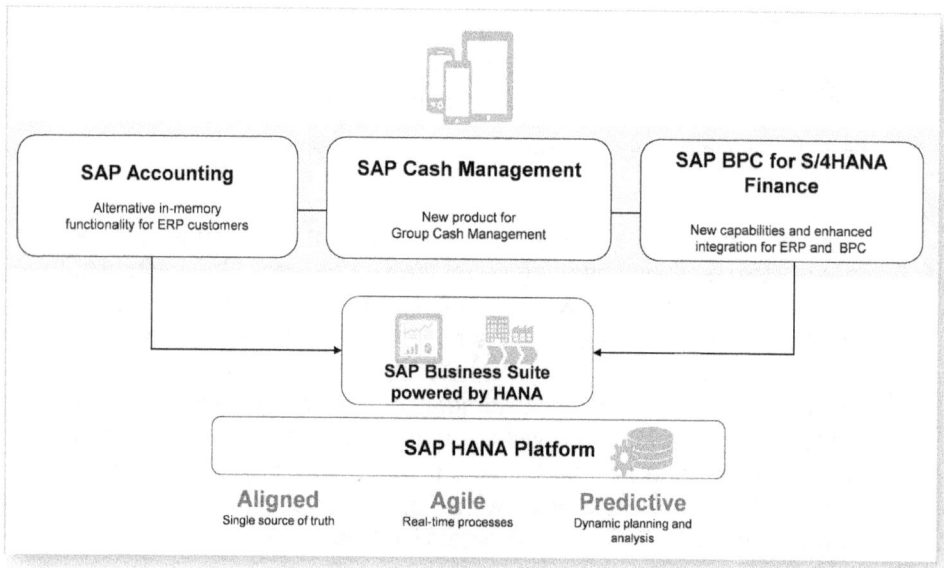

Figure 1.7: The three pillars of SAP S/4HANA Finance

At this stage, it also makes sense to run through the software evolution:

▶ SAP Business Suite powered by HANA was introduced in 2012 and uses an SAP HANA database instead of a standard database. There are some optimizations to make use of the SAP HANA database.

► SAP Simple Finance Add-On for SAP Business Suite powered by HANA was introduced in 2014 and simplifies the data structure in Financials by removing the index tables and totals tables for many of the key finance tables. You can access the documentation via this link: *http://help.sap.com/sfin100*.

► SAP S/4HANA Finance was introduced in March 2015 and brings together the transactional tables for General Ledger Accounting, Asset Accounting, Controlling, and the Material Ledger into a single table, the universal journal. You can access the documentation via this link: *http://help.sap.com/sfin200*.

► SAP S/4HANA was introduced in November 2015 and includes new tables for inventory valuation. You can access the documentation via this link: *https://help.sap.com/s4hana*. It offers both on premise and cloud editions.

In this context, it also makes sense to explain the naming conventions. There are currently two versions of SAP S/4HANA Finance on the market:

► SAP S/4HANA Finance 1503, introduced in March (03) 2015 (15) as SAP Simple Finance and requiring SAP ERP 6.0 EHP 7

► SAP S/4HANA Finance 1605, introduced in May (05) 2016 (16) and requiring SAP ERP 6.0 EHP 8

What is important here is the word **Finance**. With these software versions you have access to the universal journal, new Cash Management, and the connectors for Central Finance, but the logistics modules (Production Planning, Plant Maintenance, Sales and Distribution) and the industry solutions do not change.

There are also two versions of SAP S/4HANA on the market:

► SAP S/4HANA 1511, introduced in November (11) 2015 (15)

► SAP S/4HANA 1610, introduced in October (10) 2016 (16)

Here, in addition to the universal journal, new Cash Management, and the connectors for Central Finance, you will find changes in the logistics modules. From a finance perspective, the major changes with SAP S/4HANA are:

- ▶ The replacement of the customer and vendor transactions by the *business partner*

- ▶ The extension of the material number (now 40 characters)

- ▶ The introduction of the new inventory management table MATDOC

- ▶ Transaction-based material ledger becomes compulsory for inventory valuation

We will come back to these changes in the chapters that follow but it is worth having a clear understanding of the relevant differences before you start to look at the details of the universal journal or new Cash Management.

2 Accounting and Controlling

The German-speaking world has long since separated the Accounting modules from the Controlling modules and the move to bring the two applications into a single journal entry is one of the most significant changes of SAP S/4HANA Finance. The goal of this move is to provide internal and external reporting from the same data source. If you have struggled in the past to make sense of the SAP approach, the idea of having accounts, cost centers, profit centers, and so on in a single posting string, the universal journal, will make immediate sense.

2.1   Introducing the universal journal

The universal journal (table ACDOCA) significantly changes the way transactional data is stored for financial reporting. It offers huge benefits in terms of the ability to harmonize internal and external reporting requirements by having both read from the same document store where the account is the unifying element. You will still need to understand the different applications to the extent that you need to perform different business transactions in each application. This means that you still have to create general journal entries in General Ledger Accounting, acquire and retire assets in Asset Accounting, run allocations and settlement in Controlling, capitalize research and development costs in Investment Management, and so on, but in reporting, you read from one source, regardless of whether you want to supply data to your consolidation system, report to the tax authorities, or make internal management decisions.

Figure 2.1 illustrates the way the universal journal combines reporting dimensions from the separate applications (General Ledger Accounting, Profitability Analysis, Controlling, Asset Accounting, and Material Ledger) to provide a unified data structure for reporting that includes all relevant dimensions.

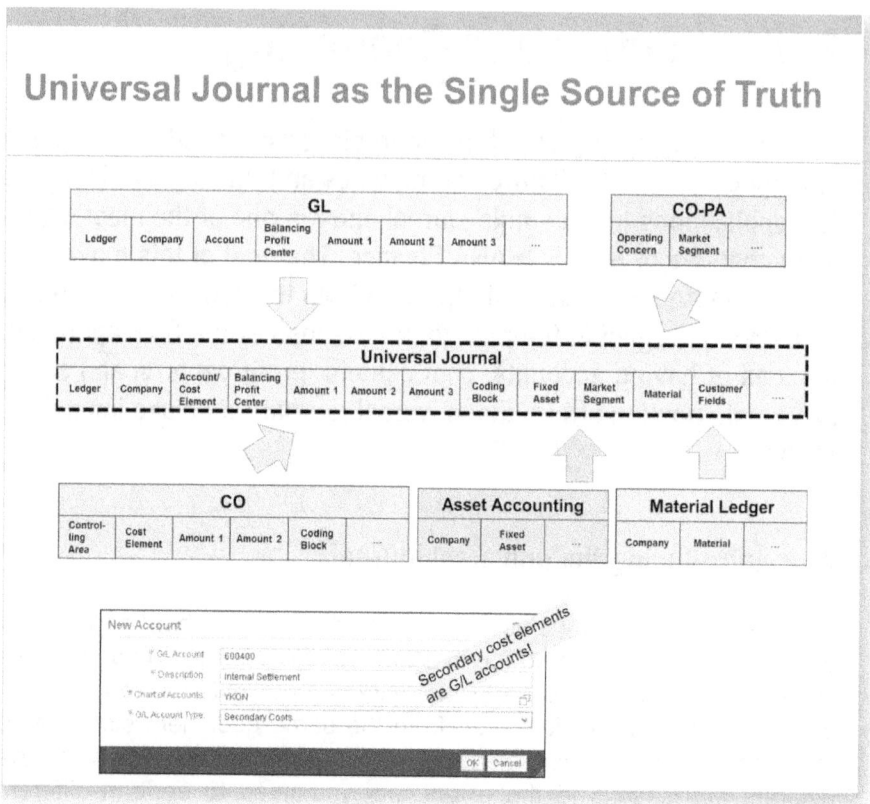

Figure 2.1: Combining reporting dimensions in the universal journal

The massive simplification inherent in this structure is that instead of having a separate set of revenue lines in Profitability Analysis, Profit Center Accounting, and Financial Accounting, you can report from a single *source document* in table ACDOCA. For internal reporting for example, you might select revenue lines for a particular product or customer (information captured as characteristics that you can choose when you generate your operating concern in Profitability Analysis) and for external reporting, you select the same revenue lines based on the profit center or company code in the document. When we talk about a *single source of truth*, what we mean is that instead of looking at datasets in multiple applications, we are looking at different aggregations of the same dataset. Here, the idea of the column store is significant. We may have hundreds of company codes, thousands of profit centers, and tens of thousands of customers, but these can be queried much more efficiently than in the past when each application built its own data store for these entities.

In this context, it is also worth understanding how the different applications used to aggregate their data in the past. Even though many of the relevant fields were available in table BSEG, organizations would configure their Financial Accounting applications to remove the individual cost centers from a large payroll document using *summarization*, or to remove the individual materials from a large invoice and only keep the cost center detail in Cost Center Accounting and the material detail in Profitability Analysis. This different granularity provided its own challenges when reconciling the various applications.

Before we look at what is new, let us remind ourselves of the high-level differences between the datasets in the various applications. However, if you are new to SAP S/4HANA Finance, you can skip straight to the next section because you do not have to worry about the historical differences between the various applications. All the Financials applications aggregate by period and fiscal year, but the other reporting dimensions are different in each application, making reconciliation tricky and meaning that management meetings are often spent discussing whose version of the truth is correct rather than what to do about the business situation the figures are showing.

2.1.1 Structure of General Ledger Accounting

Depending on which version of the SAP software you are using, there are actually two General Ledger Accounting options available:

▶ *Classic General Ledger Accounting* available from SAP R/3 onwards stores data by account, company code, and business area, as we saw when we looked at table GLT0 in Figure 1.2. If you needed reporting dimensions other than company code and business area, you could activate additional applications for Profit Center Accounting and Consolidation Preparation or build your own special ledger applications for Cost of Goods Sold Reporting, Segment Reporting, and so on. In addition to these ledgers, a *reconciliation ledger* stored the results of any allocations or settlements in Controlling that crossed company code boundaries and had to be reflected in General Ledger Accounting at period close by running transaction KALC to generate the appropriate journal entries. Moving to the universal journal makes the reconciliation ledger and transaction KALC obsolete because there is only one document in Accounting and Controlling.

▶ *SAP ERP General Ledger Accounting* (formerly known as *new General Ledger Accounting*) available from SAP ERP onwards allowed you to extend the basic account, company code, business area approach by activating additional scenarios to support Profit Center Accounting, Cost of Goods Sold Reporting, Consolidation Preparation, Segment Reporting, and so on. Activating these scenarios extends table FAGLFLEXA to store details of the profit centers and partner profit centers, functional areas and partner functional areas, trading partners and partner trading partners, segments and partner segments, and so on. What the scenarios enable is essentially drill-down reporting for these dimensions within the general ledger. Technically, you were creating additional aggregates for each of the scenarios that you added to the general ledger. The reconciliation ledger became obsolete if you activated real-time integration with CO so that any allocation or settlement that crosses a company code boundary (or a profit center boundary, a functional area boundary, and so on) would trigger a posting in the general ledger to reflect the change. This was progress compared to classic General Ledger Accounting, but there were limits to the number of dimensions that you could safely add to aggregate table FAGLFLEXA. With the universal journal, you no longer need to activate the various reporting scenarios separately—the columns are automatically updated if you maintain the proper assignments in your master data and you can add further dimensions to the coding block as required.

2.1.2   Structure of Asset Accounting

SAP S/4HANA Finance includes new Asset Accounting. The new asset accounting functions were first introduced as the business functions FIN_AA_CI_1 in EhP6 and FIN_AA_PARALLEL_VAL in EhP7. The original motivation was the need to switch between accounting principles as it became increasingly common for US customers to switch their leading valuation from US GAAP to IFRS. If you refer back to Figure 2.1, you will notice that the *ledger* is one of the key fields in the universal journal. This means that the asset valuations for IFRS and for local GAAP are stored in separate ledgers which are independent of each other, whereas in early versions of the software, the second valuation was stored as a delta or difference to the first valuation.

While Asset Accounting was always integrated with General Ledger Accounting in the sense that journal entries were created for the acquisition, retirement, and revaluation of an asset, or to account for the depreciation of the fixed asset in the general ledger, this did not mean that the account, the profit center, or any of the items we listed for the general ledger were included in the line item table for Asset Accounting (table ANEP) or conversely that the asset was available in Financial Accounting or Controlling. The only reporting dimension **common** to General Ledger Accounting and Asset Accounting other than the period and year is the company code. Reconciliation between the applications involved finding the postings in the general ledger that applied to fixed assets (those of account type A) and comparing them against the sum of the items in the Asset Accounting application. If you created a manual journal entry to an asset account, then the two would not match because this manual posting would not exist in the asset accounting table. Now, the asset is simply an additional dimension in the general ledger and sits alongside the company code, cost center, profit center, and so on in the posting string, which makes it substantially easier to report across applications than in the past.

2.1.3   Account assignments in Controlling

Although Cost Center Accounting, Order Accounting, and Project Accounting are generally considered to be separate applications in Controlling, the basic principle of assigning costs to an account assignment (a cost center, order, WBS element, and so on) is the same in each application.

In general, Controlling involves two types of posting for actual costs:

> ▶ The first type of posting is a *primary cost posting*. This simply means that the general ledger posting also includes an assignment to the cost center, order, or project responsible for the costs—for example, payroll postings and asset depreciation

might be assigned to a cost center and material expenses to an order or project. Each G/L account used to record these postings is linked with a sister *primary cost element* in Controlling that captures such costs. There is a one-to-one relationship between the primary cost postings and the appropriate profit and loss entries in the general ledger but the posting line items in the two applications are not necessarily at the same level of granularity. This is because the general ledger items are often configured such that the cost center, order, or project is summarized (in other words, **removed**) in order to reduce data volumes. This is frequently the case for the material items in the invoice, which are often summarized so that the 999 line item limit is not exceeded.

▶ The second type of posting is a *secondary cost posting*. This means that these costs are allocated or settled further. In our example, the payroll and depreciation costs assigned to the cost center might be allocated to orders and projects using time recording or order confirmation, resulting in the cost center being credited and the order or project debited under a *secondary cost element*. The order and project costs might be settled to CO-PA, resulting in the order or project being credited and the CO-PA characteristics debited, again under a secondary cost element. There was never a one-to-one relationship between these cost elements and the G/L accounts because they were aggregated to a single reconciliation account for the relevant business transaction, irrespective of whether you use transaction KALC or the real-time integration functions in SAP ERP General Ledger Accounting.

In addition, where project and order costs are to be capitalized as work in process or assets under construction, separate accounts exist that do not match one-to-one with the cost elements used to calculate work in process.

2.1.4 Profitability Analysis

Profitability Analysis (CO-PA) was generally also considered a separate application within Controlling. SAP ERP supports two types of Profitability Analysis: account-based Profitability Analysis and costing-based Profitability Analysis. However, for performance reasons, most organizations used only costing-based Profitability Analysis in the days before SAP HANA:

▶ *Account-based Profitability Analysis* captures the revenues and sales deductions under primary cost elements and the result of allocations and settlement under secondary cost elements. The difference compared to Cost Center Accounting, Order Accounting, or Project Accounting is that the account assignment is not a one-dimensional cost center or order but a multidimensional group of characteristics, such as the product sold, the customer who bought the product, the sales office, the distribution channel, and so on. The operating concern is configurable and therefore, every organization uses its own special set of CO-PA characteristics. As you move to the universal journal, a column is created for each of the characteristics in your operating concern and reporting dimensions such as the customer, product, and sales office are on an equal level with company code, profit center, and functional area.

▶ *Costing-based Profitability Analysis*, by contrast, uses the same characteristics but transforms the accounts/cost elements into *value fields*. Because there is a technical limitation which means that only 200 value fields are supported (in earlier releases it was 120), there are typically far fewer value fields than there are accounts and value fields exist for items without an account assignment, such as statistical freight costs or sales deductions. Because it is common practice to summarize (or remove) not just the cost center but also the material number in invoices, there is often a different granularity between the lines in General Ledger Accounting and the lines in Profitability Analysis. Costing-based Profitability Analysis continues to be supported in SAP S/4HANA Finance but because of the value fields, the data cannot be subsumed into the universal journal and table CE1 continues to exist alongside the universal journal. There is no migration service to switch from a costing-based model to an account-based model because the two models are fundamentally different approaches (accounts vs key figures).

2.1.5 Structures in the Material Ledger

The use of the Material Ledger in SAP S/4HANA is a source of some confusion. In the SAP Financials Add-on and SAP S/4HANA Finance, the use of the Material Ledger is **optional**, but with SAP S/4HANA, the use of the transactional Material Ledger becomes **compulsory**. As we saw with Profitability Analysis, SAP ERP supports two approaches to the Material Ledger (the transactional Material Ledger and Actual Costing), although when most organizations talk about the Material Ledger they actually mean that they use the second option, Actual Costing:

▶ The *transactional Material Ledger* is a subledger like Asset Accounting but structured by company code, valuation area, and material. From a Material Ledger perspective, materials have *price determination 2*, which simply means that inventory-related transactions are captured in different currencies and valuation approaches (group valuation, legal valuation, and profit center valuation). You can continue to work with the moving average price that is calculated with each transaction update and you do **not** require a costing run at period close. This option becomes **compulsory** with SAP S/4HANA on-premise edition 1511, although it has been available since SAP R/3 Release 4.0.

▶ *Actual Costing*, by contrast, is used in geographies and industries where there is a legal or business requirement to assign purchase price variances, production variances, and so on to the goods sold and goods in inventory at period close. This option requires you to execute one or more costing runs to calculate actual costs at period close. Actual Costing continues to be supported as an **option** in SAP S/4HANA. The data cannot be subsumed entirely into the universal journal and the material ledger tables continue to exist alongside the universal journal. Indeed, SAP S/4HANA 1610 includes a new optimized version of Actual Costing.

2.1.6 Other Subledgers

You will notice in Figure 2.1 that while the asset subledger and material subledger merge with the general ledger, some key subledgers remain separate. *Accounts Receivable* and *Accounts Payable* continue as separate subledgers for open item management and the clearing of payments. All you will find in the general ledger is the *reconciliation account* for the supplier or the customer. This is partly to do with the clearing logic in Accounts Payable and Accounts Receivable, where multiple accounting principles and multiple currencies actually get in the way if you are trying to clear an open item for a given amount. *Contract Accounts Receivable and Payable* also remains separate to store all details for utility billing and so on. Some industry solutions also have their own subledgers, such as SAP Bank Analyzer or SAP Insurance Analyzer for financial service organizations, or the SAP Customer Activity Repository (CAR) in Retail. These continue to integrate with the general ledger at the level of the account and some key reporting dimensions.

Of course, there are more differences between the applications than the reporting dimensions listed above. Historically, Financial Accounting worked with three currencies, while Controlling offered only two currencies. Accounting principles were also handled differently in each application (ledgers in General Ledger Accounting, charts of depreciation in Asset Accounting, versions in Controlling, currency types in the Material Ledger). Many of these differences are also being addressed in SAP S/4HANA Finance and we will discuss the relevant changes in the sections that follow.

2.2 General Ledger Accounting

We looked at the new table (ACDOCA) for storing transaction data in Chapter 1. However, it makes sense to look at some of the reports delivered to get a sense of what the universal journal enables simply because the data is in a long string rather than in chunks for each application. Of course, this does not mean that the whole of financial reporting can be performed using one table. There are still separate reports for viewing the open items in Accounts Payable and Accounts Receivable and reports for individual stakeholders—such as cost center managers and project managers—that select by cost center, WBS element, and so on, but we will see in the examples that follow how one simple report, the trial balance, can satisfy many reporting requirements if you use the appropriate drill-downs.

2.2.1 Trial balance

Figure 2.2 shows a *trial balance*—a list of accounts together with the opening balance, closing balance, and the debits and credits for the current accounting period for each account. The right-hand part of the screen (the results) will look familiar but what is powerful is the ability to drill down not just by segment, profit center, functional area, business area, and so on, as was possible with the drill-down reports in General Ledger Accounting, but also by any of the list of reporting dimensions that we see on the left of the screen. There are many new options compared to SAP R/3 and SAP ERP. In alphabetical order, in Figure 2.2 we see the following:

- ▶ The ACCOUNT TYPE allows us to quickly segregate accounts for assets, materials, customers, suppliers, and the general ledger. Having selected the asset accounts, we can then drill down to the associated assets, and so the journey continues. We might select the material accounts and drill down to the associated materials.

- ▶ The ACCOUNTING DOCUMENT NUMBER gives you an idea of the granularity of the data feeding into the trial balance. You may still want to drill back from this accounting document to use the *Document Relationship Browser* to understand what business transactions initiated that transaction.

- ▶ The ACTIVITY TYPE is a reporting dimension that was previously only visible in Cost Center Accounting.

- ▶ The ASSET SUBNUMBER is a reporting dimension that was previously only visible in Asset Accounting.

We could continue down the list, to see cost centers, orders, WBS elements and all the CO-PA characteristics, but it makes most sense just to start exploring the drill-down options to get a sense of what navigating through the universal journal means in the context of this report. To drill down, select the icons to the left of the reporting dimensions, which determine whether the drill-down is vertical or horizontal.

Figure 2.3 shows a very simple example where, under AVAILABLE FIELDS, we have scrolled down to COST CENTER (not visible in Figure 2.2) and then selected the drill-down icon beside COST CENTER to understand the material costs and the associated cost centers. The result is that the general ledger postings are broken down and you see a new column COST CENTER on the right and the material costs broken down by cost center. In the past, you would have had to navigate to a separate report in Cost Center Accounting to see the material costs by cost center.

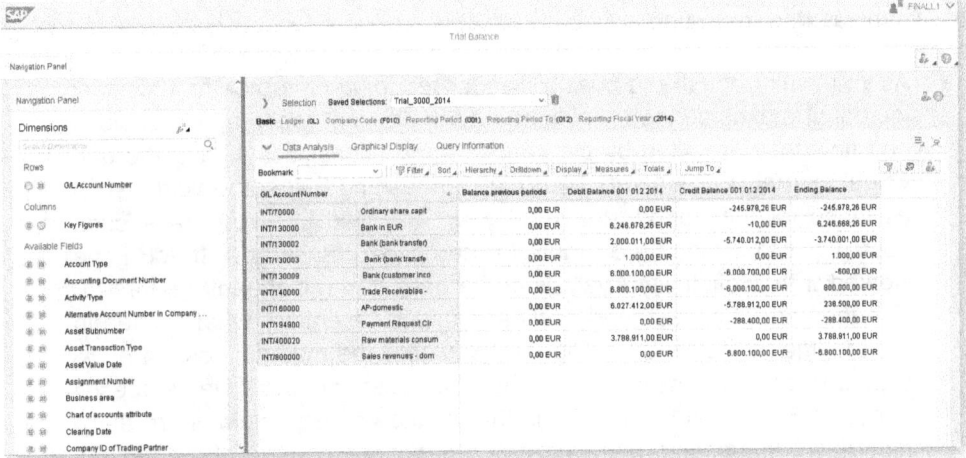

Figure 2.2: Trial balance

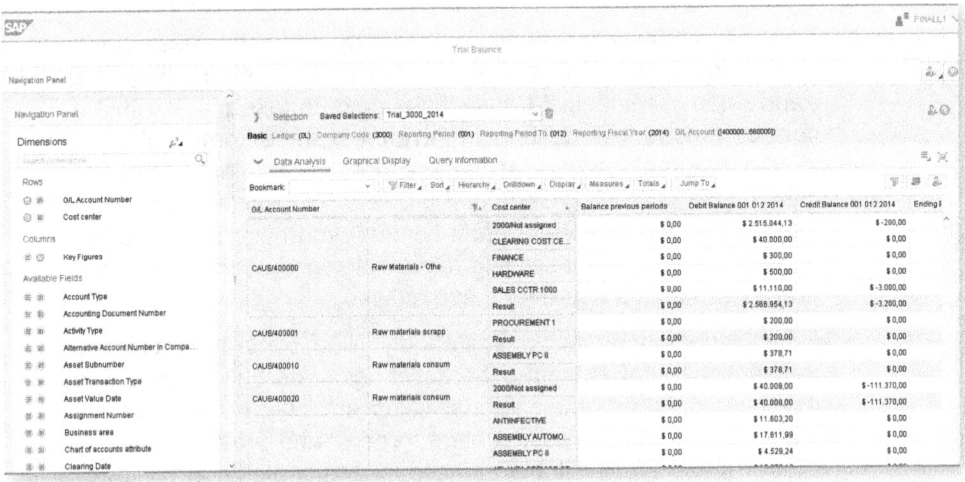

Figure 2.3: Trial balance with drill-down by cost center

Note also that the first line containing raw material costs shows the cost center as being Not assigned. This is because this account also captures postings to orders, projects, and so on. This line contains the raw material costs assigned to account assignments other than the cost center. To see these account assignments, we would have to change our drill-down dimensions again and add orders or projects alongside the cost center. As we work our way through the applications that feed into the universal journal, we will look at how each of these dimensions are populated for reporting.

As you think through the possibilities for reporting on top of the universal journal, it makes sense to think about the different reporting dimensions and how they are filled by the various applications. Essentially, the universal journal is a *sparsely filled matrix*, meaning that some fields, such as those for the period and fiscal year, are filled by every transaction posted but that many are empty for any given transaction. If you have worked with Profitability Analysis in the past, you will already be familiar with the idea of *unassigned costs* and this is essentially what we see in the top line of the report in Figure 2.3, where the material costs are assigned to account assignments other than cost centers. What is special about an SAP HANA database is that all the unfilled columns are automatically *compressed*, meaning that it is not a problem if the database includes fields that are only rarely filled because they do not occupy space in the database.

▶ Reporting dimensions such as company code, business area, profit center, segment, and so on are filled by **every** business transaction. All financial transactions have to take place within a company code. All costs and revenues are automatically assigned to profit centers, using the derivation rules in the assigned cost centers, orders, and projects. To assign the balance sheet items to the correct profit centers, you have to set up the appropriate document splitting rules. This ensures that the report always contains a figure for these entities.

▶ Other reporting dimensions are only filled by **some** business transactions—for example, the asset fields are only filled by the asset transactions, the material fields are only filled by goods movements, and the cost centers, orders, and projects are only filled if these are available as account assignments in the business transaction. The trading partner is only filled during an intercompany transaction. If the field is not filled, you will simply see the word Not assigned in the report line.

2.2.2   Reporting dimensions in General Ledger Accounting

The universal journal contains all account assignments from General Ledger Accounting, so if you scroll to the appropriate section of table ACDOCA, you will recognize the fields shown in Figure 2.4. These are the same as the general ledger scenarios (Segment Reporting, Profit Center Reporting, Cost of Goods Sold Reporting, and Consolidation Preparation) but the fields are always available in the universal journal and you do not have to activate them separately. This is a good example of the difference between SAP S/4HANA Finance and the former applications.

▶ With SAP S/4HANA Finance, there is no totals table and these fields are **always** filled, provided that you have made the correct assignments to your profit centers, business areas, and functional areas in your master data.

▶ What happened previously during the activation step was that the system would generate the relevant fields in the former totals table FAGLFLEXA. Any change to the assignment in the reporting dimensions meant that you had to correct the totals in table FAGLFLEXA.

Dictionary: Display Table

Technical Settings   Indexes...   Append Structure...

| Transparent Table | ACDOCA | Active |
| Short Description | Universal Journal Entry Line Items | |

Attributes   Delivery and Maintenance   Fields   Entry help/check   Currency/Quantity Fields

Srch Help   Predefined Type   50 / 372

Field	Key	Ini...	Data element	Data Type	Length	Deci...	Short Description	Group
RACCT		✓	RACCT	CHAR	10		0 Account Number	
.INCLUDE		✓	ACDOC_SI_GL_ACC...	STRU	0		0 Universal Journal Entry: G/L additional account assignments	ACCT_ASSIGNMENT
RCNTR			KOSTL	CHAR	10		0 Cost Center	
PRCTR			PRCTR	CHAR	10		0 Profit Center	
RFAREA			FKBER	CHAR	16		0 Functional Area	
RBUSA			GSBER	CHAR	4		0 Business Area	
KOKRS			KOKRS	CHAR	4		0 Controlling Area	
SEGMENT			FB_SEGMENT	CHAR	10		0 Segment for Segmental Reporting	
SCNTR			SKOST	CHAR	10		0 Sender cost center	
PPRCTR			PPRCTR	CHAR	10		0 Partner Profit Center	
SFAREA			SFKBER	CHAR	16		0 Partner Functional Area	
SBUSA			PARGB	CHAR	4		0 Trading partner's business area	
RASSC			RASSC	CHAR	6		0 Company ID of trading partner	
PSEGMENT			FB_PSEGMENT	CHAR	10		0 Partner Segment for Segmental Reporting	

Figure 2.4: Account assignment part of the universal journal table

Note that for every reporting dimension you also have the equivalent *partner dimension*, so you will see dimension pairs (profit center and partner profit center, functional area and partner functional area, and so

41

on). We will see this in more detail when we look at allocations because an allocation from cost center to cost center can also impact the associated profit centers, functional areas, and so on and this allocation updates the appropriate partner information.

Note that these fields are part of the general ledger. If you have handled Profit Center Accounting via a separate set of tables or used Special Ledger to handle functional areas for Cost of Goods Sold Reporting in the past, these interfaces are still supported and the data will be updated in these tables. However, if you are starting afresh, it makes sense to use the universal journal to handle these reporting dimensions rather than creating additional ledgers. In the case of the cost center, the line item table COEP is no longer updated during actual postings from Financial Accounting and all new reporting applications use table ACDOCA table directly. Statistical postings continue to be recorded in COEP and you can identify statistical postings in the new reports by selecting the flag IS STATISTICAL in the navigation block.

There are, of course, more reporting fields in the universal journal table. If you scroll through the table, you will also find the fields needed for Public Sector Accounting, Joint Venture Accounting, and Real Estate Management, with further fields being added with each release. The universal journal can also handle coding block extensions via the customer include CI_COBL. You can find details of how to implement this customer include in SAP Note 2143232 (*https://launchpad.support.sap .com/#/notes/0002143232*) and related notes.

Availability of industry solutions with SAP S/4HANA Finance

The fields that are available in the universal journal vary with the industry solution that you are using. To be sure that your industry solution is released for SAP S/4HANA Finance, please refer to SAP Note 2119188 (*https:// launchpad.support.sap.com/#/notes/000219188*).

2.2.3 Accounts and cost elements

In Figure 2.3, we drilled down by account and cost center. One of the other key aspects of the merging of Financial Accounting and Controlling is that we no longer transform G/L accounts into cost elements but rather merge the two. Figure 2.5 shows the G/L account that we looked at in Figure 2.3. In the past, the ACCOUNT TYPE field offered the options Balance Sheet and Profit and Loss. The account type Primary Costs or Revenue shown in Figure 2.5 applies to all profit and loss accounts that used to have a separate cost element or revenue element. You will still typically have some profit and loss accounts without a sister cost element and these will have the account type Non-Operating Expense or Income. The difference is that non-operating accounts cannot be assigned to a cost center, order, project, and so on (although they can be used to record work in process for an order or project). If you flag an account as being of account type Primary Costs or Revenue, you have to assign the relevant accounting item to a cost center, order, or project if it is a cost item, or to a combination of CO-PA characteristics if it is a revenue or sales deduction item. If you are setting up accounts in a greenfield project, be sure to activate the correct account assignments via the *field status groups* for each G/L account and set up default account assignments just in case the material costs cannot be automatically assigned within the business transaction.

While the account and cost element are technically merged in the ACCOUNT field in the universal journal, you can still find the familiar COST ELEMENT CATEGORY setting by navigating to the CONTROL DATA tab in Figure 2.5. Figure 2.6 shows that in this case, the material costs are Primary Costs. Note that you can only post material costs under account 400000 if you also update a cost center, order, project, or other CO object.

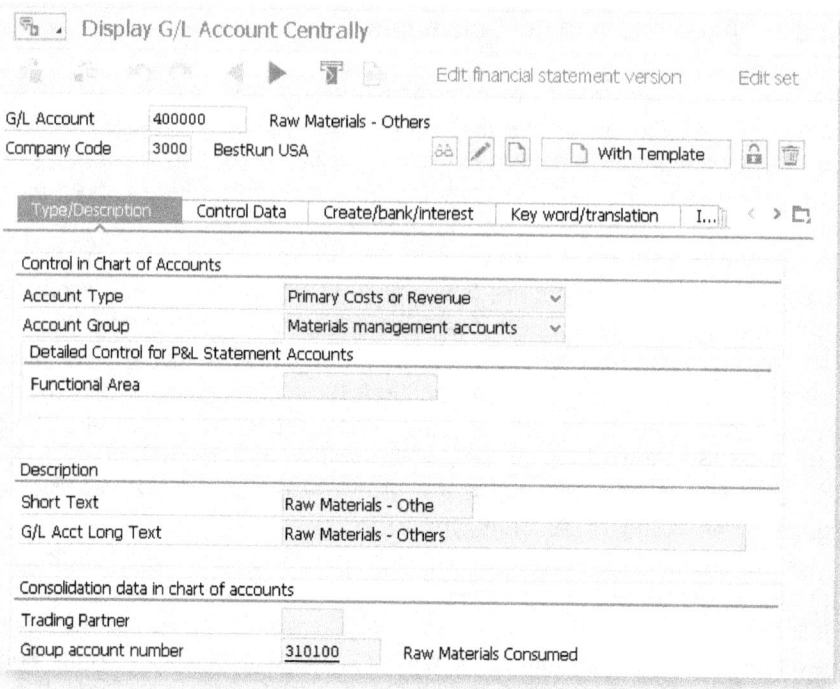

Figure 2.5: G/L account for primary costs or revenues

While these links make reporting simpler, note that in a few cases, the system still treats the account dimension as an account and a sister cost element.

► When you design your authorizations, you have to make sure that you have authorization for both the account (authorization object F_SKA_BUK) and the cost element (authorization object K_CSKB) before you can change the master data.

► When you design your period close processes, you need to be aware that each account must be allowed/locked in Financial Accounting and that the relevant business transactions (primary posting, allocation, settlement) must be explicitly allowed in Controlling.

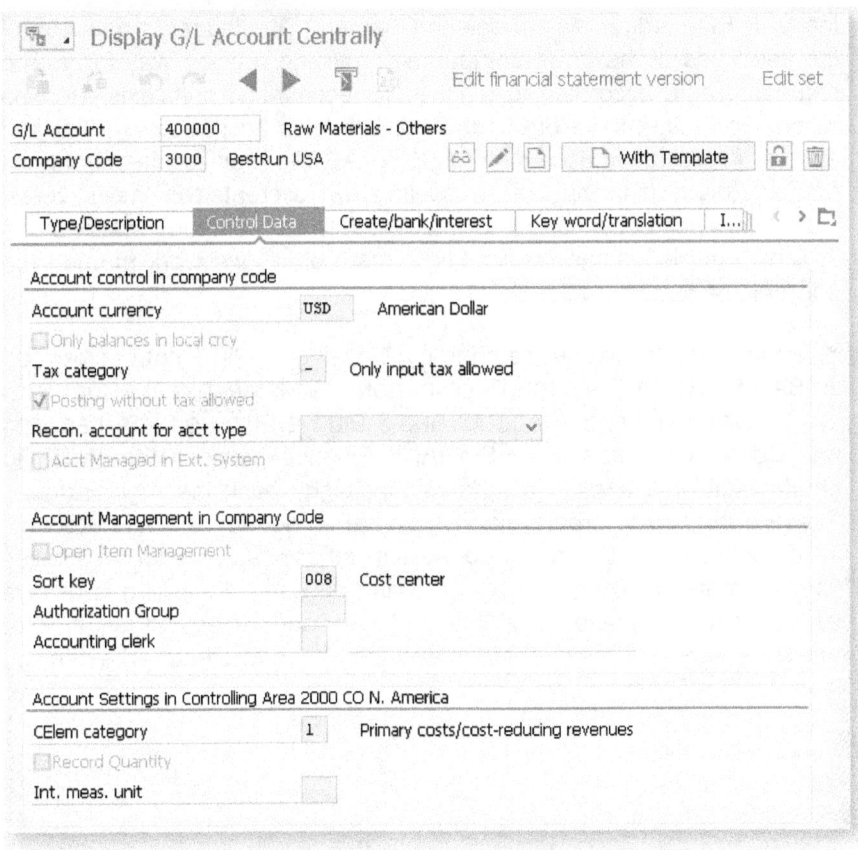

Figure 2.6: G/L account showing the cost element category

2.2.4 Types of ledger

If we now return to the business reasons for moving to SAP S/4HANA Finance, one reason is often the need to handle multiple *accounting principles*. In fact, customers have been doing this for years by using different number ranges in their charts of accounts to separate common accounts, IFRS accounts, and accounts that only apply to another accounting principle and then selecting the appropriate account groups during an allocation or in reporting (you may hear this referred to as the Mickey Mouse approach, with the common accounts being the mouse's head and the special accounts the mouse's ears). The *ledger* approach was originally introduced with the Special Ledger and then adopted in the SAP ERP ledger. As we saw in Chapter 1, the ledger is now one of the key fields of the universal journal, providing a clean way for you to segregate data according to the various accounting principles—for example, you might have one ledger for valuation according to IFRS and another for valuation according to US GAAP. From an architectural point of view, this means that a new posting line is created in the universal journal for each accounting principle. We will look at the implications of a switch to the ledger as the leading dimension as we work through the applications that follow.

You can reach the ledger settings by following the IMG path MIGRATION TO SAP S/4HANA FINANCE • PREPARATIONS AND MIGRATION OF CUSTOMIZING TO GENERAL LEDGER ACCOUNTING • DEFINE SETTINGS FOR LEDGERS AND CURRENCY TYPES. SAP S/4HANA Finance provides the option to create additional *extension ledgers* that piggy back the main ledgers. These allow you to create manual journal entries for special purposes. This would allow you to refine your profit center postings after an acquisition or create correcting entries following an audit. Reporting is always based on a combination of extension ledger and underlying ledger. Figure 2.7 shows the ledger settings and the option to create an extension ledger that references a standard ledger.

Display View "Ledger": Overview

Ledger	Ledger Name	Leading	Ledger Type	Extens. Ledger...	Underlying Ledger
0D			Standard Ledger		
0L	Leading Ledger	✓	Standard Ledger		
0M	Export ledger to 0G		Standard Ledger		
1D			Standard Ledger		
1L	Leading Ledger		Standard Ledger		
BZ	Brazil		Standard Ledger		
GF	demo		Standard Ledger		
L5	IAS		Standard Ledger		
L6	local		Standard Ledger		
			Standard Ledger		
			Extension Ledger		

Dialog Structure
- Currency Types
- Global Currency Conversion Settings
- Currency Conversion Settings for Comp
- Ledger
  - Company Code Settings for the Le
    - Accounting Principles for Ledge

Figure 2.7: Settings for standard ledgers and extension ledgers

If, in the past, you have used *group valuation* to eliminate intercompany profit, or *profit center valuation* to treat postings between profit centers with arm's length price conditions, you will remember that these valuations were always considered part of the leading ledger 0L. This idea is retained in the universal journal in that the column for group valuation and the column for profit center valuation become additional columns in the ledger line as you migrate.

Alternatively, in a greenfield project, you can set up additional ledgers to represent each valuation approach. Figure 2.8 shows the two options, with ledger L1 being used to represent all three valuations as different columns and ledgers L2, L3, and L4 being used to capture the legal valuation, group valuation, and profit center valuation separately.

Change View "Ledger": Overview

New Entries   All Table Views

Dialog Structure	Ledger						
	Ledger	Ledger Name	Leading	Ledger Type	Extens. Ledger... Underlying Ledger	Valuation View	
• Currency Types	L1	Multiple Valuation Ledger	☑	Standard Ledger ▾			▾
• Global Currency Conversi	L2	Legal Valuation	☐	Standard Ledger ▾		Legal Valuation ▾	
• Currency Conversion Set	L3	Group Valuation	☐	Standard Ledger ▾		Group Valuation ▾	
▾ Ledger	L4	Profit Center Valuation	☐	Standard Ledger ▾		Profit Center Val_ ▾	
▾ Company Code Setti							
• Accounting Princ							

Figure 2.8: Ledger settings for group, legal, and profit center valuation

The other key setting associated with the ledgers relates to the *currencies*. In SAP S/4HANA Finance edition 1503, you could assign the group currency, a local currency for the company code, and one additional currency to each ledger. This was extended in the 1602 edition to cover eight additional currencies, meaning that you can easily add a functional currency, an index currency, and so on to each ledger if you need it in that country. Figure 2.9 shows the familiar currency settings: 00 as document currency, 10 as company code currency, 20 as controlling area currency, 30 as group currency, 40 as the hard currency, and so on, plus new options Y2 to Y4 in our example. Note also the familiar currency combinations: 11 for group valuation (eliminated intercompany profits) in company code currency, 31 for group valuation in group currency, and 32 for profit center valuation in group currency where you see the link back to the original currency type in the BASE CURRENCY TYPE column. Note also the new options used with Y2, Y3 and Y4, where we have set up a functional currency Y2 and then combined it with the valuation options for group valuation and profit center valuation by entering Y2 in the BASE CURRENCY TYPE column. This is useful if you have an entity that is operating using Canadian dollars as the local currency in Canada, but doing most of its business with the USA and therefore has a requirement to report in US dollars as the functional currency in parallel.

47

Change View "Currency Types": Overview

New Entries ⬚ 🗐 ⟳ 🗒 🗒 🗐 All Table Views

Currency Type	Description	Short Description	Valuation View	Base Currency Type	Maintenance level
00	Document Currency	Doc Crcy	Legal Valuation ▾		Global ▾
10	Company Code Currency	CCde Crcy	Legal Valuation ▾		Global ▾
11	CoCode Crcy, Group Valuation	CoCo, Grp	Group Valuation ▾	10	Global ▾
12	CoCode Crcy, PrCtr Valuation	CoCo, PrC	Profit Center Val. ▾	10	Global ▾
20	Controlling Area Currency	CArea Crcy	Legal Valuation ▾		Global ▾
30	Group Currency	Group Crcy	Legal Valuation ▾		Company code... ▾
31	Group Crcy, Group Valuation	Grp, Grp	Group Valuation ▾	30	Company code... ▾
32	Group Crcy, PrCtr Valuation	Grp, PrCtr	Profit Center Val. ▾	30	Company code... ▾
40	Hard Currency	Hard Crcy	Legal Valuation ▾		Company code... ▾
50	Index-Based Currency	Index Crcy	Legal Valuation ▾		Company code... ▾
60	Global Company Currency	GloCo Crcy	Legal Valuation ▾		Company code... ▾
70	CO Object Currency	COObjCrcy	Legal Valuation ▾		Global ▾
Y2	Function Currency in legal	Func Crcy	Legal Valuation ▾		Company code... ▾
Y3	Function Currency in Gr Val	FuncCr Gr	Group Valuation ▾	Y2	Company code... ▾
Y4	Function Currency in PrCtr Val	FuncCr PC	Profit Center Val. ▾	Y2	Company code... ▾

Figure 2.9: Currency types and associated settings

The challenge now is to change the business processes to update all the currency columns with the appropriate logic over subsequent releases. At the time of writing, the currencies that are not carried in the operational process are filled as the journal entry is created.

2.3　New Asset Accounting

New Asset Accounting was introduced as an optional business function (FIN_AA_PARALLEL_VAL) in SAP Enhancement Package 7 for SAP ERP 6.0, which means that you can potentially already use it even if you are not yet using SAP S/4HANA. With SAP S/4HANA Finance, new Asset Accounting becomes compulsory, so be sure to include time for it in your project plan. Even if you are not yet ready to go to SAP S/4HANA Finance but use ERP General Ledger Accounting, consider activating new Asset Accounting if you are on a modern Enhancement Package, as documented in SAP Note 1776828 (*https://launchpad.support.sap.com/ – /notes/0001776828*), because it offers some key functional benefits and will make the move to SAP S/4HANA easier later.

2.3.1   Reporting dimensions in Asset Accounting

The first thing that changes is that the data model in Asset Accounting is simplified in order to merge with the universal journal. Figure 2.10 shows the asset-related fields in the universal journal. What we see here is the transactional data formerly stored in tables ANEK, ANEP, ANEA, ANLP, and ANLC that is now part of table ACDOCA. The naming convention for the compatibility views in Asset Accounting is FAAV_ANEK and so on for the old structures and FAAV_ANEA_ORI and so on for access to the old tables. Statistical data (for example, for tax purposes) previously stored in ANEP, ANEA, ANLP, ANLC is now stored in table FAAT_DOC_IT. Plan data previously stored in ANLP and ANLC is now stored in FAAT_PLAN_VALUES.

Figure 2.10: Asset-related fields in the universal journal

We can see how these fields are used if we return to the trial balance and drill down by the MAIN ASSET NUMBER as shown in Figure 2.11. You can easily drill down further to cover the ASSET SUBNUMBER, ASSET VALUE DATE, and ASSET TRANSACTION TYPE. By doing this, we have combined general ledger information by account with asset-related information.

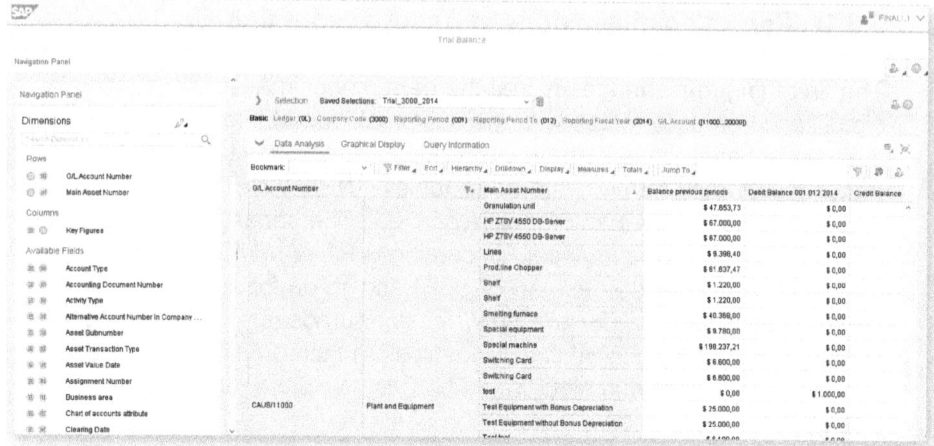

Figure 2.11: Trial balance with drill-down by asset

Because each asset is also assigned to a cost center, we can now go further and cross the old component barriers to drill down by COST CENTER, as shown in Figure 2.12, to understand how the acquisition costs for the asset affect the cost center. In the past, you would have seen this information in the asset reports, which included asset balances by asset class, by cost center, by plant, and so on, but not in the general ledger or in the cost center reports. Gradually, we start to see how a single report radically simplifies the reporting environment and potentially removes many spreadsheets with lookup tables from your reporting processes.

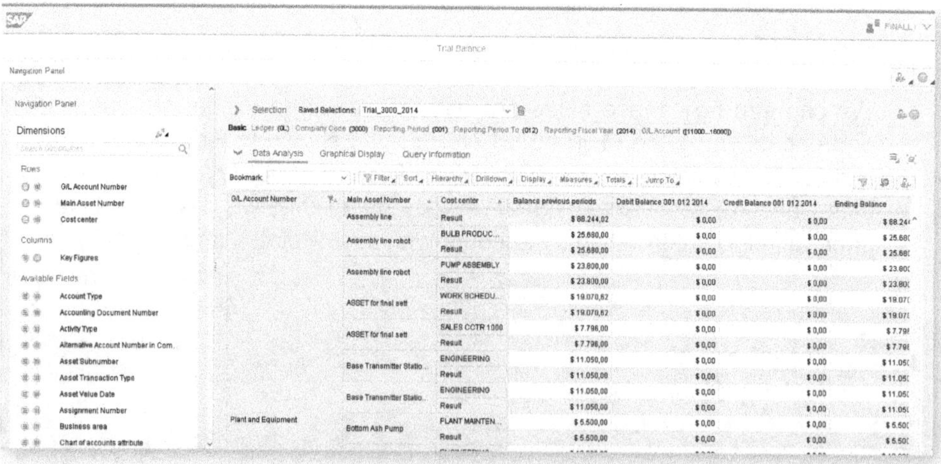

Figure 2.12: Trial balance with drill-down by asset and cost center

What does not change is the asset itself. The assignment from the asset to the account and the time-dependent link to the associated cost center is the key to this report. Clean master data is vital to fill the reporting dimensions of the universal journal, and therefore, it is important to check these settings to ensure that they are correct and that the correct profit center and segment can be derived.

Convert batch input programs for transaction AB01 into BAPIs

 If you are planning to create new assets via batch input, please note that batch input programs for AB01 are no longer supported in new Asset Accounting. If you are using customer-defined programs with batch input, you must convert these to BAPIs before you can generate new assets.

2.3.2 Ledgers and depreciation areas

Historically, Asset Accounting has always used *depreciation areas* to handle different valuations and you will be used to seeing multiple depreciation areas associated with a single asset in the *Asset Explorer*. What changes with new Asset Accounting is that depreciation area 01 is no longer hard-wired to the leading ledger and you can now easily assign the depreciation areas to the relevant ledgers. Technically, the depreciation areas are managed as full ledgers rather than delta ledgers, which makes for a much cleaner reporting process. There is now a step in the IMG that allows you to link the depreciation area with the relevant ledger and to determine whether the posting takes place in real time or periodically. Note, however, that at the time of writing, this brings its own constraints. Because you cannot add a ledger to the universal journal and fill it with historical data, you cannot add a depreciation area in Asset Accounting that is linked with the universal journal retrospectively.

It is also possible to treat assets as assets according to some accounting principles but to exclude them from other ledgers (one-sided postings).

If you have used SAP ERP General Ledger Accounting, you are probably already familiar with the idea of an *entry view*, which shows the data supplied by the delivering application, and the *general ledger view*, which shows the enriched data (where the profit center and segment are filled). New Asset Accounting picks up this same idea so that the invoice for a purchased asset delivers its data as before but posts initially to a technical *clearing account*. Figure 2.13 shows the DATA ENTRY VIEW for a sample asset acquisition from an external vendor. This entry document triggers the creation of multiple accounting documents, one for each active accounting principle. The accounting-principle specific documents clear the technical clearing account (199909) to give a zero balance. You can then manually adjust one of the accounting principles—for example, to account for freight costs differently in each accounting principle.

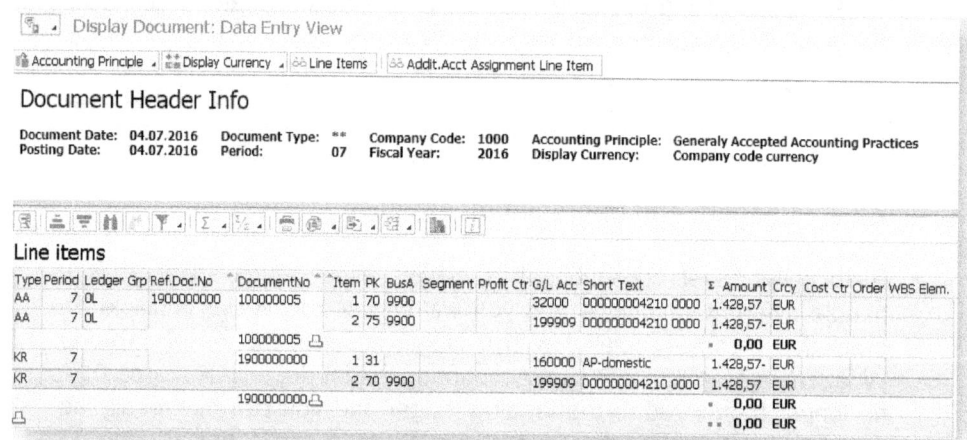

Figure 2.13: Data entry view showing clearing account 199909

2.4 Cost Center Accounting, Order Accounting, and Project Accounting

New General Ledger Accounting offered an option to include the cost center in FAGLFLEXA but orders, projects, business processes, networks, and other account assignments required organizations to report separately in Controlling. We have already looked at the drill-down by cost center in the trial balance in Section 2.2.1 but this is only half the story. We also need to understand how these costs are charged on to other cost objects in the system. We will also look at the role of the object number and partner object number and how this changes with SAP S/4HANA Finance.

2.4.1 Reporting dimensions in Cost Center Accounting, Order Accounting, and Project Accounting

We began to discuss this topic in Section 2.2.1, where we showed how to drill down from the trial balance to the cost centers. The same basic principles apply to costs assigned to orders, work breakdown structure (WBS) elements, networks, network activities, business processes, and any of the objects that have previously been considered CO objects. It is also possible to capture statistical postings to orders and projects and report on these by selecting the Is STATISTICAL flag in the new reports.

Cost objects and cost object hierarchies are the major exception in terms of backward compatibility. They will **not** be supported going forward, so you will find that all functions for cost object hierarchies have been removed from the PRODUCT COST BY PERIOD menu and that the GENERAL COST OBJECT CONTROLLING menu has been removed from the SAP EASY ACCESS MENU. For cost object hierarchies that are used primarily for reporting, the recommendation is to use *summarization hierarchies* instead. For those used to capture costs that will later be distributed to the assigned product cost collectors and orders, the recommendation is to use the *distribution of usage variances* functions in the Material Ledger menu instead (these do not require use of Actual Costing but are often used in this context).

In Figure 2.14, note that the universal journal continues to contain the object number and the partner object number for reasons of backwards compatibility, but it also breaks out the object number to fill the new AC-CAS (ACCOUNT ASSIGNMENT) and ACCASTY (OBJECT TYPE) fields so that we now have a separate column containing KS for cost center, OR for order, PS for project, and so on. In reporting, you use the object type in combination with the related field, such as AUFNR for the order number and PS_POSID for the work breakdown structure (WBS) element to select the relevant lines for reporting. What this means is that it is now substantially easier to create reports on the account assignments because you no longer have to unpack the CO object number as was the case in the classic line item reports and as costs were extracted to SAP

BW. You will also notice that every object has its equivalent *partner object*. This means that you can easily report the way an allocation cycle charges costs from one cost center to the next, or time recording is used to charge cost center costs to a network, order, or project.

Field	Key	Ini...	Data element	Data Type	Length	Deci...	Short Description
OBJNR_HK			OBJNR_HK	CHAR	22	0	Object Number of Origin Object
AUFNR_ORG			AUFNR_HK	CHAR	12	0	Origin Order Number
UKOSTL			USP_KOSTL	CHAR	10	0	Origin cost center
ULSTAR			USP_LSTAR	CHAR	6	0	Origin activity
UPPRZNR			USP_PRZNR	CHAR	12	0	Source: Business Process
ACCAS			ACCAS	CHAR	30	0	Account Assignment
ACCASTY			J_OBART	CHAR	2	0	Object Type
LSTAR			LSTAR	CHAR	6	0	Activity Type
AUFNR			AUFNR	CHAR	12	0	Order Number
AUTYP			AUFTYP	NUMC	2	0	Order category
PS_POSID			PS_POSID	CHAR	24	0	Work Breakdown Structure Element (WBS Element)
PS_PSPID			PS_PSPID	CHAR	24	0	Project Definition
NPLNR			NPLNR	CHAR	12	0	Network Number for Account Assignment
NPLNR_VORGN			VORNR	CHAR	4	0	Operation/Activity Number
PRZNR			CO_PRZNR	CHAR	12	0	Business Process
KSTRG			KSTRG	CHAR	12	0	Cost Object
BEMOT			BEMOT	CHAR	2	0	Accounting Indicator
QMNUM			QMNUM	CHAR	12	0	Notification No
ERKRS			ERKRS	CHAR	4	0	Operating concern
PACCAS			PACCAS	CHAR	30	0	Partner Account Assignment
PACCASTY			CO_POBART	CHAR	2	0	Partner object type
PLSTAR			PAR_LSTAR	CHAR	6	0	Partner activity
PAUFNR			PAR_AUFNR	CHAR	12	0	Partner order number

Figure 2.14: Fields for CO account assignments in the universal journal

If you compare Figure 2.15 with Figure 2.3, you will notice that we are again looking at an account/cost center combination but that this time, we are looking at how those costs are charged to a partner receiver (in this case, an order) via an activity type. The material cost posting in Figure 2.3 was offset against an open item for a vendor payment but here we have an internal posting, where one cost center is credited and another receiver debited under what used to be known as a secondary cost element. In many cases, the charge is from cost center to an order or project and therefore, the partner cost center is unassigned. However, for the DAA machine costs item, we can see both the debit and credit sides of the allocation as the cost center Corporate Services charges costs to Pump Assembly.

We see this pattern whenever a direct activity allocation is posted (as here, either via time recording or order confirmation), overheads are applied, allocation cycles are run, or orders and projects are settled. There will always be a *sender* and a *receiver* (or indeed senders and receivers) and the value flow will be captured in an account. This sender-receiver relationship takes us back to Figure 2.4, where we looked at the account assignment pairs—profit center and partner profit center, functional area and partner functional area, and so on. A simple allocation credits one cost center and debits another cost center but also potentially triggers a shift in profit centers, functional areas, and so on based on the cost center master data. These dimensions are also updated in the universal journal. What this means is that an allocation is no longer a posting that happens in Controlling and is subsequently represented in Financial Accounting, either by running transaction KALC or initiating a journal entry of type COFI, but that the allocation is simply a special type of journal entry.

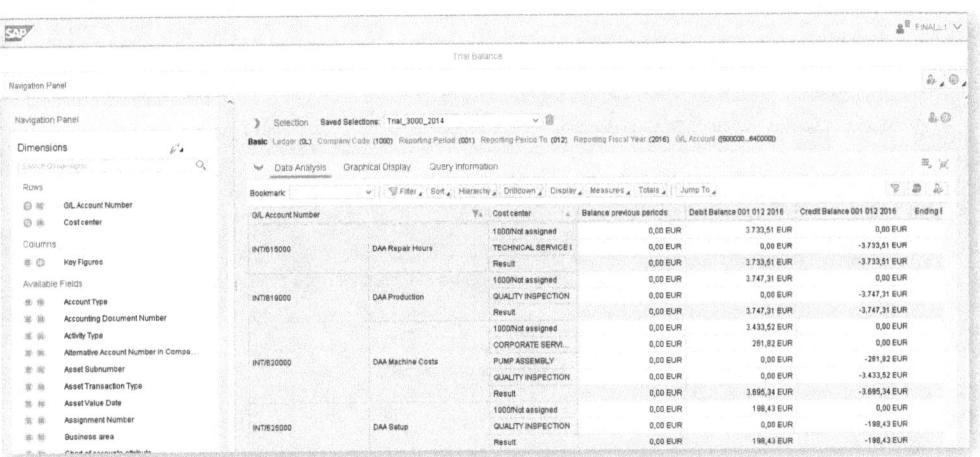

Figure 2.15: Trial balance showing the allocation for machine time

2.4.2 Cost elements and the general ledger

One of the fundamental changes with SAP S/4HANA Finance is that the secondary cost elements no longer exist in isolation but are themselves G/L accounts. The old transaction KA06 (Create Secondary Cost Element) now redirects you to transaction FS00 (Change G/L Account), as does the old transaction KA01 (Create Primary Cost Element). During migration, secondary cost elements are migrated to the G/L account tables (SKA1, SKB1, and SKAT) for all company codes assigned to the CO area. Figure 2.16 shows the G/L account master data for a secondary cost element for the allocation of machine costs (Cost Element Category 43). Each of the sender-receiver relationships that can occur as a result of an allocation are represented as before by a cost element category, giving you 43 for internal activity allocation (as shown in Figure 2.16), 21 for internal settlement, 41 for overhead rates, and 42 for assessment. The fundamental change with SAP S/4HANA Finance is that the document that records this value flow (cost center to order in Figure 2.15) credits the cost center and debits the order under a G/L account of type secondary cost element. It also updates any affected profit centers, segments, functional areas, and so on in a single sweep rather than generating a CO document and a reconciliation document in FI if the reporting dimensions change.

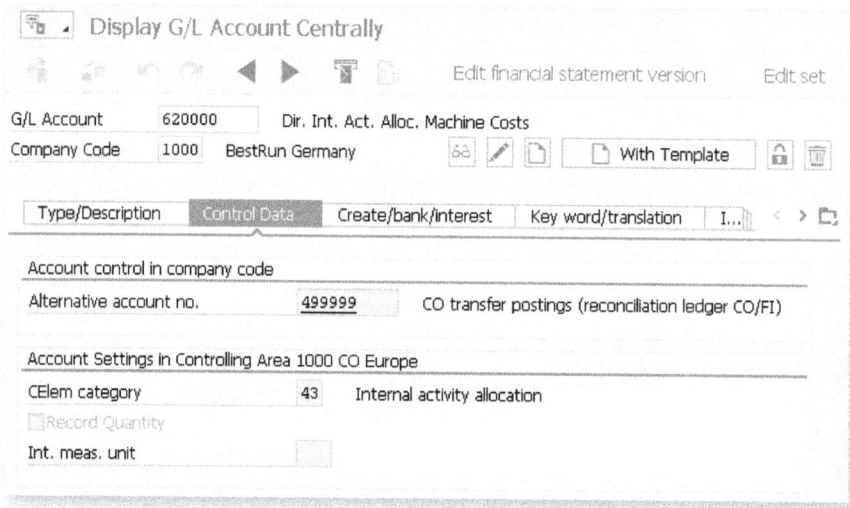

Figure 2.16: G/L account for a secondary cost element showing a cost element category

This link simplifies the closing process by ensuring that you do not need to reconcile to ensure the consistency of the FI and CO data. As you think about a *soft close*, consider activating an additional business function CO_ALLOCATIONS so that you can allocate overhead in real time. This will ensure that as you post material costs to a project, for example, the system checks the conditions in the costing sheet and assigns material overhead as appropriate, generating a double posting—one for the material costs and one for the overhead. The same principle applies to direct activity allocations and repostings where the appropriate overhead is calculated as a double posting to follow up from the allocation.

We have shown how all primary cost elements and most secondary cost elements are simply G/L accounts of the appropriate account type. The cost elements used to record work in process, results analysis, earned value, and so on must be considered an exception to this logic. Here, the calculated work in process is updated using a work in process cost element of cost element category 31 (Results Analysis) but settlement updates a WIP account of account type Non-Operating Expense or Income.

2.4.3 Ledgers and versions

We will come back to the version used in planning in Chapter 5, but for actual costs, versions were used for four purposes in Controlling:

- ► To handle group valuation (currency type 31)
- ► To handle profit center valuation (currency type 12 or 32)
- ► To handle parallel cost of goods manufactured (currency type 10)
- ► To handle parallel activity-based costing

With SAP S/4HANA Finance, the versions continue to be used for planning and to store target costs, variances, and results analysis data but there has been a fundamental redesign for the actual costs. As we discussed in Section 2.2.4, we can now use the **ledger** to handle all differences associated with the different accounting principles and the different valuation approaches. Note that this function is only available from edition 1605 and parallel cost of goods manufactured (business function FIN_CO_COGM) and parallel activity-based costing are not available at the time of writing, although parallel cost of goods manufactured should be released shortly.

2.5 Profitability Analysis

We have just looked at how cost centers, orders, projects, business processes, networks, and so on are recorded in the universal journal for reporting purposes. Account-based Profitability Analysis is based on the same idea, but the account assignment is **multidimensional**, being a combination of the various characteristics selected in your operating concern (typically, the product, customer, sales organization, and so on). If you have already worked with costing-based Profitability Analysis, the configuration steps will look similar in that you select the characteristics that you want to report against and set up derivation rules for those characteristics (such as product group, customer group, and region) that cannot be read straight from the invoice or delivery document but must be **derived** from the associated master data using look up tables and so on. What changes as Profitability Analysis becomes part of the universal journal is that you work with **accounts/cost elements** rather than value fields, so you have to make sure that all the relevant revenue accounts, sales deduction accounts, and cost of goods sold accounts that you want to see in your financial statements are defined as primary cost elements of the appropriate category (see Figure 2.6). This represents a significant change in the handling of cost of goods sold, since this account becomes a cost element and derives the CO-PA characteristics at the time of delivery rather than invoice. You must also check secondary cost elements (see Figure 2.16) that you use to settle or allocate to CO-PA to make sure that they provide sufficient transparency and that you are not just using a single settlement cost element to clear all orders and projects when you really want to distinguish the type of costs that are being selected for settlement.

2.5.1 Reporting dimensions in Profitability Analysis

A standard operating concern can have up to 50 characteristics (this limit still holds with SAP S/4HANA Finance) and as you activate the operating concern or migrate, the system generates a column in the universal journal for each of these characteristics. You can identify these postings by the entry E0 in the new ACCASTY (account assignment) field. Many are already available as standard characteristics but each industry generally has its own handful of characteristics (such as brand and category in the consumer goods industry) that are added to the operating concern and for which a column is generated in the universal journal. While it is generally considered best practice to have a single operating concern, if you do have multiple operating concerns, the system generates a column for every different characteristic but only fills lines for that operating concern.

Figure 2.17 shows the fields for the CO-PA characteristics in the universal journal. Remember that when you report, you can use *SAP Core Data Service (CDS)* views to include additional master data attributes, so do not try to put fields for every eventuality into the universal journal. If you used account-based Profitability Analysis in the past, you will know that there used to be settings to reduce the number of characteristics used in account-based Profitability Analysis compared to costing-based Profitability Analysis. Those settings are now obsolete and **all** characteristics in the operating concern are automatically in the universal journal. Table CE4 (with the characteristics) continues to exist for compatibility reasons, so classic reports, such as KE30, will continue to read it, but the new reports read directly from the universal journal. Remember also that the currency settings for Profitability Analysis are driven by the ledger, so you always have group currency and local currency and the option to add additional currencies as we discussed in Section 2.2.4.

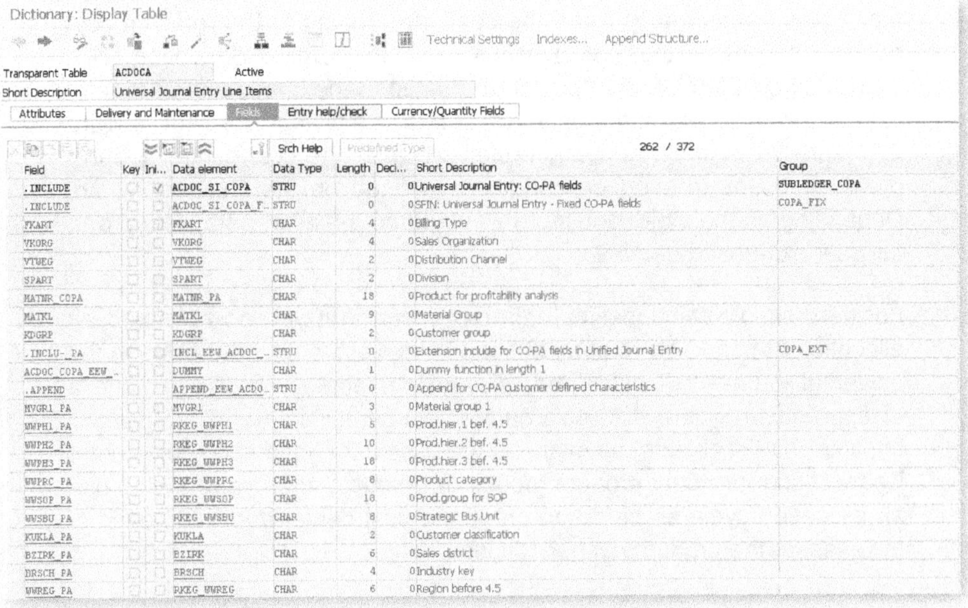

Dictionary: Display Table

Technical Settings   Indexes...   Append Structure...

Transparent Table: ACDOCA   Active
Short Description: Universal Journal Entry Line Items

Attributes | Delivery and Maintenance | Fields | Entry help/check | Currency/Quantity Fields

Srch Help   Predefined Type   262 / 372

Field	Key	Ini...	Data element	Data Type	Length	Deci...	Short Description	Group
.INCLUDE		✓	ACDOC_SI_COPA	STRU	0	0	Universal Journal Entry: CO-PA fields	SUBLEDGER_COPA
.INCLUDE			ACDOC_SI_COPA_F...	STRU	0	0	SFIN: Universal Journal Entry - Fixed CO-PA fields	COPA_FIX
FKART			FKART	CHAR	4	0	Billing Type	
VKORG			VKORG	CHAR	4	0	Sales Organization	
VTWEG			VTWEG	CHAR	2	0	Distribution Channel	
SPART			SPART	CHAR	2	0	Division	
MATNR_COPA			MATNR_PA	CHAR	18	0	Product for profitability analysis	
MATKL			MATKL	CHAR	9	0	Material Group	
KDGRP			KDGRP	CHAR	2	0	Customer group	
.INCLU-_PA			INCL_EEW_ACDOC_...	STRU	0	0	Extension include for CO-PA fields in Unified Journal Entry	COPA_EXT
ACDOC_COPA_EEW_...			DUMMY	CHAR	1	0	Dummy function in length 1	
.APPEND			APPEND_EEW_ACDO...	STRU	0	0	Append for CO-PA customer defined characteristics	
MVGR1_PA			MVGR1	CHAR	3	0	Material group 1	
WWPH1_PA			RKEG_WWPH1	CHAR	5	0	Prod.hier.1 bef. 4.5	
WWPH2_PA			RKEG_WWPH2	CHAR	10	0	Prod.hier.2 bef. 4.5	
WWPH3_PA			RKEG_WWPH3	CHAR	18	0	Prod.hier.3 bef. 4.5	
WWPRC_PA			RKEG_WWPRC	CHAR	8	0	Product category	
WWSOP_PA			RKEG_WWSOP	CHAR	18	0	Prod.group for SOP	
WWSBU_PA			RKEG_WWSBU	CHAR	8	0	Strategic Bus.Unit	
KUKLA_PA			KUKLA	CHAR	2	0	Customer classification	
BZIRK_PA			BZIRK	CHAR	6	0	Sales district	
BRSCH_PA			BRSCH	CHAR	4	0	Industry key	
WWREG_PA			RKEG_WWREG	CHAR	6	0	Region before 4.5	

Figure 2.17: Fields for CO-PA characteristics in the universal journal

As you think about the fields that you want to include in the universal journal, it also makes sense to think about what can be filled when. Usually, the richest information comes from the billing document, where you have full details of the customer, the product, and so on in the invoice. It is common to use summarization to remove the material detail from the invoice in the accounting document because it is not needed for open item management. By contrast, the universal journal can handle the detail of thousands of material lines. Derivation rules can populate additional fields for these material lines as before. For reporting purposes, what you effectively see is the document view **as posted**. If you need to change these assignments later, please be aware that a tool for reassigning characteristic values retrospectively (reorganization) is available from edition 1610. You can use this to make corrections if your organizational structure changes or to adjust the CO-PA characteristics after the fact.

As you think about other lines for settlement, allocation, and so on, it is worth investigating the new options for *real-time derivation* for cost centers, orders, and projects. The idea is that instead of waiting for period close and running an allocation to bring costs from the marketing cost center to the region it serves, you can set up derivation rules to update the region **immediately** when the costs are posted to the relevant cost center. You set up these derivations using the familiar derivation rules (transaction KEDR). As the costs are posted to the cost center, the relevant CO-PA columns in the universal journal are filled accordingly. Figure 2.18 shows a sample derivation rule that takes the cost center and derives the country based on conditions defined on the CONDITION tab. Depending on the logic required, this might be a master data lookup or a full user exit-based derivation.

For very simple relationships, this can mean that you do not need an allocation at period close at all but can immediately extend the line in the universal journal to include the relevant characteristics. If you have a *disaggregation* where the costs on the cost center are to be assigned to multiple CO-PA objects, as might be the case if the marketing cost center was working for many product groups or products, then you have to use an allocation cycle as before to credit the cost center and debit each of the lines for the products at period close.

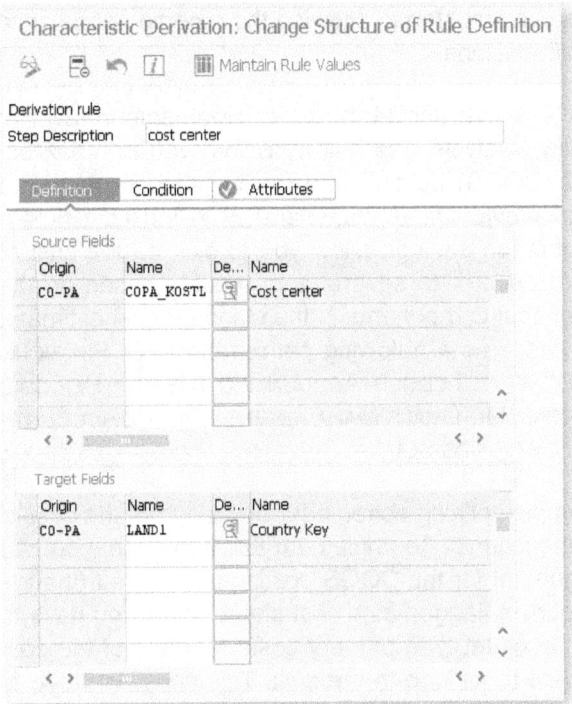

Figure 2.18: Derivation rule for deriving the country from the cost center

This approach works extremely well for project costs, where the CO-PA characteristics such as customer and product can easily be derived from the associated sales order item, meaning that you do not have to settle at all. Again, this only works if you have a single settlement receiver in CO-PA. If you want to settle to multiple receivers, you have to settle using distribution rules containing the relevant receiver objects as before.

If you capture work in process or reserves for unrealized costs for commercial projects, settlement creates a journal entry at period close that does not update CO-PA because these items are considered period costs rather than cost of goods sold. If you want to assign the work in process to the CO-PA dimensions, you can set up a derivation rule to read the settlement rule for the WBS element and derive the relevant customer, product, and so on. Classic reports, such as transaction KE30, will not show the work in process because the account assignment is not EO, but the new project reports will show the work in process by customer and product. This is a first step to allowing the reporting of balance sheet items by CO-PA dimensions.

Prior to SAP S/4HANA Finance, one of the other arguments in favor of costing-based Profitability Analysis was that it allowed you to break out the cost of goods sold (COGS) posting and the variance posting into separate value fields to provide more transparency in the cost break-down. Now, new configuration settings allow you to pick up the cost of goods sold posting and repost it to several subaccounts based on the weighting of the different cost components in the standard cost estimate. To configure this split, choose the following path in the IMG: FINANCIAL ACCOUNTING (NEW) • GENERAL LEDGER ACCOUNTING (NEW) • PERIODIC PROCESSING • INTEGRATION • MATERIALS MANAGEMENT • DEFINE ACCOUNTS FOR SPLITTING THE COST OF GOODS SOLD.

Figure 2.19 shows a sample splitting scheme for breaking out the cost of goods sold into four subaccounts. To implement this approach, you can leave the account assignment for the COGS posting unchanged (though make sure that the account is flagged as a cost element) but you have to create new accounts of account type primary costs for each of the cost components that you want to include in the split. This does not have to be a 1:1 assignment—you can also assign multiple cost components to one account.

Change View "Detailed COGS Accounts": Overview

New Entries

Splitting of Cost of Goods Sold		
Splitting Scheme	COGS Split Scheme	SCHEME1
Detailed COGS Accounts	Chart of Accts	CAUS
Company Code Assignment	Cost Comp. Str.	01

Detailed COGS Accounts

COGS Acct	CComp	Name of Cost Compon...	Target Acc	Short Text	Default
893015	10	Raw Materials	893017	GS-Material	☐
893015	30	Production Labor	893016	COGS-Labour	☐
893015	80	Material Overhead	893018	COGS-Overhead	
893015	120	Other Costs	893019	COGS-Others	☑
893115	10	Raw Materials	893117	COGS-Material	☐
893115	30	Production Labor	893116	COGS-Labour	☐
893115	80	Material Overhead	893118	COGS-Overhead	☐
893115	120	Other Costs	893119	COGS-Others	☑

Figure 2.19: Splitting scheme for COGS accounts

Figure 2.20 shows a COGS posting based on these settings. Note that the account assignment is always to the market segment in CO-PA. We see that the delivery is posted as before and then reversed. The total COGS value is then split according to the configuration in Figure 2.19 to create four new posting line items under the appropriate accounts/cost elements.

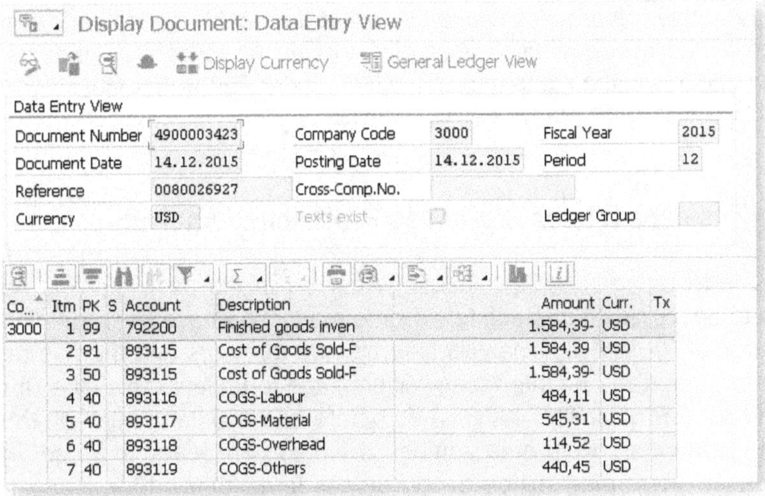

Co...	Itm	PK	S	Account	Description	Amount	Curr.	Tx
3000	1	99		792200	Finished goods inven	1.584,39-	USD	
	2	81		893115	Cost of Goods Sold-F	1.584,39	USD	
	3	50		893115	Cost of Goods Sold-F	1.584,39-	USD	
	4	40		893116	COGS-Labour	484,11	USD	
	5	40		893117	COGS-Material	545,31	USD	
	6	40		893118	COGS-Overhead	114,52	USD	
	7	40		893119	COGS-Others	440,45	USD	

Figure 2.20: Cost document for splitting

While this might seem like a new way of implementing the valuation strategy with which you could assign the standard cost component split to value fields in costing-based Profitability Analysis, there is a critical difference: note at the top of the screen in Figure 2.19 that we can use exactly **one** cost component structure (COST COMP. STR.). In an account view, we can explain the cost of goods sold either in terms of the cost of goods manufactured (the main cost component split) or in terms of the primary cost components (the auxiliary cost component split) but not both. In account-based CO-PA, you have to opt for **one** cost component structure.

Further new settings allow you to break out the production variances and repost to several subaccounts. Again, choose the following path in the IMG: FINANCIAL ACCOUNTING (NEW) • GENERAL LEDGER ACCOUNTING (NEW) • PERIODIC PROCESSING • INTEGRATION • MATERIALS MANAGEMENT • DEFINE ACCOUNTS FOR SPLITTING PRICE DIFFERENCES.

In the past, you were also only able to capture the delivery quantity in the delivery unit of measure. The universal journal also includes new columns for extra quantities if you need them for your sales reporting. To access the configuration, choose CONTROLLING • GENERAL CONTROLLING • ADDITIO-NAL QUANTITIES • DEFINE ADDITIONAL QUANTITY FIELDS in the IMG. You can then use a BADI to convert the delivery quantity into the unit of measure of your choice. A sample BADI FCO_HOME_COEP_QUANTITY is delivered to illustrate how the process works but you will probably create your own BADI to fill the new quantities according to your business requirements. You can find this in the same part of the IMG under ADDITIONAL QUANTITIES • BADI: INTERFACE FOR ADDITIONAL QUANTITIES.

2.5.2 The case for costing-based Profitability Analysis

If you used costing-based Profitability Analysis in the past, there is no reason to deactivate it immediately. Some customers have been running both types of Profitability Analysis side by side for years and there is no reason to stop now. The interfaces will continue to update table CE1 (for costing-based Profitability Analysis) as before and you can switch off the update via the controlling area settings when you are ready to do so. In some cases, there may still be good reasons for continuing to use cost-ing-based Profitability Analysis.

▶ Account-based Profitability Analysis captures record types F (billing), B (direct posting from FI), C (order and project settle-ment) and D (allocations), so if you are using other record types, such as A (sales order entry), you may want to continue using costing-based Profitability Analysis.

▶ Account-based Profitability Analysis, as the name implies, cap-tures accounts, so if you have sales conditions that map to value fields but not to accounts, you either need to change your ac-count determination to find true accounts or if they should remain statistical, such as statistical freight costs or sales deductions, you may want to continue using costing-based Profitability Anal-ysis.

▶ Account-based Profitability Analysis is inherently reconciled with General Ledger Accounting so the cost estimate will always be the one used to value the goods movement. If you capture multi-ple cost estimates to represent different planning assumptions, you may want to continue using costing-based Profitability Anal-ysis.

▶ At the time of writing, the settlement of actual costs from Actual Costing updates a single account rather than subaccounts for the various cost components.

Certainly, no one approach is better than the other. The approaches are different and complement one another. The account approach is inherently reconciled with General Ledger Accounting so there is always one revenue line item with the associated CO-PA characteristics, whereas the costing-based approach gives you more freedom in that you can capture different assumptions and statistical costs in your profitability model. If you run only costing-based Profitability Analysis without account-based Profitability Analysis, then allocations and settlements are not assigned to profitability segments (account assignment type EO) but only to reconciliation objects (account assignment type AO). These simply ensure that all secondary cost postings balance but do not give you the full details you need for analysis.

2.6 Material Ledger

Just as there are two types of Profitability Analysis, there are two types of Material Ledger.

▶ When most people talk about the Material Ledger, they mean *Actual Costing*. The Material Ledger is used to track goods movements, invoices, and order settlements and then calculate a *weighted average cost* (the periodic unit price) using one or more costing runs at period close. This option continues to be supported in SAP S/4HANA for industries that regularly use Actual Costing, such as chemicals, pharmaceuticals, and food, and countries that require Actual Costing, such as Brazil, but the use of Actual Costing is **not** compulsory in SAP S/4HANA.

▶ The other option is to use the Material Ledger as an *inventory subledger* that captures inventory values in multiple currencies. This inventory subledger is also needed to store group valuations and transfer prices based on standard costs. This option is **compulsory** in SAP S/4HANA and is activated during migration, writing the inventory values in multiple currencies to the universal journal.

Figure 2.21 shows the fields for the Material Ledger in the universal journal. Note that the fields include all types of special stocks relating to the material.

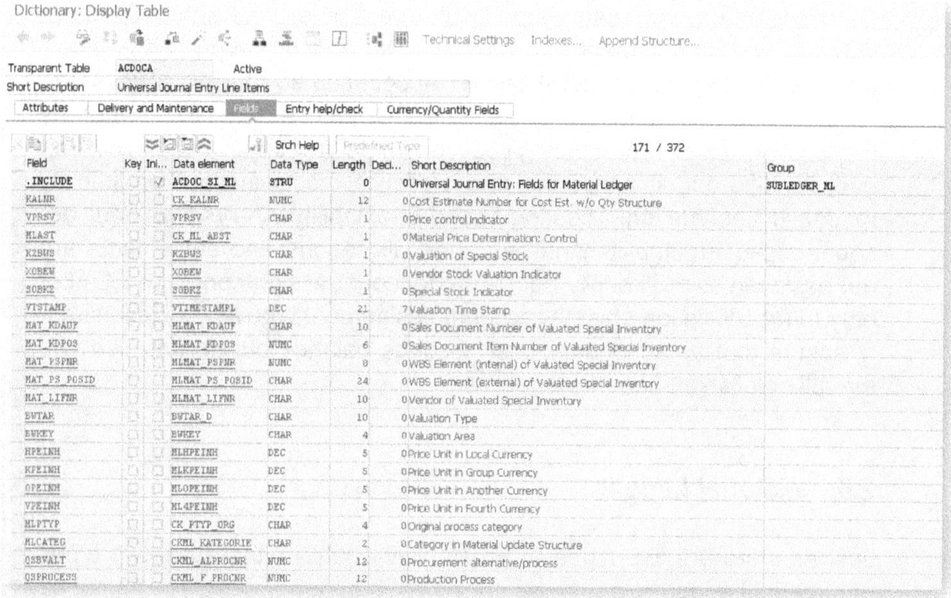
Dictionary: Display Table

Technical Settings Indexes... Append Structure...

Transparent Table ACDOCA Active

Short Description Universal Journal Entry Line Items

Attributes | Delivery and Maintenance | Fields | Entry help/check | Currency/Quantity Fields

Srch Help Predefined Type 171 / 372

Field	Key	Ini...	Data element	Data Type	Length	Deci...	Short Description	Group
.INCLUDE		✓	ACDOC_SI_ML	STRU	0	0	Universal Journal Entry: Fields for Material Ledger	SUBLEDGER_ML
KALNR			CK_KALNR	NUMC	12	0	Cost Estimate Number for Cost Est. w/o Qty Structure	
VPRSV			VPRSV	CHAR	1	0	Price control Indicator	
MLAST			CK_ML_ABST	CHAR	1	0	Material Price Determination: Control	
KZBWS			KZBWS	CHAR	1	0	Valuation of Special Stock	
XOBEW			XOBEW	CHAR	1	0	Vendor Stock Valuation Indicator	
SOBKZ			SOBKZ	CHAR	1	0	Special Stock Indicator	
VTSTAMP			VTIMESTAMPL	DEC	21	7	Valuation Time Stamp	
MAT_KDAUF			MLMAT_KDAUF	CHAR	10	0	Sales Document Number of Valuated Special Inventory	
MAT_KDPOS			MLMAT_KDPOS	NUMC	6	0	Sales Document Item Number of Valuated Special Inventory	
MAT_PSPNR			MLMAT_PSPNR	NUMC	8	0	WBS Element (internal) of Valuated Special Inventory	
MAT_PS_POSID			MLMAT_PS_POSID	CHAR	24	0	WBS Element (external) of Valuated Special Inventory	
MAT_LIFNR			MLMAT_LIFNR	CHAR	10	0	Vendor of Valuated Special Inventory	
BWTAR			BWTAR_D	CHAR	10	0	Valuation Type	
BWKEY			BWKEY	CHAR	4	0	Valuation Area	
HPEINH			MLHPEINH	DEC	5	0	Price Unit in Local Currency	
KPEINH			MLKPEINH	DEC	5	0	Price Unit in Group Currency	
OPEINH			MLOPEINH	DEC	5	0	Price Unit in Another Currency	
VPEINH			ML4PEINH	DEC	5	0	Price Unit in Fourth Currency	
MLPTYP			CK_PTYP_ORG	CHAR	4	0	Original process category	
MLCATEG			CKML_KATEGORIE	CHAR	2	0	Category in Material Update Structure	
QSBVALT			CKML_ALPROCNR	NUMC	12	0	Procurement alternative/process	
QSPROCESS			CKML_F_PROCNR	NUMC	12	0	Production Process	

Figure 2.21: Fields for the Material Ledger in the universal journal

As you think about the impact of collecting inventory data in the universal journal, you should also be aware that from SAP S/4HANA 1511, the data model for Inventory Management (MM-IM) changes radically. With the switch to the Material Ledger, the inventory valuation tables in MM that used to be accessed directly from the ACCOUNTING view material master, such as EBEW and EBEWH (Sales Order Stock Valuation), MBEW and MBEWH (Material Valuation), OBEW and OBEWH (Subcontractor Stock Valuation), and QBEW and QBEWH (Project Stock Valuation), are replaced and the stock values read directly from the Material Ledger. What we see here is an example of the *principle of one* applied to inventory valuation, where we used to have two documents, one in MM-IM (Inventory Management) and one in ML (Material Ledger), and now have a single document.

The removal of aggregates that began in Finance continues in Inventory Management, so where totals tables were used to store the inventory figures for a plant, a storage location, or to store the values of special stocks—such as project stock, sales order stock, stock in transit, and so on—we now find these values being aggregated on the fly from the new transactional table MATDOC. Pure aggregate tables that store the values by stock type have been removed completely, while others remain where they are needed to store genuine master data (such as the name and description, the weight, the assignment to a profit center, and so on) but aggregate the total inventory figures on the fly. These are known as *hybrid tables* on account of their dual purpose in former releases.

- ▶ There is a new document table MATDOC which records all goods movements. Just as we learnt in Chapter 1 when we looked at the case for removing aggregate tables in Finance, this new table accelerates processing because you can now record a goods movement simply by inserting a new document into the database without locking the associated master data tables.

- ▶ Tables such as MARC (Plant Data for Material), MARD (Storage Location Data for Material), and MCHB (Batch Stocks) still exist to store product attributes which do not change regularly. However, they are no longer used to store aggregated stock values and instead, the data is aggregated on the fly from the new table MATDOC.

- ▶ The tables for vendor stock, sales order stock, project stock, and stock in transit have been removed completely and all inventory values are aggregated on the fly from the new table MATDOC.

- ▶ The extra history tables that used to exist for all the inventory tables MARCH, MARDH, MCHBH, and so on have been removed.

Details of new Inventory Management

 Because the new Inventory Management is very new, check out the requirements and watch for updates via SAP Note 2267788. (*https://launchpad.support.sap.com/#/notes/0002194618*)

If you have not worked with the Material Ledger before, Figure 2.22 shows the material master for a raw material using the transaction-based Material Ledger (PRICE DETERMINATION 2). Inventory values are stored in three currencies: company code currency, group currency, and in this case a hard currency. We will use this example to understand the implications of the new Inventory Management.

- ▶ Fields such as DIVISION, VALUATION CLASS, VALUATION CATEGORY, PRICE CONTROL, and so on are *product attributes* and will continue to be stored in the old master data tables.

- ▶ The STANDARD PRICE and PERIODIC UNIT PRICE fields are stored in the Material Ledger. Note that if you use transaction-based price determination, you can still use a moving average price that recalculates the price with every goods movement and invoice receipt.

- ▶ Inventory levels are calculated on the fly from the new table MATDOC.

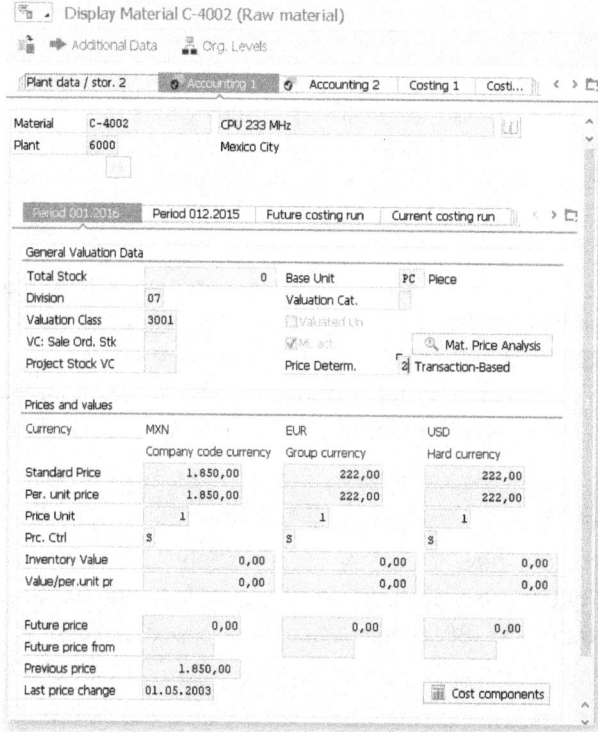

Figure 2.22: Material master using transaction-based Material Ledger

Now that we have looked at the main aspects of SAP Accounting, we will turn our attention to SAP Cash Management.

3 SAP Cash Management powered by SAP HANA

With SAP HANA, the SAP component Cash Management has also been completely revised and adapted to the requirements of a modern finance organization. In this chapter, you learn how the *Bank Account Management* component can support you in organizing your bank accounts in the company. You also learn about the enhanced functionalities and new features in *Cash Operations* and get an insight into SAP's *Liquidity Management* component.

The requirements in the financial services area have changed significantly in recent years. One of the reasons for this was almost certainly the introduction of the Single Euro Payments Area. As well as introducing standardized legal framework conditions, SEPA was a first step towards harmonizing standardized payment media within Europe.

European standards were developed based on ISO 20022 formats. These standards have since been supplemented by the global formats of the Common Global Implementation Market Practice (CGI-MP).

Common Global Implementation Market Practice (CGI-MP)

 The CGI-MP is based on the numerous ISO 20022 format standards. The guidelines for defining the formats were developed in different working groups. Existing standards are subject to continuous further development and are published on an ongoing basis. For more information about the tasks and content of the CGI-MP, see *www.swift.com/cgi*.

In addition to this further development of payment media, new business models are coming to the forefront. In the future, instant payments should make payments significantly faster than was previously possible via bank and payment service providers.

Alongside existing banks, new companies are being founded from the field of financial technology (FinTech). These companies are pushing onto the market with products and services that classic banks currently do not offer in their solution portfolio. Thanks to this diversification, the companies can derive numerous strategies for improved cash and liquidity management and improve their internal payment transaction processes sustainably.

However, the downside to all these new features is the difficulty in implementing them in an efficient and modern cash management solution. Today, information from payment flows is available much more quickly than even just a couple of years ago. The resulting data volumes have grown and require a higher maintenance effort in ERP systems. The ISO 20022 formats are a further contributory factor to this growth in data volume.

With *SAP Cash Management powered by SAP HANA* (hereinafter referred to as *Cash Management*), many of the demands arising from these new framework conditions for payment transactions have been addressed and implemented: the required data models have been adapted and the solution portfolio for payment transactions and cash management extended. For example, since edition 1503, in addition to electronic bank statement processing, the SAP Treasury solution map offers the following solutions in the area of cash and liquidity management:

- ▶ Bank Account Management
- ▶ Cash Operations
- ▶ Liquidity Management

The conceptual design for the applications in Cash Management has been implemented almost completely with Fiori apps. Numerous transactional and analytical (SAP Smart Business) apps can be assigned to users from catalogs or based on roles.

Fiori apps reference library

The Fiori apps reference library provides an overview of all available applications. It contains information about installation and configuration, as well as documentation and examples for the respective application software. You can access the library here:

https://fioriappslibrary.hana.ondemand.com/sap/fix/externalViewer/#

The apps in Cash Management have a clear and simple structure and thus support the user in time-critical tasks such as the daily checking and planning of open item accounts. There is also significantly more flexibility in the design and execution of evaluations for this area in comparison to classic Cash Management.

Configuration guide for SAP Cash Management powered by SAP HANA

SAP Note 2233404 provides a configuration guide for SAP Cash Management powered by SAP HANA with the required Customizing and configuration steps. Note 2233405 contains the related data setup guide for SAP Cash Management powered by SAP HANA.

The following pages provide an initial overview of the new functionalities in the following areas:

▶ Bank account management

▶ Liquidity management

▶ Daily cash transactions

We will use examples to illustrate the information.

Development and scope of functions

Even though we are currently experiencing rapid development in the field of SAP HANA, it is still worth noting that in some areas, we are only just at the very beginning of fully comprehensive solutions. The scope of functions in SAP Cash Management powered by SAP HANA is subject to ongoing further development in the development cycles. Any existing gaps in this area are therefore constantly being closed and the functionalities adapted to the needs of a modern cash management function. Therefore, in your system, you may encounter slight variations to the functions presented below.

3.1 Bank Account Management

In addition to the core cash management tasks, such as planning liquid funds or controlling payment flows, today, companies are faced with a greater effort for managing bank accounts.

The *Bank Account Management (BAM)* component from SAP provides a solution that allows you to map the management of bank accounts in one integrated process. A central account administration ensures that all of a company's bank accounts can be managed efficiently and transparently from one point.

Electronic Bank Account Management (eBAM)

In addition to organizing bank accounts on a paper basis, you can also use the ISO 20022 message types to manage accounts electronically. Via *eBAM*, banks and companies can exchange standardized XML messages. The Working Group (WG4) of the *Common Global Implementation Market Practice Initiative (CGI-MP)* is responsible for the further development and harmonization of the *acmt* message standard. For further details and information on this message type, see the SWIFT website: *www.swift.com/cgi*. There are currently no plans to extend SAP Bank Account Management to support eBAM.

If you have activated SAP Cash Management powered by SAP HANA in your system, BAM takes over the central role in managing your bank accounts. Compared to classic bank account management, in BAM, a bank account can only be used if it has been previously activated via a workflow process.

This ensures that bank accounts can only be opened, changed, or closed from one central point.

There are numerous SAP standard functionalities that support you in these processes. If you need further or different logic in your overall process, or want to use your own logic, you can implement this using enhancement options available in Customizing, such as Business Add-Ins (BAdIs) or workflow templates.

In contrast to the primarily consistent use of apps in SAP Cash Management powered by SAP HANA, you can also access BAM via NetWeaver Business Client (NWBC) (see Figure 3.1).

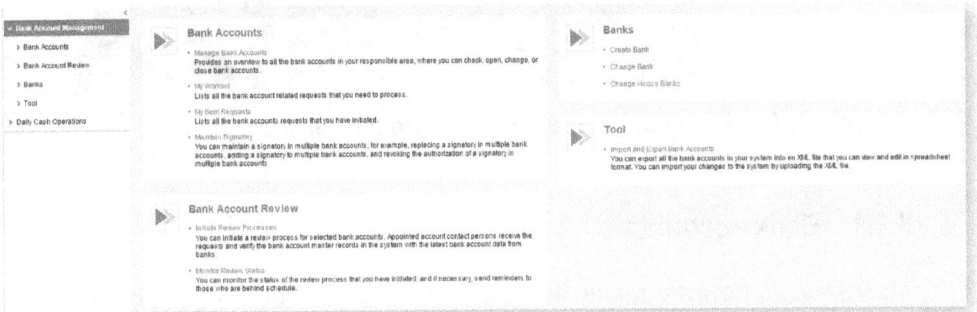

Figure 3.1: Bank Account Management in NetWeaver Business Client

Parallel to managing bank accounts via NWBC, the required apps are also displayed via the tile catalog (see Figure 3.2). For the examples in this book, we use Bank Account Management via NWBC.

With NWBC, you can currently use both portal-based and classic SAP GUI-based transactions regardless of the release you are using. For example, the creation of memo records (transaction FF63) for daily cash transactions has been integrated into the BAM functionalities. In the sections below, we will look at the relevant menu items in NWBC.

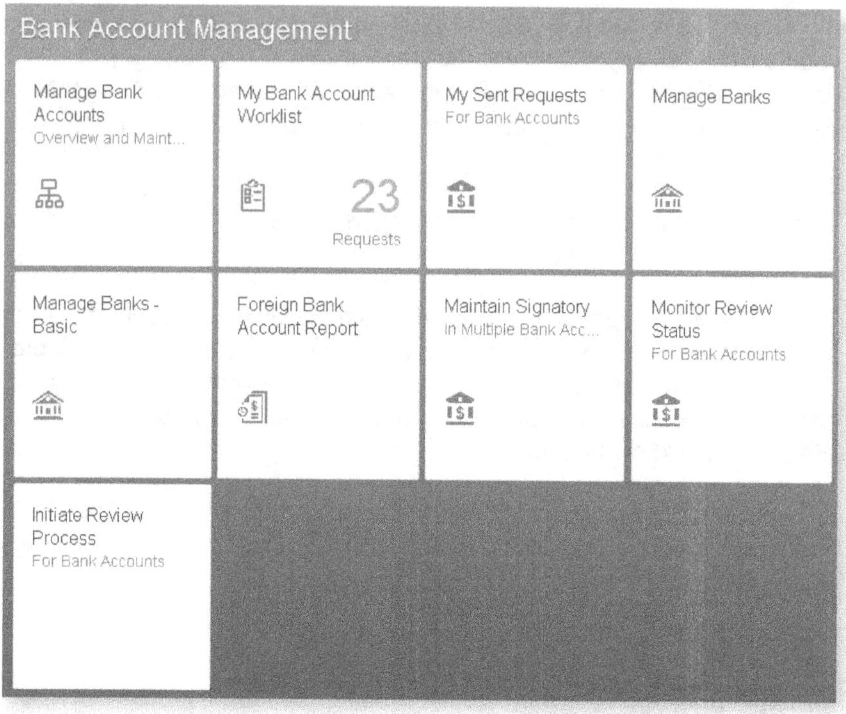

Figure 3.2: Bank Account Management in the tile catalog

3.1.1 Bank accounts

The BANK ACCOUNTS menu item contains the central components of Bank Account Management, such as opening or changing accounts. Here you will find various worklists for bank account requests and you can also maintain the signatories for your bank accounts. We will now look at the options available under this menu item.

Manage Bank Accounts

First click the MANAGE BANK ACCOUNTS menu item. A standard view of all accounts currently managed in Bank Account Management is displayed (see Figure 3.3).

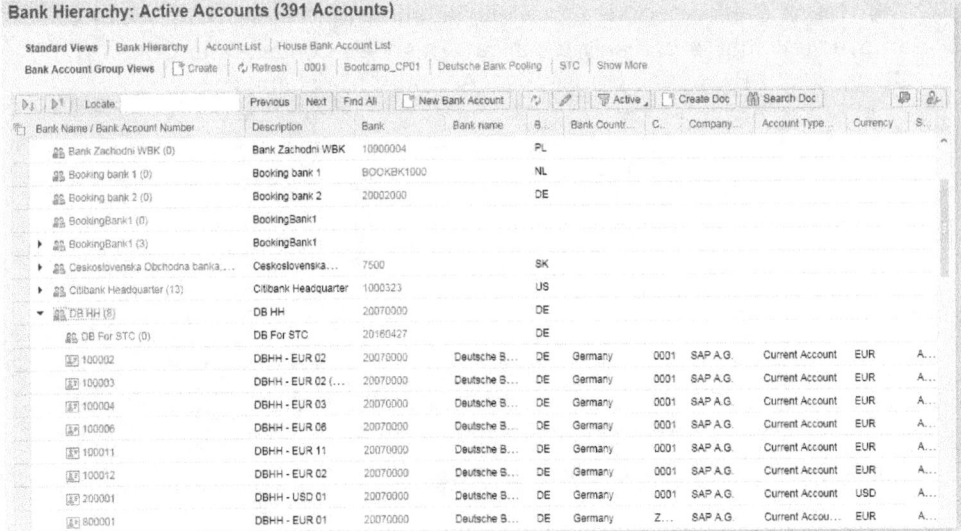

Figure 3.3: Overview of the Bank Hierarchy

Here, you can switch between the different standard views by selecting:

▶ Bank Hierarchy

▶ Account List

▶ House Bank Account List

The Bank Hierarchy has a tree structure. As shown in Figure 3.3, the accounts assigned are presented by bank in the Bank Name column. In the Account List view, the accounts are merely presented in a list form (see Figure 3.4). Here you can use the Fuzzy Search field to search for banks. The columns provide further flexible sorting and grouping options.

Account Number	Description	Bank	Bank Number	Bank name	Bank Country
000432725	Account test	123-456	123-456	ANZ Banking Corporation	AU
000432725	Migrated from BAM	0032044	0032044	Westpac Banking Corporation	AU
000432756	Migrated from BAM	0032044	0032044	Westpac Banking Corporation	AU
000812202	Migrated from BAM	0032091	0032091	Westpac Banking Corporation	AU

Figure 3.4: Display of active accounts

The HOUSE BANK ACCOUNT LIST view, as shown in Figure 3.5, provides an overview that is primarily technical. This view contains the COMPANY CODE, HOUSE BANK, and HOUSE BANK ACCOUNT ID columns.

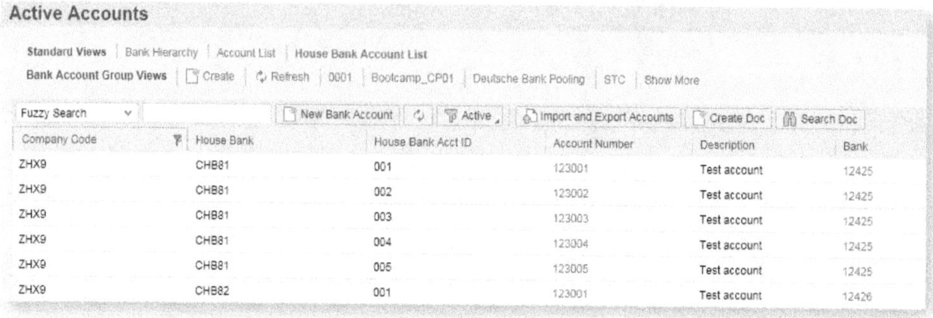

Active Accounts

Standard Views | Bank Hierarchy | Account List | **House Bank Account List**
Bank Account Group Views | Create | Refresh | 0001 | Bootcamp_CP01 | Deutsche Bank Pooling | STC | Show More

Fuzzy Search | | New Bank Account | | Active | Import and Export Accounts | Create Doc | Search Doc

Company Code	House Bank	House Bank Acct ID	Account Number	Description	Bank
ZHX9	CHB81	001	123001	Test account	12425
ZHX9	CHB81	002	123002	Test account	12425
ZHX9	CHB81	003	123003	Test account	12425
ZHX9	CHB81	004	123004	Test account	12425
ZHX9	CHB81	005	123005	Test account	12425
ZHX9	CHB82	001	123001	Test account	12426

Figure 3.5: HOUSE BANK ACCOUNT LIST view

All of these presentation options give you a global or higher level view of the bank accounts in the company or group. In some cases, however, these views may be too extensive. If you need a regional or bank-based view of your accounts instead, you can define your own, user-based views via the BANK ACCOUNT GROUP VIEWS menu item. To do so, click Create to access the BANK ACCOUNT GROUP menu item as shown in Figure 3.6 and then enter a name for the group in the BANK ACCOUNT GROUP field in the header.

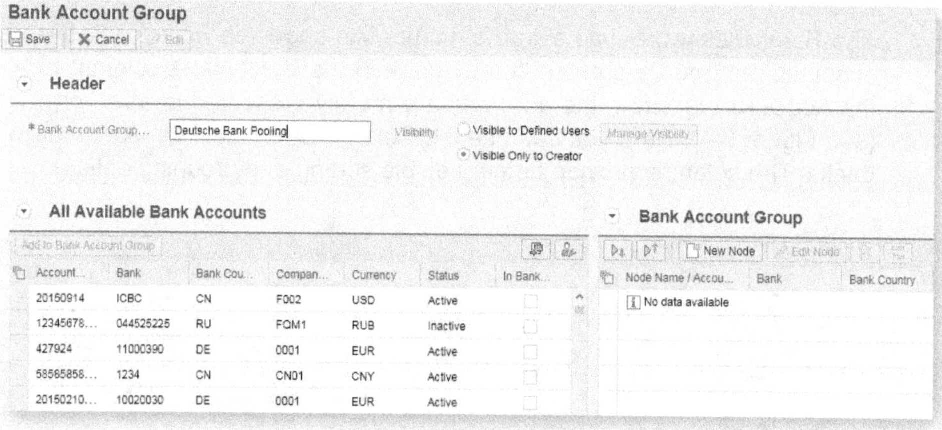

Bank Account Group

Save | Cancel | Edit

▾ **Header**

* Bank Account Group... | Deutsche Bank Pooling | Visibility: ○ Visible to Defined Users | Manage Visibility
● Visible Only to Creator

▾ **All Available Bank Accounts**   ▾ **Bank Account Group**

Add to Bank Account Group

Account...	Bank	Bank Cou...	Compan...	Currency	Status	In Bank...
20150914	ICBC	CN	F002	USD	Active	
12345678...	044525225	RU	FQM1	RUB	Inactive	
427924	11000390	DE	0001	EUR	Active	
58565858...	1234	CN	CN01	CNY	Active	
20150210...	10020030	DE	0001	EUR	Active	

Node Name / Accou...	Bank	Bank Country
No data available		

New Node | Edit Node

Figure 3.6: Defining an individual bank account group

In the next step, define whether the group should be visible for you alone or for other users as well. Then click ⬚ New Node in the right-hand part of the screen under BANK ACCOUNT GROUP to create a node that will contain your accounts (see Figure 3.7). Confirm your entry by clicking OK.

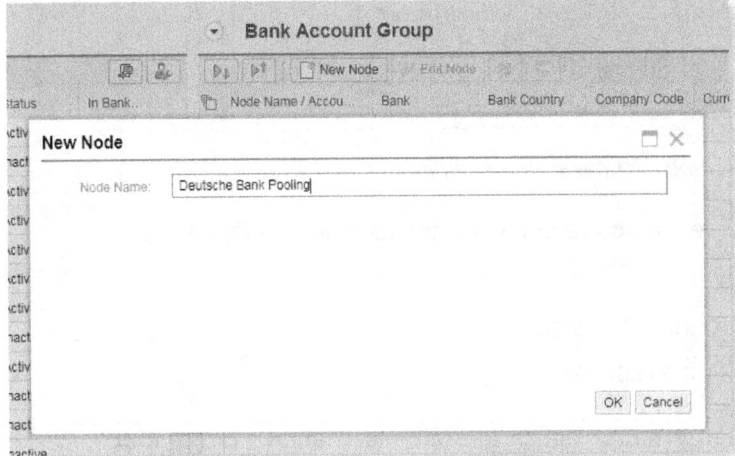

Figure 3.7: Creating a new node in a bank account group

The system takes you back to the view shown in Figure 3.6. In the BANK ACCOUNT GROUP area, select the node you have just created and in the left-hand area, ALL AVAILABLE BANK ACCOUNTS, identify the accounts to be included under the node. Click ⬚ Add to Bank Account Group to add the accounts to your list. Save your entries by clicking ⬚ Save .

Once you have refreshed the view, the account group that you defined in the menu for the bank account groups is displayed (see Figure 3.8).

Deutsche Bank Pooling: Active Accounts (2 Accounts)						
Standard Views	Bank Hierarchy	Account List	House Bank Account List			
Bank Account Group Views	Create	Refresh	0001	Bootcamp_CP01	Deutsche Bank Pooling	STC
Locate:		Previous	Next	Find All		Active	Cash Pool
Bank Name / Bank Account Number	Description	Bank	Bank name	B...	Bank C
▼					
123456789	Girokonto in Euro...	12070000	Deutsche Bank	DE	Germa
201502100003	Test	10020030	Deutsche Bank	DE	Germa

Figure 3.8: Own bank account group views

You can navigate directly to the account details from all of the views available under the STANDARD VIEWS and BANK ACCOUNT GROUP VIEWS menu items. To do so, click an account and call up the detailed information.

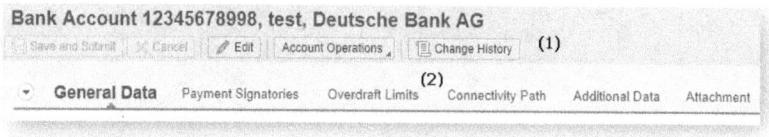

Figure 3.9: Detailed menu for a bank account

Here you see the **active** options in the toolbar (see Figure 3.9):

▶ EDIT

▶ ACCOUNT OPERATIONS

▶ CHANGE HISTORY

You can use the EDIT option to switch to change mode and then make changes to the account—for example, to adjust the overdraft limit or make changes to the general data. Via the ACCOUNT OPERATIONS option, you can start the workflow process for closing an account, for creating a new account, or for copying an existing account. Using the CHANGE HISTORY option, you can get an overview of all of the changes that have been made for the account.

Beneath the toolbar ❶, the menu bar ❷ provides you with further setting options. You can choose from the following tabs:

▶ GENERAL DATA

▶ PAYMENT SIGNATORIES

▶ OVERDRAFT LIMITS

▶ CONNECTIVITY-PATH

▶ ADDITIONAL DATA

▶ ATTACHMENT

Here, numerous fields and functions have been added to the bank master data as we know it from classic Bank Account Management (transaction FI12). We will now look at these functions in more detail.

Function: General Data

In addition to the basic data such as the account and bank details, the GENERAL DATA tab contains a number of additional fields (see Figure 3.10) which are the basis for numerous apps in Cash Operations. Via the BANK STATEMENT DATA area, for example, you control the import method and import channel for your bank statements. Using the BANK STATEMENT CHECK TIME field, you can check the status of the import operation for your bank statements in Cash Operations.

In the PAYMENT DATA area, also referred to as the **cut-off times**, you define the latest possible time of submission of a payment at your house bank. In the BANK CONTACT PERSONS and INTERNAL CONTACT PERSONS areas, you define the respective contact persons whom you can contact if necessary.

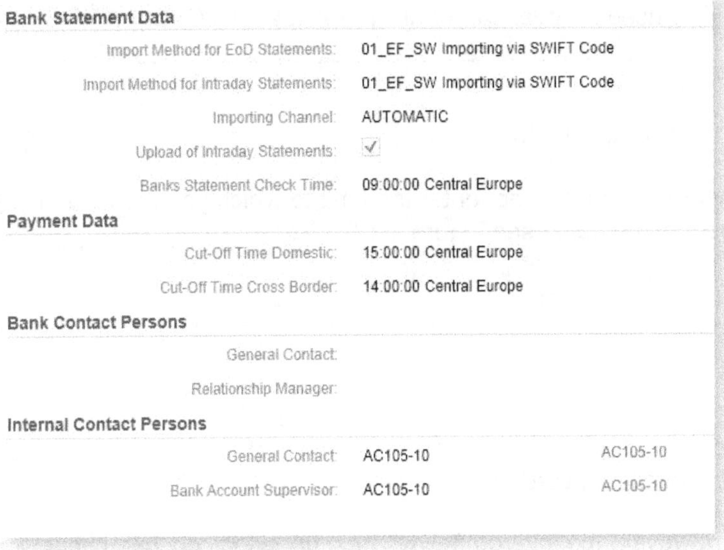

Bank Statement Data

Import Method for EoD Statements:	01_EF_SW Importing via SWIFT Code
Import Method for Intraday Statements:	01_EF_SW Importing via SWIFT Code
Importing Channel:	AUTOMATIC
Upload of Intraday Statements:	✓
Banks Statement Check Time:	09:00:00 Central Europe

Payment Data

Cut-Off Time Domestic:	15:00:00 Central Europe
Cut-Off Time Cross Border:	14:00:00 Central Europe

Bank Contact Persons

General Contact:	
Relationship Manager:	

Internal Contact Persons

General Contact:	AC105-10	AC105-10
Bank Account Supervisor:	AC105-10	AC105-10

Figure 3.10: Optional fields under GENERAL DATA

Function: Payment Signatories

On the PAYMENT SIGNATORIES tab, you can define signatories who can then subsequently authorize payments for the bank account. You can group these signatories in different groups in the SIGNATORY GROUP and under MAXIMUM AMOUNT.... columns, define maximum amounts per payment. You can also define a validity period (see Figure 3.11).

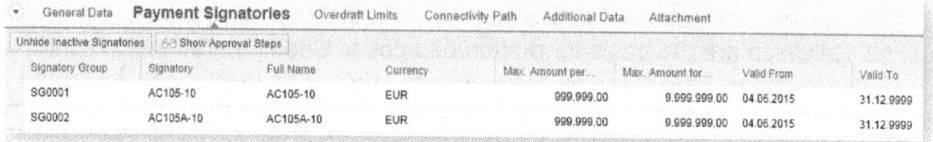

Signatory Group	Signatory	Full Name	Currency	Max. Amount per...	Max. Amount for...	Valid From	Valid To
SG0001	AC105-10	AC105-10	EUR	999.999,00	9.999.999,00	04.06.2015	31.12.9999
SG0002	AC105A-10	AC105A-10	EUR	999.999,00	9.999.999,00	04.06.2015	31.12.9999

General Data · Payment Signatories · Overdraft Limits · Connectivity Path · Additional Data · Attachment

Unhide Inactive Signatories · Show Approval Steps

Figure 3.11: Detailed view for payment signatories

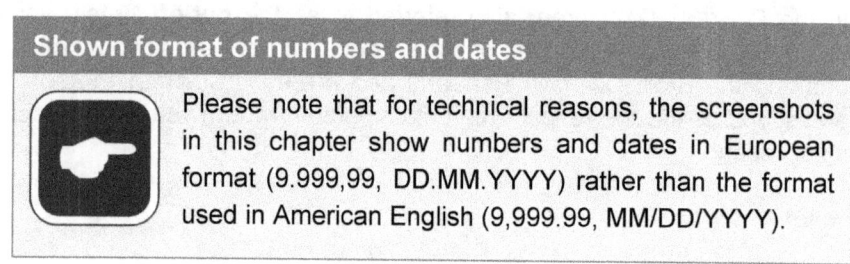

Shown format of numbers and dates

Please note that for technical reasons, the screenshots in this chapter show numbers and dates in European format (9.999,99, DD.MM.YYYY) rather than the format used in American English (9,999.99, MM/DD/YYYY).

Function: Overdraft Limits

On the OVERDRAFT LIMITS tab, enter the limit to which you may overdraw your account at the bank (see Figure 3.12).

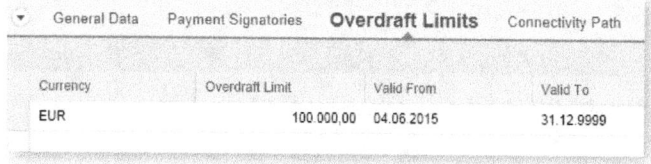

General Data · Payment Signatories · **Overdraft Limits** · Connectivity Path

Currency	Overdraft Limit	Valid From	Valid To
EUR	100.000,00	04.06.2015	31.12.9999

Figure 3.12: Account overdraft limit

In BAM, however, the overdraft limit has no effect on the check for planned amounts in the bank determination (transaction FBZP). In the current release status, the value entered here is used exclusively for the purposes of orientation in the cash position.

Function: Connectivity Path

On the CONNECTIVITY PATH tab, you define numerous items of master data for a bank account (see Figure 3.13). Via the ID CATEGORY field, you determine the system from which the bank account is to be linked. You can choose between:

▶ Central System: House Bank Account—links the bank account with a house bank account in the central system

▶ Remote System: House Bank Account—links the bank account with a house bank account in an SAP Business Suite remote system

▶ Remote System: G/L Account—links the bank account with a G/L account in an SAP Business Suite remote system

▶ Others—links the bank account with an account data record in a non-SAP system

This allows you to also control the central management of your bank accounts via remote or non-SAP systems.

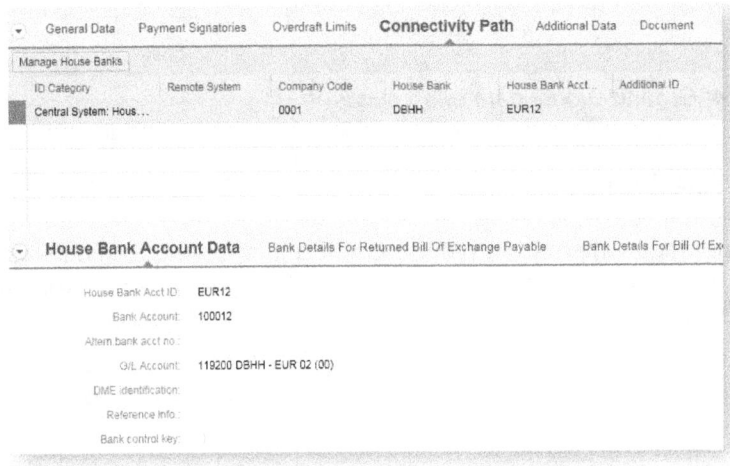

Figure 3.13: The connectivity path of a bank account

Here, via the HOUSE BANK ACCOUNT ID and the GENERAL LEDGER ACCOUNT fields, you can enter further data for your bank account. You also have the option, via the ALTERN. BANK ACCT NO. field, of defining an alternative bank account number in the master record. For bills of exchange, you have access to further fields in the following areas:

- ▶ BANK DETAILS FOR RETURNED BILL OF EXCHANGE PAYABLE
- ▶ BANK DETAILS FOR BILL OF EXCHANGE PRESENTATION

You can enter relevant information in these fields.

Function: Additional Data

On the ADDITIONAL DATA tab, under ORGANIZATIONAL DATA, you can define a profit center and a segment for the account (see Figure 3.14) if required.

Organizational Data

Controlling Area:	1000 CO Europe
Profit Center:	
Business Area:	
Segment:	

Technical Data

Technical ID:	0000000022

Figure 3.14: Organizational data of an account

Function: Attachment

An important requirement for a bank account management solution was realized with the ATTACHMENT tab: the option to store documents in a central location.

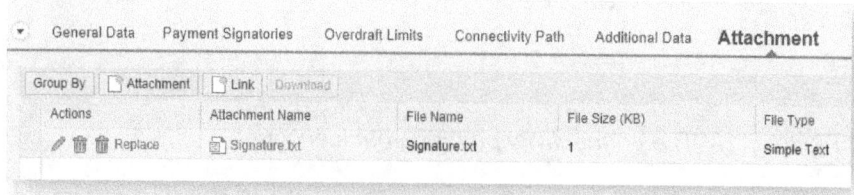

Figure 3.15: Attachment for a bank account

This means that you can now manage all internal correspondence (bank contracts) with your house banks or subsidiaries centrally (see Figure 3.15).

My Worklist

Depending on the authorizations assigned to you, you may receive a request to approve a bank account via the workflow process. To process this task, click the MY WORKLIST menu item. The list that appears contains all requests assigned to you, with the status of each request given under REQUEST STATUS (only one request is listed in Figure 3.16).

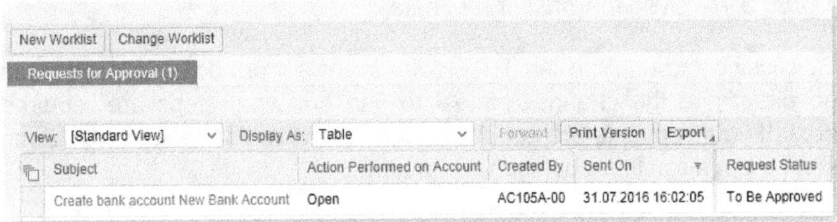

Figure 3.16: Requests for approval in the worklist

Open the document by clicking the entry in the list and then check the associated request data (see Figure 3.17).

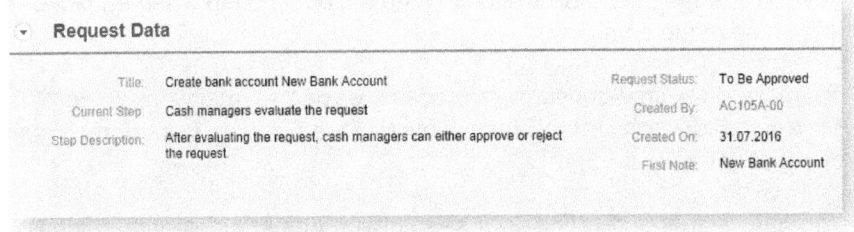

Figure 3.17: Request data for a change request

You start the next workflow processes using the buttons APPROVE or REJECT.

My Sent Requests

Via the MY SENT REQUESTS menu item, you can call up an overview of all the requests and workflow processes that you have initiated (see Figure 3.18).

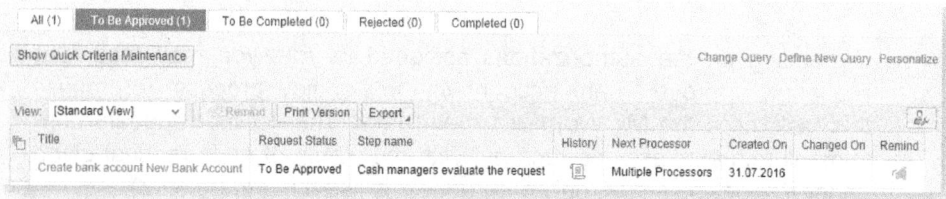

Figure 3.18: Overview of sent requests

By clicking the entry in the TITLE column for a work document, you can go directly to the change request to find out what steps are required next. If your requests are not processed in time by the recipient, you can send them a reminder using the button.

Maintain Signatory

When you create or change bank accounts, you can define employees who are authorized signatories for the accounts. In practice, you will have to change the authorizations in the accounts often when employees join or leave the company.

To make this time-consuming process easier to maintain, under the MAINTAIN SIGNATORY menu item, you have an option to perform mass changes (see Figure 3.19).

You can restrict and refine your search with numerous search criteria. A results list containing the selected accounts is then displayed and you can choose between the following options:

- ► ADD SIGNATORY
- ► CHANGE SIGNATORY
- ► REVOKE AUTHORIZATION

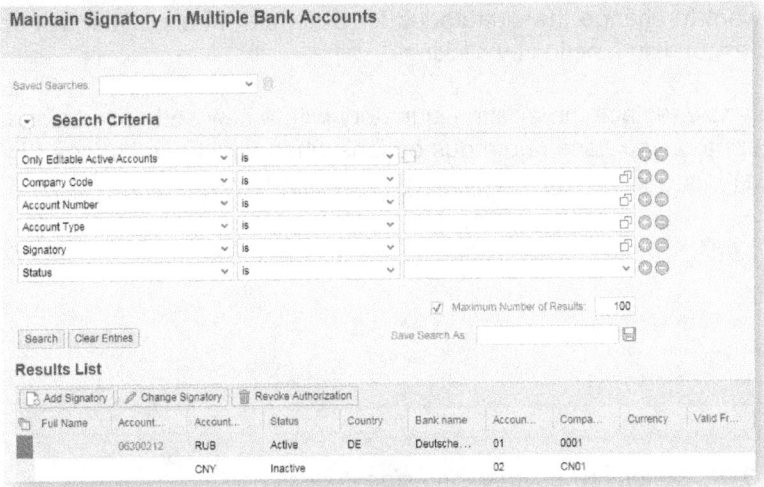

Figure 3.19: Maintaining signatories in multiple bank accounts

If you want to add further signatories for one or more accounts, select these accounts in the list and then click ⌗ Add Signatory . For the accounts selected, you can now add a new user with numerous options (see Figure 3.20).

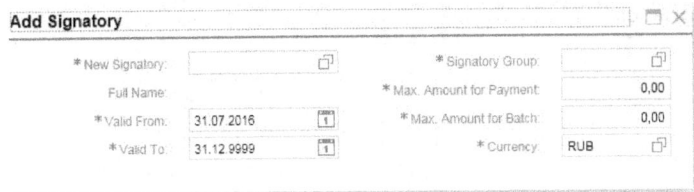

Figure 3.20: Options when adding signatories

Link to SAP Bank Communication Management (BCM)

The release process for a payment or a payment batch is controlled via the users defined in BCM. Alternatively, you can assign the authorized signatories via BAM. You use the following function modules to control this:

► FCLM_BAM_BCM_AGT_PRESEL

► FCLM_BAM_BCM_REL_PROC_CTRL

If you want to change the signatories for a number of accounts, call up the corresponding function by clicking ✎ Change Signatory .

You can now replace the existing signatory with a new authorized signatory. Here too, you have numerous options when adding users (see Figure 3.21).

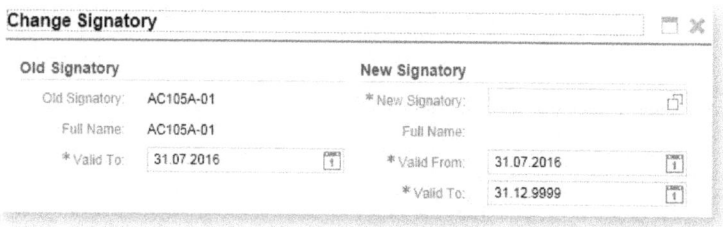

Figure 3.21: Options when changing signatories

If you want to withdraw the authorization for access to an account from a user, start this function by clicking 🗑 Revoke Authorization . From the validity date specified, the user is no longer authorized for this account (see Figure 3.22).

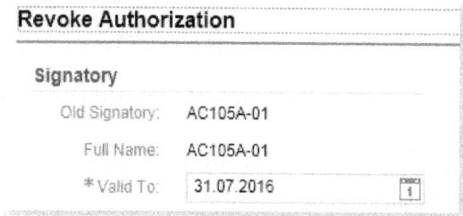

Figure 3.22: Revoking signature authorization for an account

For all changes under the MAINTAIN SIGNATORY menu item, a new change request is created and sent to the next processor via a workflow.

3.1.2   Bank account review

A further function in BAM is the *integrated bank account review*. With this functionality, SAP Cash Management powered by SAP HANA gives you the opportunity to review the house bank master data for superfluous bank accounts and bank accounts no longer used. In consultation with the relevant contact person, these accounts can then be closed and this helps to reduce the number of accounts and the level of costs involved in managing house banks. In the sections below, we will look at the options available under the Bank Account Review menu item.

Initiate Review Processes

Start the review process by clicking as follows in NWBC: BANK ACCOUNT REVIEW • INITIATE REVIEW PROCESSES. Use the search criteria available to restrict the search of your bank accounts (see Figure 3.23).

Results List

✓ Initiate Review							
Account Number	Description	Company Code	Country	Bank	Currency	Contact Person
12345678900	Current bank accou...	1000	DE	10020030	EUR	AC105-00
12345678990	Current bank accou...	1000	DE	10020030	EUR	AC105-00
12345678901	Current bank accou...	1000	DE	10020030	EUR	AC105-01
12345678902	Current bank accou...	1000	DE	10020030	EUR	AC105-02
12345678903	Current bank accou...	1000	DE	10020030	EUR	AC105-03
12345678904	Current bank accou...	1000	DE	10020030	EUR	AC105-04

Figure 3.23: Results list for the bank account review

Select the required accounts and click ✓ Initiate Review . In the dialog box that appears, enter data in the DUE DATE TITLE, and NOTE fields to complete the information required for the review.

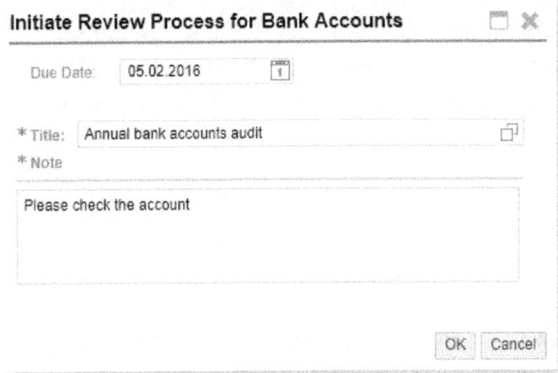

Figure 3.24: Initiating the review process for bank accounts

Confirm your entries by clicking OK (see Figure 3.24). This triggers the workflow process. The processor defined in the account is informed of the review process and the change request is stored in the sent requests.

Monitor Review Status

Via the functionality available under Monitor Review Status, you can query the processing status of the bank account review. Analog to the Initiate Review Processes function, you can also restrict the search using different search criteria. The list that is then output shows a percentage-based result for the respective progress of your queries (see Figure 3.25).

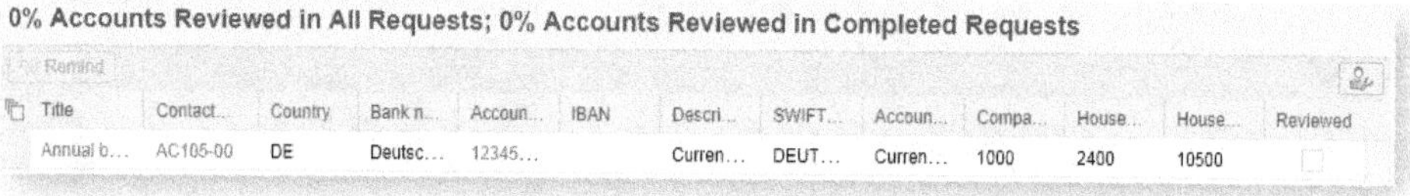

0% Accounts Reviewed in All Requests; 0% Accounts Reviewed in Completed Requests

Title	Contact..	Country	Bank n..	Accoun..	IBAN	Descri..	SWIFT..	Accoun..	Compa..	House..	House..	Reviewed
Annual b...	AC105-00	DE	Deutsc...	12345...		Curren...	DEUT...	Curren...	1000	2400	10500	

Figure 3.25: Monitoring the status of the bank account review

If the employees responsible have not processed queries on time, you can draw their attention to the delay directly from this list by clicking Remind .

3.1.3   Bank maintenance

As already discussed at the beginning of Section 3.1, the maintenance of the house banks has been added to the application menu in NWBC. Under the Banks menu item (see Figure 3.1), you have access to the following transactions:

- ▶ Create Bank (FI01)
- ▶ Change Bank (FI02)
- ▶ Change House Banks (FI12_HBANK)

You can still also maintain the banks in the SAP Easy Access Menu using the same transaction codes.

Special feature of transaction FI12_HBANK

 You can no longer maintain banks and house bank accounts using transaction FI12. Instead, you use the new transaction FI12_HBANK. You also have to use this transaction if you do not use SAP Cash Management powered by SAP HANA.

With *S/4 HANA Finance on Premise Edition 1605*, the house bank management functionalities were enhanced. Two further apps are now available for maintaining and managing the house banks:

► Manage Banks—Basic

► Manage Banks

The main difference between the two apps is that in MANAGE BANKS—BASIC, the level of detail of a house bank is restricted to the control data, whereas in MANAGE BANKS, you can also define additional information such as communications data, EDI partner profiles, and contact persons.

To start the basic house bank account management, call up the function by clicking the MANAGE BANKS—BASIC tile (see Figure 3.26).

Figure 3.26: MANAGE BANKS—BASIC tile

A list of all banks defined in the system is displayed (see Figure 3.27) and you can use numerous setting options to modify this list.

Standard ⊙

Bank Country:	Bank Number:	City:	SWIFT/BIC:	Bank Type:
				All

Banks (459) Standard * ⊙

Bank Name	Bank Country	Bank Number	Bank Hierarchy Group	Rating
1000020 (1000020)	USA (US)	1000020		10
100023 (1000021)	USA (US)	1000021		
1111 (11)	USA (US)	11		
123 (20150629)	Germany (DE)	20150629	TEst name	10
15111910 (15111910)	Germany (DE)	15111910		
15111911 (15111911)	Germany (DE)	15111911	US001001001	11
15112001 (15112001)	Germany (DE)	15112001	FI payment formats test	30
15112005 (15112005)	Germany (DE)	15112005	15112005	

Figure 3.27: Overview of the house banks created in the SAP system

For example, you can use filter functions and sorting and grouping options to classify the list further. In addition to the display functions, you also have the option to create a new house bank in the system.

If you want to see detailed information for your house banks, use the MANAGE BANKS app (see Figure 3.28).

Manage Banks

Figure 3.28: MANAGE BANKS tile

Just like in the basic bank management app, a list of all existing house banks is displayed. Again, you can use sorting and grouping options or create a new house bank directly.

In this application (see Figure 3.29), the view of the house banks has been enhanced: in addition to the general bank data, you can also see the company codes and contact persons assigned to the bank.

HOUSE BANKS

House Banks (6)

Company Name	House Bank
Cash Management SAT (FQM1)	LL61
Cash Management SAT (FQM1)	M003
Ledger LN01 copy (Z001)	DB
SAP A.G. (0001)	10101
SAP A.G. (0001)	M001
SAP A.G. (0001)	M002

CONTACT INFO

Contacts (0)

Last Name	First Name

Figure 3.29: Enhanced view of the house banks

3.1.4   Tools

If the bank account master data delivered with the SAP standard system is not sufficient for your needs, you can enhance the structures FCLM_BAM_AMD and CI_AMD_EXT. To make the necessary changes to the bank master data, use the TOOL menu item. Here you can export all existing bank accounts and edit them—for example, using Microsoft Excel. You can then re-import the work folder with the changed or supplemented data back into BAM.

Import and Export Bank Accounts

To import or export bank accounts, use the following menu: BANK AC-COUNT MANAGEMENT • TOOL • IMPORT AND EXPORT BANK ACCOUNTS. The following functions are available for the bank account export (see also Figure 3.30):

► EXPORT BANK ACCOUNTS TO AN XML FILE

► DOWNLOAD XML SPREADSHEET TEMPLATE

► DOWNLOAD XML SCHEMA FILE FOR IMPORT VALIDATION

You can use these tools to edit the bank accounts in Microsoft Excel using a template provided and validate them against an XML schema file.

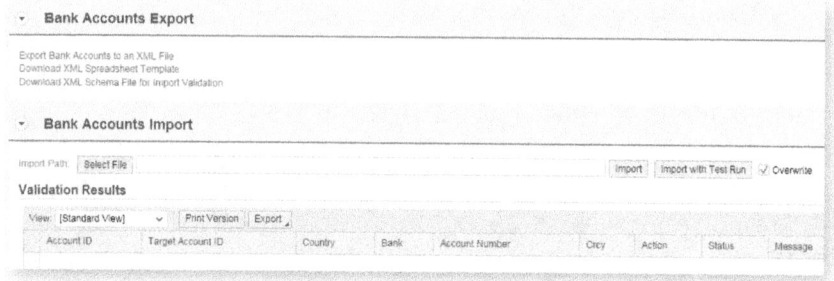

Figure 3.30: Importing and exporting bank accounts

Once you have made the changes to the bank master data, you can return it to your SAP system using the BANK ACCOUNTS IMPORT menu item.

Workflow for deactivating BAM

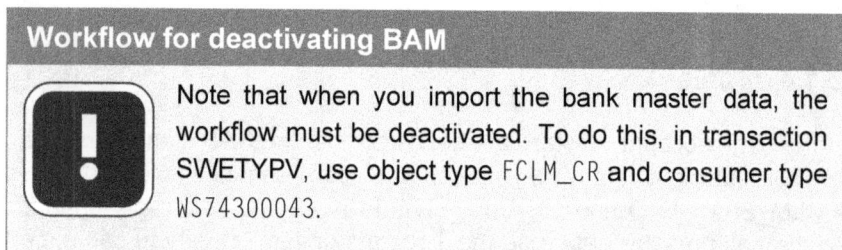

Note that when you import the bank master data, the workflow must be deactivated. To do this, in transaction SWETYPV, use object type FCLM_CR and consumer type WS74300043.

3.2 Daily cash operations

The daily tasks in cash management include the planning of incoming and outgoing liquid funds in the company. To plan your business transactions manually, in classic SAP Cash Management you can use the *Memo Records* function. This involves the following transactions:

▶ FF63: Create

▶ FF6B: Change via List.

These functionalities and transactions are also available in SAP Cash Management powered by SAP HANA. However, they are no longer displayed explicitly in the SAP application menu: instead, they are part of

Bank Account Management and you can call them up directly in the SAP Easy Access menu.

3.3 Foreign bank account report

As part of the US income tax return, there is an obligation to report foreign bank accounts and securities portfolio accounts and any financial investments owned. To do this, you have to complete the *Report of Foreign Bank and Financial Accounts* (FBAR) form in the tax return. This is a requirement when US persons have one or more foreign accounts or are authorized signatories for such accounts. The reporting obligation comes into force as soon as the (cumulative) balances of all foreign accounts affected exceeds a value of USD 10,000.00 at any point in the calendar year.

Report of Foreign Bank and Financial Accounts (FBAR)

 For more information about FBAR reporting, see *http://bsaefiling.fincen.treas.gov/main.html.*

In the SAP system, this legal requirement has been implemented in the FOREIGN BANK ACCOUNT REPORT app (see Figure 3.31).

Foreign Bank
Account Report

Figure 3.31: FOREIGN BANK ACCOUNT REPORT tile

Once you have started the application, a list appears containing the companies required to submit a report and the employees who are authorized signatories (see Figure 3.32).

Figure 3.32: Details for the foreign bank account report

Using the filter values in the HOME COUNTRY, TIME RANGE, and MINIMUM AGGREGATE VALUE fields, you can enter the required information (including the value of USD 10,000.00 and use this information to restrict the companies selected.

Bank Account Management (BAM) Lite

 BAM Lite is the basic version of Bank Account Management that you can use if you do not have a license for SAP Cash Management powered by SAP HANA. For example, it does not contain any workflow-based bank account processes. For more information on BAM Lite, see Note 2243324.

3.4   BAM summary

With the BAM function in SAP Cash Management powered by SAP HANA, you have access to an effective tool in your SAP system for managing and controlling bank accounts across the group. The account control is still strongly linked to the existing functionalities from classic house bank maintenance. As a supplement to NWBC, in the current edition 1605, the corresponding apps for managing the bank accounts are now available. This centralization of the bank account management requires advance intensive planning of the assignment of responsibilities and of the complete opening, changing, and closing processes for bank accounts.

3.5   Cash Operations

In SAP Cash Management powered by SAP HANA, the term *cash operations* covers all activities concerned with the daily management of a company's operating capital. These include:

▶ Monitoring the status of incoming bank statements

▶ Creating daily forecasts of incoming and outgoing payments and expected end balances

▶ Initiating bank transfers and payments

▶ Approving and monitoring payments

The tile catalog contains a number of apps that support you in these daily tasks (see Figure 3.33). The flexible way grouping of the apps means that you can design your workspace in your activity profile yourself to a large extent (depending on the roles assigned to you). A distinguishing feature of the apps is their easy user guidance. Via a context menu, the apps offer numerous options for navigating to further functions and apps.

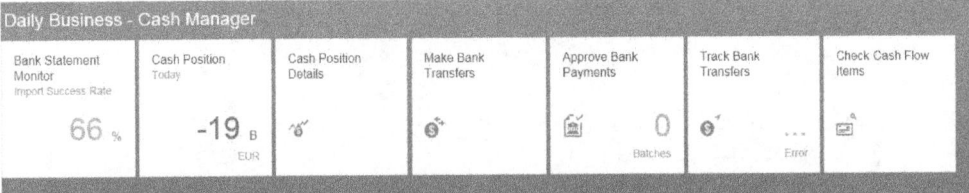

Figure 3.33: Grouping of apps in an activity profile

The data structure has also been simplified. The classic cash management tables have been replaced and most of the information is now taken directly from the following original tables:

▶ Accounting information from BSEG and BKPF

▶ Memo records from FDES

▶ Information relevant to cash and liquidity (e.g., from the components MM and SD) from the One Exposure table FQM_FLWO

▶ Information from remote systems from the One Exposure table FQM_FLOW

▶ Bank statement information from FEBKO and FEBEP

The following examples give a brief overview of a number of new functionalities in Cash Operations.

3.5.1 Bank statement monitor

One of the first tasks in everyday cash management is checking that bank statements have been transmitted completely and without any errors. This step is the basis for all further activities in Cash Operations. To perform this step, you use the *Bank Statement Monitor* analytical app (left-hand tile in Figure 3.33). The time at which a bank statement is imported is stored in BAM. This is the basis for determining and visualizing the respective import status of the bank statement in the app. Once you have called up the app, an overview of your accounts appears which you can then structure in different dimensions (see Figure 3.34).

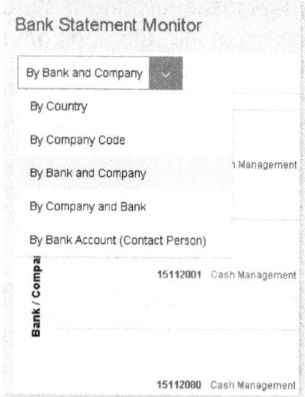

Figure 3.34: Structuring options in the Bank Statement Monitor

The colored bar diagrams (see the arrow on the right-hand side) support you in analyzing errors. Different colors represent the different processing statuses of the bank statement:

▶ Green: bank statement has been read in and processed completely

▶ Yellow: bank statement has been read in but not processed completely yet

▶ Red: bank statement has not been processed or has not been supplied by the bank yet

If necessary, you can use the context menu to access the contact partners defined in BAM directly.

To do this, as shown in Figure 3.35, select the bar for an incorrect bank entry and click, for example, the BY BANK ACCOUNT (CONTACT PERSON) option in the context menu that appears. A list of the contact persons responsible for the respective bank accounts is then displayed, allowing you to make contact with the correct person quickly and easily.

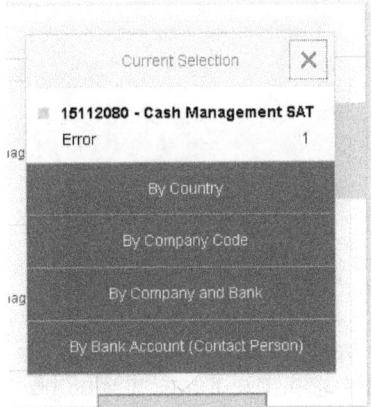

Figure 3.35: Context menu for the search for a contact person

3.5.2 Cash position

If you want to display your cash position, you can use an analytical and a transactional app to do so. The CASH POSITION TODAY app (see Figure 3.36) gives you an overview of your entire liquidity based on the current date.

Figure 3.36: CASH POSITION TODAY tile

Once you have called up the app, you can use numerous filter options to concentrate the result to certain dimensions. To do this, select an item in the list. A context menu then appears showing the numerous functions that you can navigate to from this point (Figure 3.37).

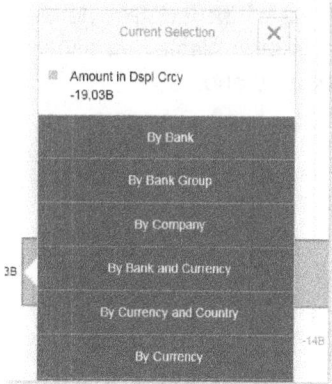

Figure 3.37: Selection options in the context menu

The options offered by the context menu vary depending on the dimension selected—the more detailed the dimension, the greater the number of options offered. For example, you can go directly to the details for the cash position or immediately initiate an account transfer if there are insufficient funds in a bank account.

Cash position time frame

 The cash position represents the short-term development of the bank and bank clearing accounts, including the planned items, based on the value date. The typical time frame in the cash position is between one and five days.

3.5.3 Cash position details

One of the most extensive apps in SAP Cash Management powered by SAP HANA is without doubt the Cash Position Details app (see Figure 3.38). Compared to the cash position function in classic Cash Management, the functions here have been enhanced significantly and offer improved evaluation options for the daily actual and planned data.

Figure 3.38: CASH POSITION DETAILS tile

In addition to the provision of numerous new dimensions and filter options, the associated database for the cash position has been enhanced. Information is now provided based on data from the following sources:

▶ Accounting

▶ Manual memo records

▶ One Exposure

You therefore have a significantly enhanced and more detailed view of your transaction data. For example, the liquidity items have been added to the cash position details, thereby providing you with additional information on the source and use of the cash flow for a selected item.

One Exposure

 One Exposure is the central storage location (table FQM_FLOW) for all operating data from Treasury and Risk Management (TRM), Loans Management (FS-CML), Contract Accounts Receivable and Payable (FI-CA), for bank account balances uploaded from Excel, and for data from remote Cash Management systems imported via IDoc.

Call up the CASH POSITION DETAILS app by clicking the corresponding tile (see Figure 3.33). An extensive list with numerous filter and sorting options appears (see Figure 3.39). The list also contains the value date, for which the default is always the current date.

Here, we will take a closer look at the structure and setting options in the app.

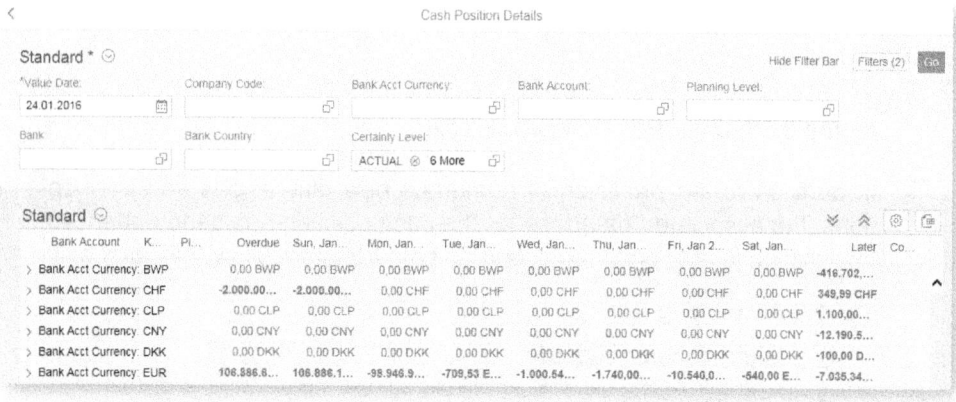

Figure 3.39: Cash position details

In the header (at the top in Figure 3.39), you have access to numerous filter options that you can use to refine the selection and presentation of the data (see Figure 3.40).

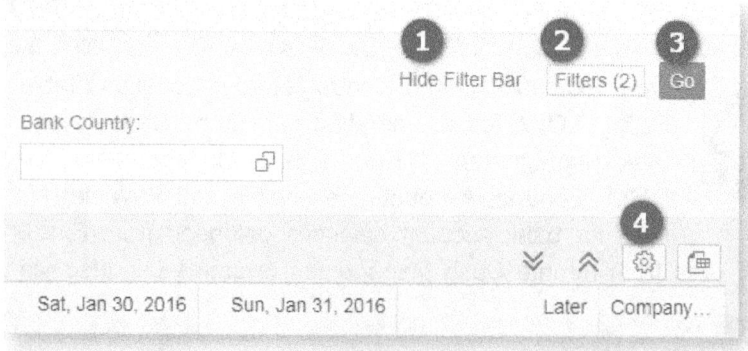

Figure 3.40: Filter bar and setting options

For example, you can:

❶ Hide the filter bar

❷ Display the filter bar

❸ Start the selection of the data with or without a filter

❹ Call up the setting options

To create an additional filter, click Filter. You can then add further basic settings to your list (see Figure 3.41).

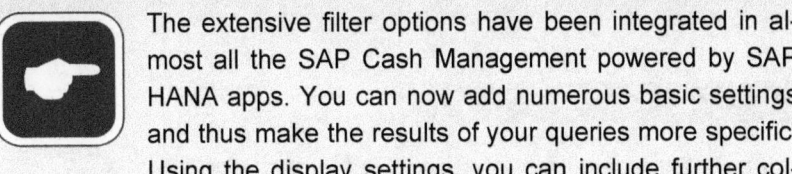

The extensive filter options have been integrated in almost all the SAP Cash Management powered by SAP HANA apps. You can now add numerous basic settings and thus make the results of your queries more specific. Using the display settings, you can include further columns in the list output and sort the list according to different criteria. This gives you a high degree of flexibility in your evaluations.

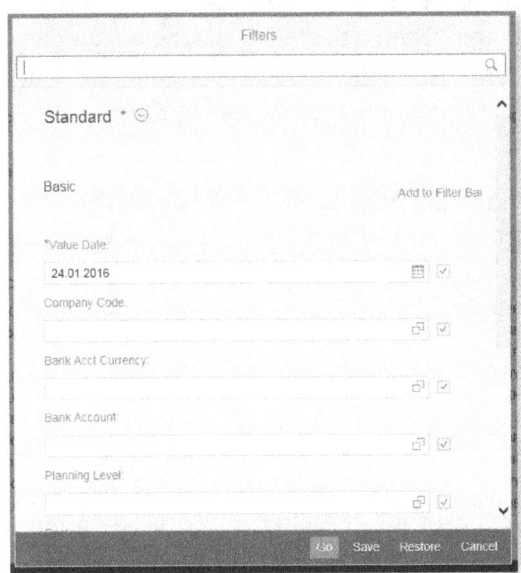

Figure 3.41: Filter options in the cash position

Now configure your desired basic settings and save them in a variant. You can then access this variant via the variant management function (see Figure 3.42) and perform the data selection again with the changed parameters.

Figure 3.42: Management of variants in the cash position

Filter options in conjunction with BAM

 In conjunction with BAM, you have access to further filter options in the cash position. For example, you can sort or filter your accounts using the bank account groups and bank account names defined in BAM.

The selected data is displayed in the cash position list output. Here too, you have numerous setting options. For example, via ☼ (see Figure 3.40, ❹), you can:

▶ Select columns

▶ Sort fields

▶ Filter data

▶ Group data

Let us now look at the structure of the selected or filtered data more closely.

Define whether you want to see all data or only the delta data by selecting your preferred presentation via the button Filter at the bottom right of the list output (see Figure 1.39). The view is updated and you can navigate to the required information by clicking ⚙ to the left of one of the items in the list to display further details (see Figure 3.43).

Bank Acct...	Bank Account	Overdue	Sat, Jan 23, 2016	Sun, Jan 24,...	Mon, Jan 25, 2016
> Bank Acct Currency: BWP		0,00 BWP	0,00 BWP	0,00 BWP	0,00 BWP
> Bank Acct Currency: CHF		-2.000.098,00 CHF	-2.000.098,00 CHF	0,00 CHF	0,00 CHF
> Bank Acct Currency: CLP		0,00 CLP	0,00 CLP	0,00 CLP	0,00 CLP
> Bank Acct Currency: CNY		-31.783,74 CNY	-31.783,74 CNY	0,00 CNY	0,00 CNY
> Bank Acct Currency: DKK		0,00 DKK	0,00 DKK	0,00 DKK	0,00 DKK
⌄ Bank Acct Currency: EUR					
⌄ Company Code: 0001					
⌄ Bank Account:					
EUR	Not Assigned	-97.168.195,90 EUR	-97.168.195,90 EUR	0,00 EUR	20,00 EUR
> Bank Account: 000002		0,00 EUR	0,00 EUR	0,00 EUR	0,00 EUR
> Bank Account: 000004		0,00 EUR	0,00 EUR	0,00 EUR	0,00 EUR

Bank Account - Currency ⌄

Figure 3.43: Detailed view of the bank account currency

The amounts and balances are presented as hyperlinks. If you would like to call up further navigation options for an amount or balance in the cash position, simply click the respective item to activate the hyperlink. This gives you a context menu from which you can trigger further transactions (see Figure 3.44)

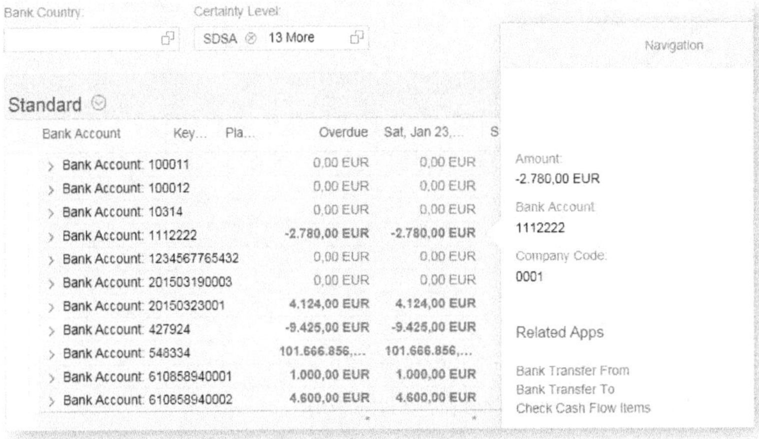

Bank Country: Certainty Level:

SDSA ⊗ 13 More

Navigation

Standard ⌄

Bank Account	Key...	Pla...	Overdue	Sat, Jan 23,...	S
> Bank Account: 100011			0,00 EUR	0,00 EUR	
> Bank Account: 100012			0,00 EUR	0,00 EUR	
> Bank Account: 10314			0,00 EUR	0,00 EUR	
> Bank Account: 1112222			-2.780,00 EUR	-2.780,00 EUR	
> Bank Account: 1234567765432			0,00 EUR	0,00 EUR	
> Bank Account: 201503190003			0,00 EUR	0,00 EUR	
> Bank Account: 20150323001			4.124,00 EUR	4.124,00 EUR	
> Bank Account: 427924			-9.425,00 EUR	-9.425,00 EUR	
> Bank Account: 548334			101.666.856,...	101.666.856,...	
> Bank Account: 610858940001			1.000,00 EUR	1.000,00 EUR	
> Bank Account: 610858940002			4.600,00 EUR	4.600,00 EUR	

Amount:
-2.780,00 EUR

Bank Account:
1112222

Company Code:
0001

Related Apps

Bank Transfer From
Bank Transfer To
Check Cash Flow Items

Figure 3.44: Context menu in the cash position

For example, if there is too much or too little money in your accounts, you can initiate a bank transfer immediately or go directly to the cash flow items without having to leave the transaction.

Numerous icons (see the KEY FIGURE column) support you in viewing your balances, incoming money, and outgoing money (see Figure 3.45). Depending on the variant selected, further columns such as PLANNING LEVEL or the liquidity item are displayed to the right of the key figure.

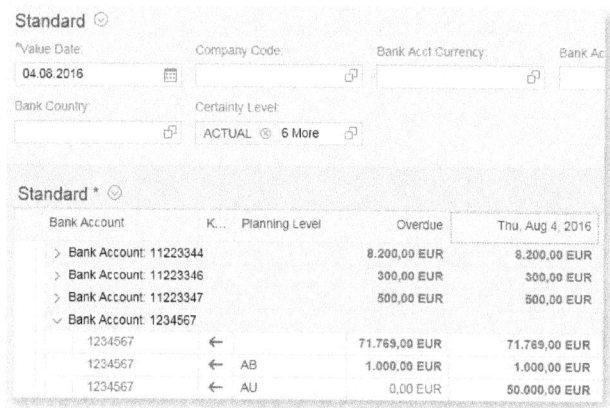

Figure 3.45: Key figures and the planning level in the detailed view

To obtain further information or details for a line item (planned item or bank statement), click the amount in the line item. The context menu opens and from here, you can go directly to the details of the cash flow item (see Figure 3.46).

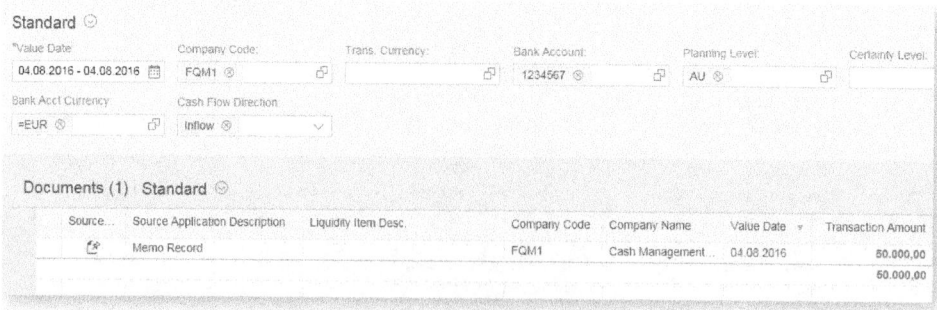

Figure 3.46: Detailed information for a line item

At this level, you can also go directly to the memo record details and derive further information for the document.

3.5.4 Making bank transfers

Another aspect of daily cash management and forecast is the *bank account transfer*. In this process, surplus liquidity in an account is transferred to accounts with a lower credit limit or a shortage of funds. Once all the balances from the previous day have been reconciled and the planned values for the next day recorded via the memo records, you can execute the transfer between the sending account and the target account. To do this, call up the MAKE BANK TRANSFERS app (see Figure 3.33).

A simple overview appears with all possible bank accounts for which you can execute a transfer (see Figure 3.47). Here, in the header, you can use the AMOUNT, TRANSFER DATE, and PAYMENT METHOD fields to enter the required information for the planned transfer. Via the NOTE field, you can also enter any additional, optional information for your transfer.

In the next step, select the sending bank in the left-hand column (FROM field) and the receiving bank in the right-hand column (TO field). You can also use the search function to determine the sending and target bank.

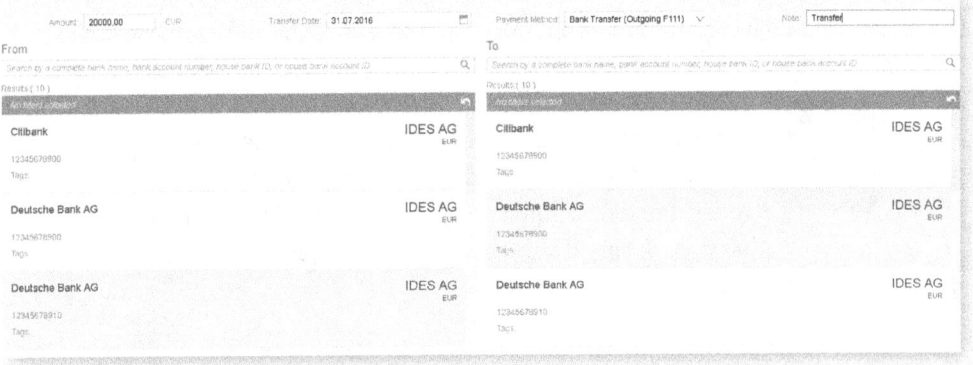

Figure 3.47: Making bank transfers

The accounts selected are now highlighted in a different color and you can execute the transfer. To do this, in the footer of the app, click MAKE

BANK TRANSFER. A dialog box appears, showing the details of your transfer. You can enter information for the note in the data medium again (see Figure 3.48).

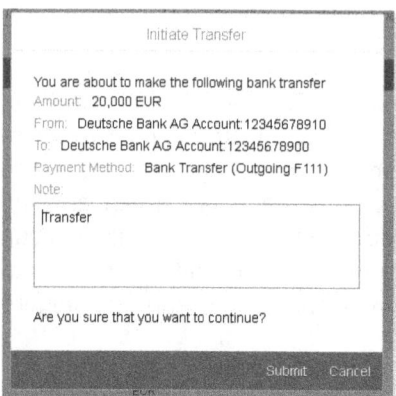

Figure 3.48: Confirming the account transfer

Finally, confirm the transfer by clicking SUBMIT. In conjunction with the component BCM, a *payment batch* is created which is subsequently used to release the payment. For this purpose, grouping rules are defined in BCM so that the payments can be grouped in individual packets. Report SAPFPAYM_MERGE is scheduled periodically for the subsequent merging of the payments in BCM. You also have to make a reservation for cross-payment run payment media in transaction OBPM5.

SAP BCM functions in Cash Operations

 Some functionalities in Cash Operations are closely linked with SAP BCM. In addition to the bank statement monitor, the approval and grouping processes also access the basic functions from this module. In this context, a follow-on project is often required to create access to the SWIFT network or EBICS.

You also define a number of authorized signatories in your company for the subsequent release of the payment. The authorization can be via BAM or you can link the release using the release strategies and release objects of BCM.

3.5.5 Approving bank payments

In a next step, you can authorize the bank account transfers previously executed or release them for payment. To do this, call up the APPROVE BANK PAYMENTS app (see Figure 3.49).

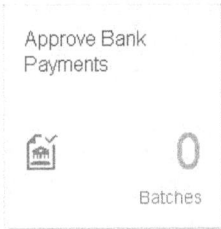

Figure 3.49: APPROVE BANK PAYMENTS tile

You now see an overview of all payment batches that have been assigned to you via the rules in BAM or BCM (see Figure 3.50). The left-hand side contains the overview of the batches awaiting your approval. The FOR REVIEW tab contains all the new, unprocessed batches. The PROCESSED tab contains all batches for which an approval step has already taken place. On this tab, you can see the total of the payment as well as the current approval step for the batch.

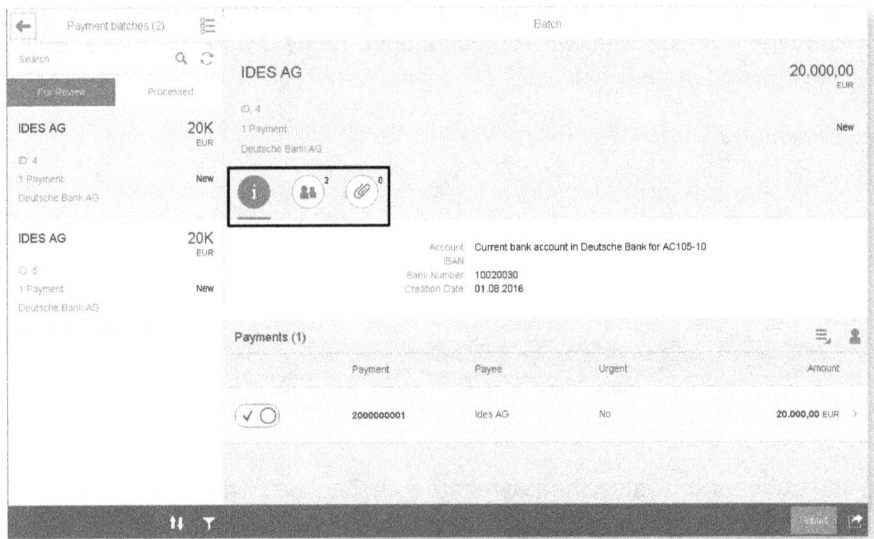

Figure 3.50: First approval step in a payment batch

Using the toolbar outlined in Figure 3.50, you can call up detailed information.

Click one of the icons to get further information about the account data of the receiving bank, the individual workflow steps (see Figure 3.51), or call up attachments which you can attach to the payment if required.

Figure 3.51: Process steps in a payment batch

The lower area of the app contains detailed information about the payment document in the PAYEE column, for example, or possible instruction keys (e.g. rapid money transfer) in the URGENT column. Using the buttons APPROVE or DECLINE, you can trigger the next workflow steps for the batch (see Figure 3.52).

	Payment	Payee	Urgent	Amount
✓ ○	2000000001	Ides AG	No	20.000,00 EUR >

Figure 3.52: Details for the payment document

If you want to refuse the payment, click DECLINE. The batch is then returned to the previous group of possible authorized signatories (see Figure 3.53) and presented for signature again. If you are the first approver for a batch, the document or payment is canceled and has to be executed again.

Figure 3.53: Declining a payment batch

To release the payment, click APPROVE. In the dialog box that appears, enter your password and, optionally, a note for the payment. Confirm your entry by clicking OK (see Figure 3.54).

Figure 3.54: Approving a payment batch

When you release the payment the workflow continues. If you are the first approver in the entire process, the batch is forwarded to the next processor. If you are the final approver, the data medium is created and sent to the bank.

3.5.6 Tracking bank transfers

With the transactional app TRACK BANK TRANSFERS (see Figure 3.33), you can track your bank transfer from the time you send it to the time the final confirmation is received from the bank.

When you call up the app, an overview showing the status or progress of the process for your payment batches appears. The payment transfers are grouped in the header according to the respective status (see Figure 3.55).

Figure 3.55: Overview for tracking bank transfers

A payment batch goes through the following stages:

1. NEW: initial batches that have not yet been approved
2. IN APPROVAL: batches that are currently in the approval process
3. APPROVED: batches that have been released for payment with the final signature
4. SENT TO BANK: payment batches that have been sent to the bank
5. COMPLETED: confirmation has been received from the bank

All transfers and payments that are not merged using report SAP-FPAYM_MERGE are listed on the EXCEPTIONS tab.

The list beneath the header shows the details for the payment, such as the sending and receiving banks, the payment method, and the transfer amount. For more details about the payment, click the corresponding line in the list. As shown in Figure 3.56, this reveals additional information for the selected batch.

Here you can navigate to the ANALYZE PAYMENT DETAILS app by clicking the corresponding hyperlink. You can then perform additional analyses for the payment.

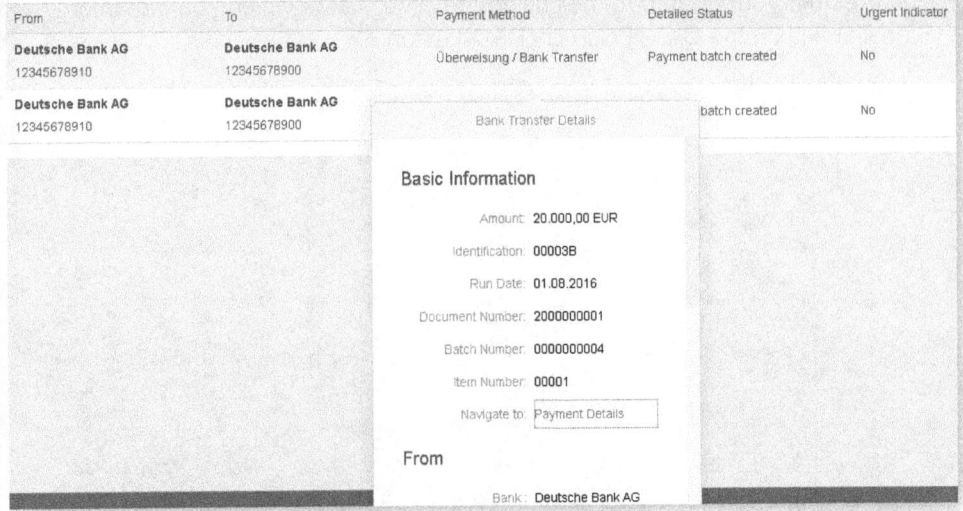

From	To	Payment Method	Detailed Status	Urgent Indicator
Deutsche Bank AG 12345678910	**Deutsche Bank AG** 12345678900	Überweisung / Bank Transfer	Payment batch created	No
Deutsche Bank AG 12345678910	**Deutsche Bank AG** 12345678900		batch created	No

Bank Transfer Details

Basic Information

Amount:	20.000,00 EUR
Identification:	00003B
Run Date:	01.08.2016
Document Number:	2000000001
Batch Number:	0000000004
Item Number:	00001
Navigate to:	Payment Details

From

Bank: **Deutsche Bank AG**

Figure 3.56: Transfer details for a payment batch

3.5.7   Checking cash flow items

Another task in cash management is looking at and assessing the cash flows in the entire company. To do this, you need all incoming and outgoing movements (actual and planned data) in chronological order. To take a detailed look at your cash flows, use the CHECK CASH FLOW ITEMS app, which is another analytical app (see Figure 3.57).

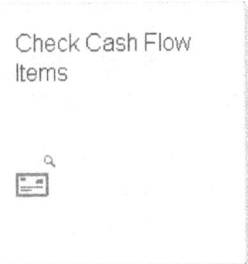

Check Cash Flow Items

Figure 3.57: CHECK CASH FLOW ITEMS tile

Call up the app and in the filter area, under VALUE DATE, define a period for which you want to evaluate your cash flows (see Figure 3.58). You can restrict your search further using the other filters which you became familiar with in the CASH POSITION DETAILS app.

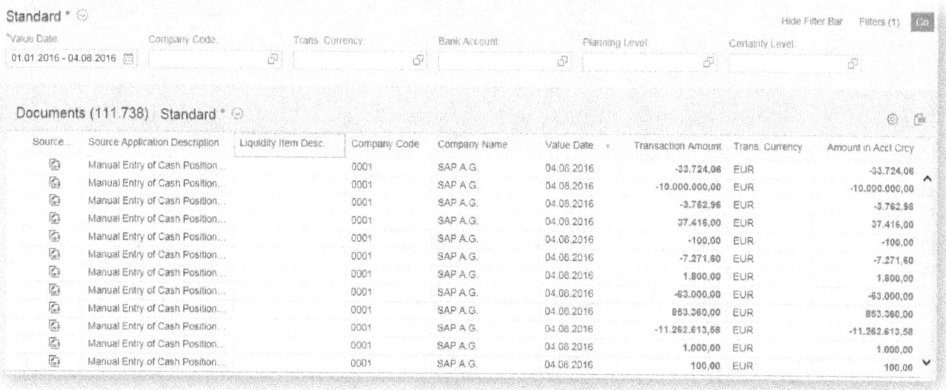

Source...	Source Application Description	Liquidity Item Desc.	Company Code	Company Name	Value Date	Transaction Amount	Trans. Currency	Amount in Acct Crcy
	Manual Entry of Cash Position...		0001	SAP A.G.	04.08.2016	-33.724,06	EUR	-33.724,06
	Manual Entry of Cash Position...		0001	SAP A.G.	04.08.2016	-10.000.000,00	EUR	-10.000.000,00
	Manual Entry of Cash Position...		0001	SAP A.G.	04.08.2016	-3.762,96	EUR	-3.762,96
	Manual Entry of Cash Position...		0001	SAP A.G.	04.08.2016	37.416,00	EUR	37.416,00
	Manual Entry of Cash Position...		0001	SAP A.G.	04.08.2016	-100,00	EUR	-100,00
	Manual Entry of Cash Position...		0001	SAP A.G.	04.08.2016	-7.271,60	EUR	-7.271,60
	Manual Entry of Cash Position...		0001	SAP A.G.	04.08.2016	1.800,00	EUR	1.800,00
	Manual Entry of Cash Position...		0001	SAP A.G.	04.08.2016	-63.000,00	EUR	-63.000,00
	Manual Entry of Cash Position...		0001	SAP A.G.	04.08.2016	853.360,00	EUR	853.360,00
	Manual Entry of Cash Position...		0001	SAP A.G.	04.08.2016	-11.262.613,58	EUR	-11.262.613,58
	Manual Entry of Cash Position...		0001	SAP A.G.	04.08.2016	1.000,00	EUR	1.000,00
	Manual Entry of Cash Position...		0001	SAP A.G.	04.08.2016	100,00	EUR	100,00

Figure 3.58: List with information about the cash flow

For example, you can restrict your search to planning levels or liquidity items, or search specifically for documents for certain business partners, customers, and vendors (you can see one possible result of this selection in Figure 3.61). Via the source application displayed, you can always derive the source of the document or the transaction from the cash flow item.

You can also sort the results using the settings familiar from the CASH POSITION DETAILS app (see Figure 3.40). To access these settings, click ⚙. A dialog box appears in which you can refine your list or view settings (see Figure 3.59).

In addition to a large selection of possible columns, you can also assign default values for the display via the SORT, FILTER, and GROUP options.

If you want further details for a document, simply click the amount, which is highlighted in the document line (see Figure 3.58). Doing this takes you to the detailed information for the cash flow item (see Figure 3.60).

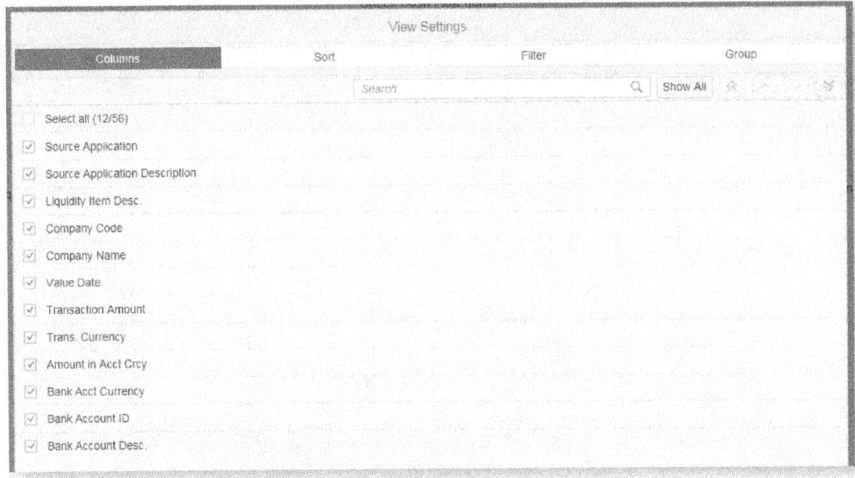

Figure 3.59: View settings for sorting the list

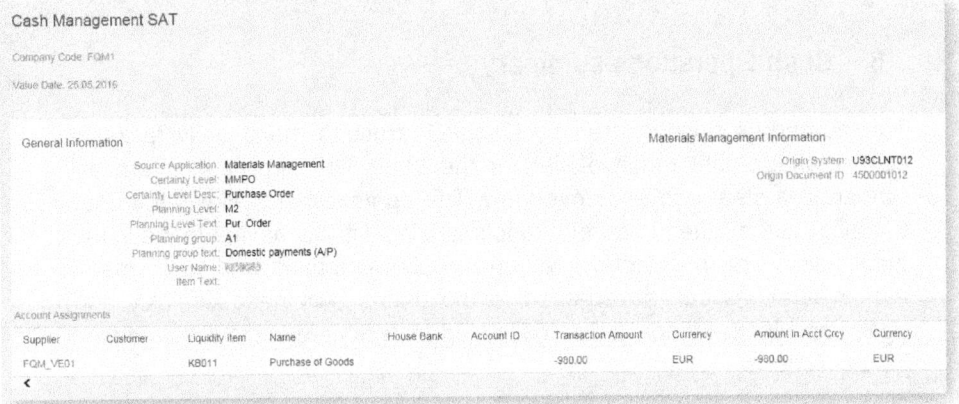

Figure 3.60: Detailed information for a cash flow item

Here too, you can navigate further to the source document—for example, to view the details of the materials management information (see Figure 3.61).

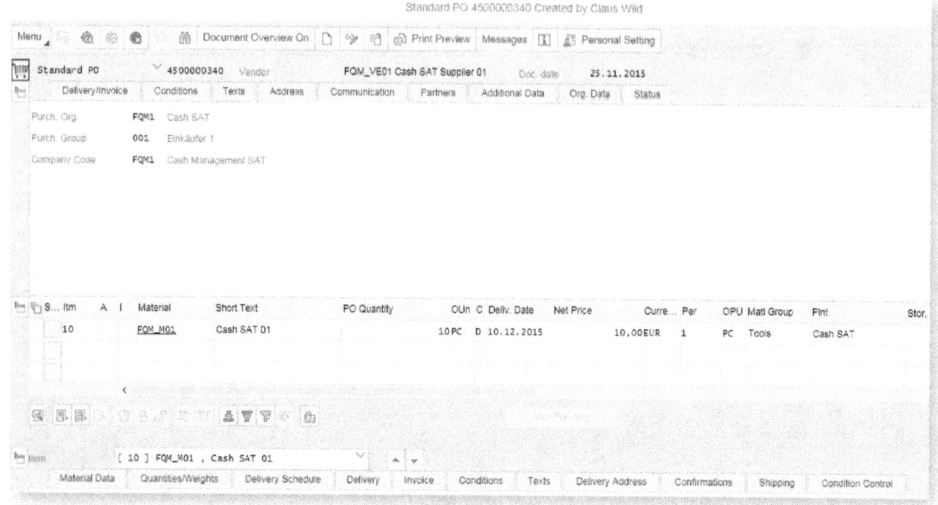

Figure 3.61: Details of a purchase order

3.6 Cash Operations summary

The numerous apps offered by Cash Operations make daily tasks in cash management much easier for the user. The applications are arranged in a clear and easy overview. The context menu allows the user to navigate to further, important functionalities without having to leave the application. The numerous filter and analysis options and tools mean that evaluations can be adapted to the user's own needs quickly and easily and information can be called up in real time without scheduling jobs or reports.

3.7 Liquidity management

With SAP Cash Management powered by SAP HANA, the SAP Liquidity Management component has also been revised with regard to strategic company development. Functionalities have been added in the following areas:

▶ *Liquidity planning*

▶ *Liquidity analysis*

The new SAP Liquidity Management contains numerous tools which, on the one hand, plan, monitor, and control a company's short-term and long-term ability to pay. On the other hand, these tools indicate possible risks (inability to pay) and impending financial bottlenecks transparently.

In this section, we focus on the **liquidity analysis**. This is supported, for example, by the following analytical apps:

- ▶ Liquidity Forecast
- ▶ Actual Cash Flow

3.7.1 Liquidity forecast

In classic Cash Management, the liquidity forecast covers the expected liquidity development of the subledger accounts. The integration of the cash position means that you can see the overall liquidity of your company.

Liquidity forecast time frame

The liquidity forecast shows the future liquidity development based on subledger accounts. It also contains the expected payment flows as well as manual planned items. The typical time frame of the liquidity forecast is one to fifteen weeks.

In SAP Cash Management powered by SAP HANA, the evaluation options of the liquidity forecast (analysis) have been significantly enhanced. For example, you have access to further default reports which you can use to start numerous additional evaluations. We will look at some of these in more detail.

Call up the LIQUIDITY FORECAST app via the now familiar tiles (see Figure 3.62). An overview of your expected payment flows appears. It also shows the probable development of your bank accounts for the next 90 days based on the current date.

Figure 3.62: LIQUIDITY FORECAST tile

A diagram displays the probable incoming and outgoing movements on your subledgers as bars—at the same time, the lines give you an overview of the closing balances to be expected for your bank accounts (see Figure 3.63).

If you want more detailed information about a cash flow, click one of the elements in the diagram (bar or line point) or directly on the date in the footer. This opens up a context menu from which you can navigate to further display variants or directly to the associated cash flow item.

The cash flow item shows you the respective detailed information for the documents for your selected value date (see also Figure 3.58).

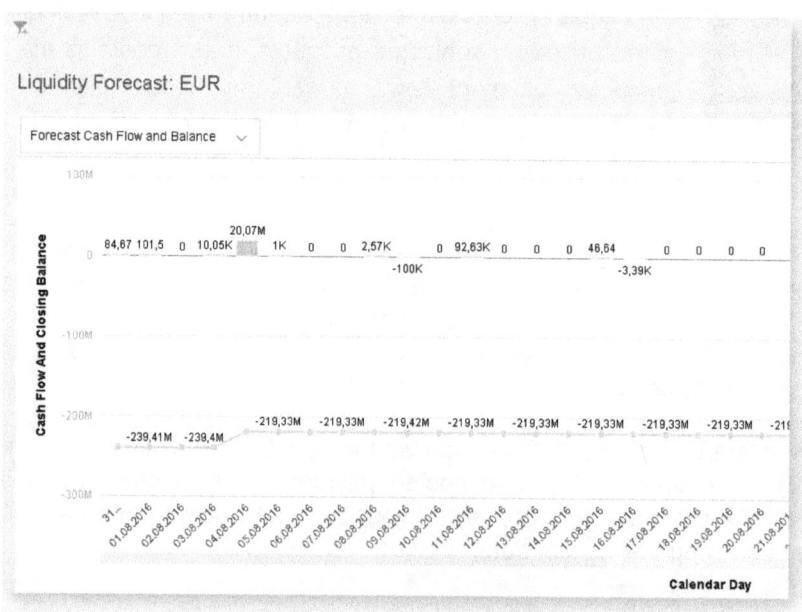

Figure 3.63: Detailed view of the liquidity forecast

As already shown for the apps for the cash position, in the liquidity forecast you also have access to numerous filters for detailed analyses. At the moment, you also have access to the following preconfigured reports:

▶ Forecast Flow and Balance

▶ Operating Cash Flow

▶ Investing Cash Flow

▶ Financing Cash Flow

▶ Cash Flow by Liquidity Item

▶ Cash Flow by Company Code

You can create evaluations for your specific needs based on these dimensions quickly and easily.

3.7.2 Actual cash flow

Just like the CASH POSITION app, the ACTUAL CASH FLOW app opens up a number of evaluation options that you can use to analyze your cash flow in more detail (see Figure 3.64). In contrast to the liquidity forecast, however, a retrospective consideration of your actual cash flow over the last 90 days is output for the evaluation of the payment flows.

Figure 3.64: ACTUAL CASH FLOW tile

When you start the Actual Cash Flow app, just like in the Liquidity Forecast app, you have access to numerous preconfigured reports:

▶ Aggregated Cash Flow

▶ Operating Cash Flow

▶ Investing Cash Flow

▶ Financing Cash Flow

▶ Cash Flow by Liquidity Item

▶ Cash Flow by Company Code

Select one of the reports for a detailed view. Click one of the items or a calendar day to open a context menu (see Figure 3.65) via which you can navigate to one of the other reports or directly to the cash flow item (see also Figure 3.58).

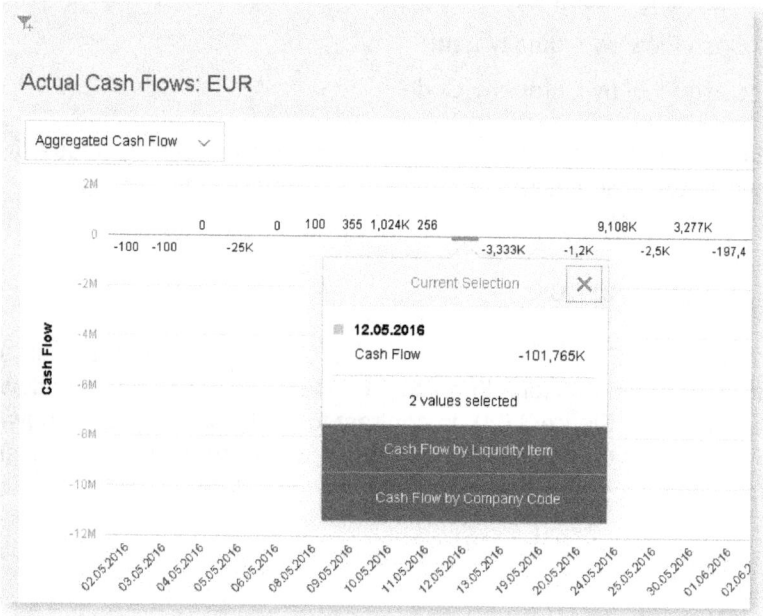

Figure 3.65: Details of the actual cash flow

3.8 Summary

In SAP Cash Management powered by SAP HANA, the SAP Liquidity Management component has been changed fundamentally. For example, the liquidity planning based on *SAP Business Planning & Consolidation* (BPC) has been redesigned and thus replaces the *Liquidity Planner* in classic Cash Management. As already mentioned at the beginning of this chapter, we are still at the very beginning of some new features. The new liquidity planning already has an extensive scope of functions to which further functions will continue to be added during the development cycles. It is therefore worth looking at the *SAP Note & Knowledge Base Article Search* regularly to get information about the new features and developments in the SAP Release Notes.

Numerous apps support you in the central development, monitoring, and reporting of your liquidity plans. The functionalities for evaluating the actual cash flow and the liquidity forecast have also been enhanced, and we have presented some of the templates for these functionalities. Here too, the concept of drilling down to the single document is continued consistently, which gives you extensive insights into your business transactions.

4 Instant payments

Guest contribution: Christian Fink, NTT DATA Deutschland

Instant payments are coming in 2017 and will revolutionize payment transactions. In this chapter you will learn about the opportunities and challenges that real-time processing of payments offers for retail, companies, and banks.

4.1 Why it makes sense to accelerate SEPA transfers to near time

The retail trade has changed enormously in recent years. For many customers, a life without e-commerce is no longer imaginable. Twenty-four hour accessibility, fast and easy processing from home, and an unbeatable selection of products are just some of the reasons for the online boom which is completely reshaping existing retail structures. Over-the-counter trade is looking for additional instruments to tie customers in during the payment process without losing data sovereignty to third parties. And the calls from politicians for cash transactions to be completely removed—or at least restricted—are increasing in intensity. The German government, for example, is currently pushing for a common limit for cash payments in Europe.

These and other innovative trends, such as the increasing use of mobile end devices, pose completely new challenges for payment transactions: the classic bank transfers and debit memos no longer fit in this development, particularly due to their long clearing times; a retailer needs an immediate message about successful payment by a customer so that he can ship the goods without risk; private individuals want to be able to exchange money in real time and use it for purchases immediately.

In the past, this deficit in classic payment procedures has been increasingly compensated for by companies which are not necessarily conventional banks. These companies provide platforms for processing payments which work outside the existing bank transfer and debit memo systems. These subsystems enable fast response times due to some of them performing their own clearing between participants and then clearing through the conventional bank systems in a subsequent step. Depending on the area of application, this acceleration of the payment takes places in very different ways, ranging from a pure payment release in conjunction with an immediate confirmation to the payment recipient—as offered, for example, by the SOFORT transfer in Germany, iDEAL in The Netherlands, eNETS in Singapore, the American company Plaid with the product Auth, and Skrill in the UK with the product Rapid Transfer—up to completely autonomous clearing systems as used by PayPal or Skrill and credit card providers, for instance. For these market requirements, even the modernized transfers that are part of the SEPA migration are much too slow.

If banks were able to establish an infrastructure which brings the processing of a transfer between two checking accounts to almost real time, the process chain for the transaction between the payer and the payment recipient could be massively reduced. This would be a new basis for creating efficiency and innovation in payment transactions.

4.2   An initiative of the European Central Bank

The European Retail Payments Board (ERPB), founded in December 2013, has taken over the tasks of the SEPA Council and will continue to develop standards in European payment transactions as well as identify technical, legal, and behavioral problems and attempt to solve them. The aim is to drive forward the development of an integrated, innovative, and competitive market for mass payments in euros in the European Union. The Board is made up of representatives of financial service providers, SEPA users, and the national central banks—all with equal representation—which should ensure that the interests of all parties concerned are taken into account.

At a meeting of the ERPB on December 1, 2014, the following agreement was reached:

"The need for at least one pan-European instant payment solution for euro open to any payment service provider (PSP) in the EU."[1]

---

[1]   Statement following the second meeting of the European Retail Payments Board held on December 1, 2014, ERPB/2014/018, 1.12.2014

In mid-2015, the ERPB reiterated its requirement for a universal solution for instant payments. The European Payments Council (EPC), as representative of the European credit services sector, is responsible for designing the set of rules for an *instant SEPA transfer*—analog to the SEPA development.

Due to the disaggregation of the value creation chain in payment transactions which has taken place in recent years, as well as the different technical developments in the eurozone, the interests of the groups involved are very heterogeneous. Therefore, in the interests of creating a processing structure valid across the eurozone, all parties are called upon to cooperate in the development of a standardized solution and thereby take into account all analog as well as digital payment methods and means.

4.2.1 Definition of "instant payments"

In its proposed resolution to the ERPB meeting in December 2014, the ECB formulated the following definitions and requirements.

Instant payments are hence defined as an electronic multichannel payment transaction solution which is available constantly (24/7) and fulfills the following criteria:

Immediately or close to immediately (within seconds of payment initiation):

1. The payment message is sent to the payment recipient's bank

2. The execution of the payment is confirmed to the payer

3. The payment is credited to the account of the payment recipient

4. The recipient can access the amount credited

According to the ECB's assessment, the requirement for immediate availability to the payment recipient in particular is not fulfilled by any of the payment systems that currently exist.

It is very important to the decision-makers at the ECB that potential solutions support all channels for payment initiation. Instant payments should therefore be used not only in e-commerce, but also for point-of-sale transactions (for example, as a substitute for cash and card payments) and in the private sphere (P2P).

According to the current status of discussions, this means specifically that an infrastructure must be created which enables a transaction between two accounts to be processed within seconds. With regard to the format, a new type of transfer based on the SEPA credit transfer scheme (SCT) would be appropriate.

4.2.2 Areas of application for instant payments

The European Central Bank is calling for the introduction of at least one instant payments platform for 2017. It is still not clear how quickly the instant transfer will become accepted practice and which parts of the classic payment procedure will be replaced. We can expect numerous areas in which processes will be simplified and business models questioned or even new ideas arise. In addition to cash management and the frequently quoted person-to-person payments, we can assume two application areas which would be changed most quickly and sustainably by an instant payments (IP) initiative:

e-commerce

An instant payments procedure adapts the flow of funds to the requirements of modern retailing. This means that retailers will have less need to use interim solutions which cause additional risks and costs. In e-commerce, the retailer would thus have the option of waiting for a final payment receipt in the account held at the house bank (which takes place in seconds using IP) before he initiates the shipping of the goods. This reduces the risk of payment default. In contrast to the much-loved SEPA debit memo, which can be returned within eight weeks without specifying a reason, this incoming payment via instant payments transfer would be final from a technical perspective. On the other hand, if the customer makes a complaint, the retailer can also refund the money to the customer's bank account immediately. This simplifies processing and increases customer satisfaction and trust. For processing, retailers can work together with their own bank and do not have to use additional payment service providers. In many cases, this would reduce transaction costs.

POS in over-the-counter trade

These models from e-commerce can also be applied to POS (point-of-sale) transactions, that is, over-the-counter trade. An IP transfer could replace all other payment procedures used exclusively to initiate the transaction. At the POS, the customer could trigger a transfer from his bank on his mobile end device, with this transfer then going directly to the retailer's bank. The transaction data required for this process can be transferred from the cash register to the smartphone via various media. Established procedures such as NFC, QR code, or similar could be used here. The retailer's bank has to process the incoming payment immediately and send corresponding information to the retailer. The retailer's cash register system recognizes this as confirmation of payment and the purchase is thus completed. This would make many interim steps which are currently still required superfluous, thereby saving costs and minimizing risks.

4.2.3   Expectations of and challenges for companies

Companies which have already been looking into instant payments have clear expectations.

The retail trade in particular focuses on customer acceptance and wants to achieve this through simple handling, support for P2P payments, and simplification of small payment amounts. For the retail trade, numerous value-added services are also imaginable, such as an electronic receipt, which could be established based on open standards and practice-oriented technology. A solution for instant payments could also be advantageous for companies outside the retail trade. In the area of cash management in particular, companies expect improvements in terms of cost and flexibility. Not least the universal implementation of the specifications for 24/7 availability would contribute to achieving such improvements.

However, companies must be clear that using an instant payments infrastructure will also involve challenges for their own processes and systems. The entire logic involved in day-end closing and accounting cut-off will have to be reviewed. In theory, systems which serve follow-on processes triggered by an incoming payment also have to be accessible 24/7. Liquidity can flow in and out of accounts registered for instant payments at any hour of the day or night. Companies also have to think about how they can use the new options, such as faster purchase processing, efficiently to ensure that they do not put themselves at a competitive disadvantage to other companies investing in new instant payments-based payment procedures more quickly. The retail trade in particular is called upon to cooperate in the design of new offers which banks and other payment service providers will develop based on instant payments.

4.2.4   Opportunities and challenges for banks

Around the world, banks still process the majority of payment transactions, even though new players have increasingly taken market share away from them, above all in the retail trade (in particular, in the field of payment initiation). Therefore, a higher investment requirement can be expected for financial institutions for the implementation of a real-time or near-time payment procedure. They may have to contribute towards the costs of setting up one or more central messaging platforms. Most banks will not be able to avoid investing in their core bank systems. With regard to posting logic, in many cases these systems are not prepared for clearing in real time up to the customer account. Therefore, for banks, it is particularly important to use the advantages of an instant payments infrastructure to provide additional offerings to their customers so that they can compensate for the high investments with added value in payment transactions.

5 SAP BPC for S/4HANA Finance

SAP BPC for S/4HANA Finance is the third pillar of the new finance solution. Historically, planning was always part of the finance solution and included separate planning transactions for cost center planning, order planning, project planning, market segment planning, profit center planning, general ledger planning, and so on. The difference is that the classic planning transactions updated totals records and were connected by further transactions that transferred, for example, the planned costs for the cost center to profit center planning. SAP S/4HANA Finance provides a single planning model.

5.1 The case for a single planning model

If you have already conducted planning within core ERP, you will be familiar with the planning transactions for cost center planning (transaction KP06), order planning (transaction KPF6), project planning (transaction CJR2), market segment planning (transaction KEPM), profit center planning, general ledger planning (transaction GP12N), and so on. These are essentially detailed plans for the account assignments we discussed in Chapter 2 (cost center, order, WBS element) and the CO-PA characteristics and aggregations of these plans by profit center, company code, and so on.

These planning applications updated the totals tables, meaning that cost center planning, order planning, project planning, and CO-PA planning updated tables COSP and COSS and general ledger planning and profit center planning updated table FAGLFLEXP. With these tables declared redundant for capturing actual costs, changes were needed for storing planned costs.

The idea of the *single document* applies equally to a planning model. Just as we expect payroll costs to be assigned from the cost center to the assigned profit center, functional area, and so on, users entering plan data expect to capture wage costs per cost center and have the system update the affected functional areas, profit centers, company codes, and so on. It is the same story when we think about entering material costs for a project or order. Similarly, when planning secondary costs by entering the activity usage on the project, we expect the relevant partner objects to be updated. Only by doing this can we ensure that the plan and the actual costs are available for the same reporting dimensions.

The **difference** in planning, however, is that we sometimes plan at the most detailed level, such as the order, project, or a CO-PA characteristic, and sometimes at a higher aggregation, such as the company code or the profit center. To this extent, the planning application will always aggregate the detailed planned data to the higher aggregations. The reverse process of breaking down targets set at the higher level to cost centers and so on (a process known as *disaggregation*) is controlled using *planning functions*. It is also possible to plan not just by reporting dimension but also by node—for example, you might plan wages and salaries rather than the original accounts, something that could never happen for a journal entry which always refers to an account.

The planning model is a combination of a new planning table ACDOCP (available from SAP S/4HANA 1610) and a cube-based model that uses the technology from SAP Business Planning and Consolidation (SAP BPC). In other words, it uses SAP BPC 10.1, version for SAP NetWeaver, powered by SAP HANA and this is *embedded* in SAP S/4HANA to allow you to build powerful simulations using the faster aggregations and disaggregation that are possible with SAP BW on HANA. Do not be fooled by the mention of SAP BW here—we are not advocating building a separate data warehouse but rather only activating the relevant BW cubes on the ERP system and using these to store the planned data during planning and simulation. SAP offers business content designed specifically for use with the SAP BPC 10.1 embedded model. This business content can be extended using SAP BPC tools to build additional cubes where you have to model additional planning assumptions. For example, instead of manually entering wages and salary costs, you might build a model in SAP BPC to capture human resource-related costs in an independent cube.

Stay informed about planning updates

The planning solution is evolving with each release. Stay up to date by checking SAP Note 2081400 (*https://launchpad. support.sap.com/#/notes/0002081400*), which collects all SAP Notes relating to the solution.

5.1.1 ACDOCP—a new table for planning

In Chapters 1 and 2 we introduced table ACDOCA as the universal journal. From SAP S/4HANA, there is a new planning table, ACDOCP, shown in Figure 5.1, which stores planning data for reporting purposes once planning within SAP BPC on S/4HANA Finance has been completed. You will notice many similarities with table ACDOCA, but also that the source is different because the data is not created via business transactions within S/4HANA but from SAP BPC. Alternatively, this table can store data from external planning systems, including SAP's own Cloud for Planning solution or home-grown spreadsheets for plan/actual reporting. Over time, this planning table will be extended to capture planned data for production orders, maintenance orders, and so on, all of which continue to update the totals records in SAP S/4HANA.

Dictionary: Display Table

Technical Settings   Indexes...   Append Structure...

Transparent Table	ACDOCP	Active
Short Description	Plan Data Line Items	

| Attributes | Delivery and Maintenance | Fields | Input Help/Check | Currency/Quantity Fields |

Srch Help   Built-in Type   1 / 143

Field	Key	Ini...	Data element	Data Type	Length	Deci...	Short Description
RCLNT	✓	✓	MANDT	CLNT	3	0	Client
REQTSN	✓	✓	RSPM_REQUEST_TSN	NUMC	23	0	Request Transaction Sequence Number
DATAPAKID	✓	✓	RSDATAPID	NUMC	6	0	Data packet number
RECORD	✓	✓	RSARECORD	INT4	10	0	Data record number
RYEAR			GJAHR	NUMC	4	0	General Ledger Fiscal Year
RLDNR			FINS_LEDGER	CHAR	2	0	Ledger in General Ledger Accounting
RACCT			RACCT	CHAR	10	0	Account Number
RBUKRS			BUKRS	CHAR	4	0	Company Code
AWTYP			AWTYP	CHAR	5	0	Reference procedure
USNAM			USNAM	CHAR	12	0	User name
.INCLUDE			ACDOCP_SI_NOTIN...	STRU	0	0	ACDOCP: Fields which are not ion ACDOCA
CATEGORY			FCOM_CATEGORY	CHAR	10	0	Category
KPRICE			FINS_PLAN_KPRICE	CURR	23	2	Price in Global Currency
HPRICE			FINS_PLAN_HPRICE	CURR	23	2	Price in Company Code Currency
WPRICE			FINS_PLAN_WPRICE	CURR	23	2	Price in Transaction Currency
.INCLUDE			ACDOCP_SI_00	STRU	0	0	ACDOCP: Transaction, Currencies, Units
AWORG			AWORG	CHAR	10	0	Reference Organizational Units
AWREF			AWREF	CHAR	10	0	Reference Document Number
.INCLUDE			ACDOCP_SI_CURRK...	STRU	0	0	ACDOCP: Transaction, Currencies, Units
RWCUR			FINS_CURRW	CUKY	5	0	Transaction Currency
RHCUR			FINS_CURRH	CUKY	5	0	Company Code Currency
RKCUR			FINS_CURRK	CUKY	5	0	Global Currency

Figure 5.1: The new planning table—ACDOCP

5.1.2 Planning cubes

If the planning table is used to store data in SAP S/4HANA from edition 1610, the planning applications work with their own data store that is modelled like the old planning layouts to capture data in the appropriate level of detail. To get an idea of the complete scope of the solution, call up transaction PFCG and review the contents of the role SAP_SFIN _ACC_PLANNING. Figure 5.2 provides an overview of the various planning applications delivered with SAP S/4HANA Finance 1503.

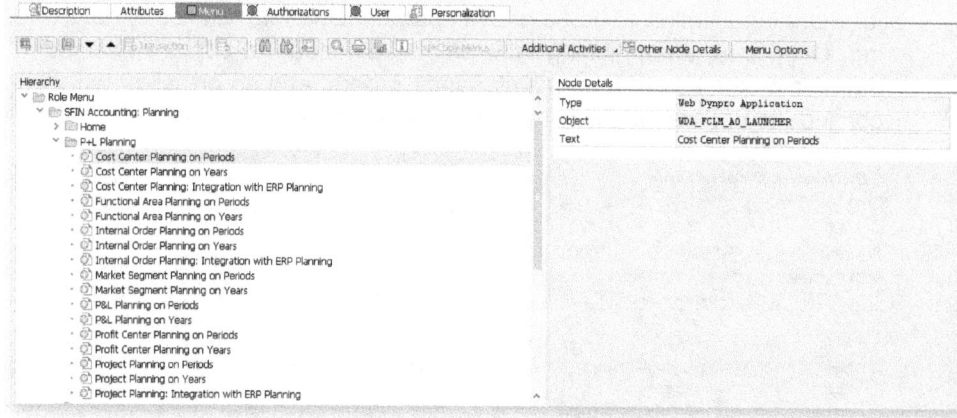

Figure 5.2: Overview of planning applications delivered with SAP S/4HANA Finance 1503

The new planning applications behave like the old planning transactions in the sense that they access actual data and master data in real time from SAP ERP **without** data replication. In other words, you pull the transactional data for previous periods and years directly from the universal journal. However, before you can work with the new planning applications, you have to generate the appropriate planning cubes to store the data entered and the planning functions that perform the various aggregations and derivations needed to enrich the data entered in planning. Figure 5.3 provides an overview of the generated planning content. You can access this view using transaction RSA1 (Administrator Workbench), which is usually part of SAP BW, but here it runs in embedded mode on an SAP S/4HANA system. Note the following elements of the planning model:

▶ *Aggregation levels* (on the right) define the entities for which planned data can be entered and planning functions update information. These are a subset of all dimensions in the cube.

▶ A *virtual InfoProvider* (center panel) acts as the data store for the relevant data from the universal journal and the relevant master data tables.

▶ The planning applications and planning functions (left) structure data entry and offer functions such as copy, distribute, or revaluate to manipulate the planning data.

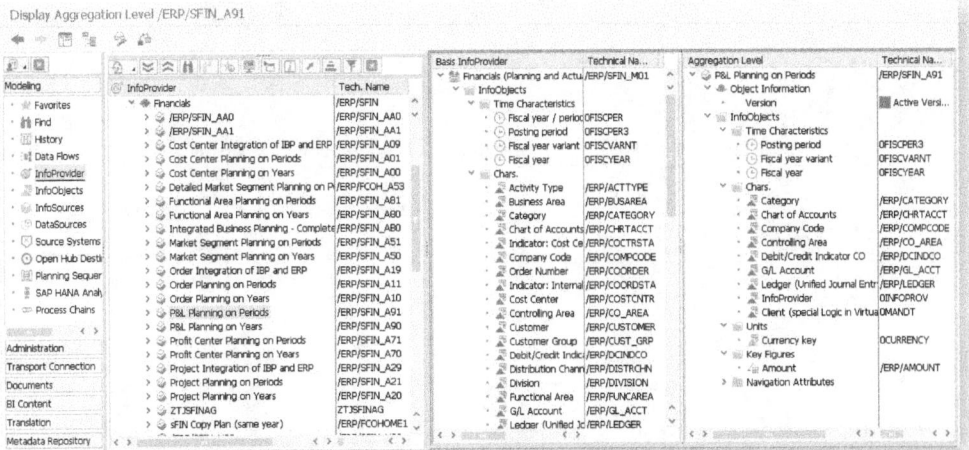

Figure 5.3: Planning model in embedded SAP BW within SAP S/4HANA

We will come back to the process of how to configure these planning cubes in Section 5.3.

5.1.3 Interaction of planning applications

To get an idea of what we mean by a single planning model, let us look at a simple example. Figure 5.4 shows the planned values by company code and account for 2016. This is essentially an aggregation of the planned values by cost center, order, project, market segment, and so on. It is roughly equivalent to the results of the general ledger planning transaction. If you prefer to stick with the old transactions instead of moving to the new solution, SAP Note 2253067 (*https://launchpad.support. sap.com/#/notes/0002253067*) explains how to reactivate the old planning transactions for the general ledger, at least for the interim. However, if you do this, you also have to run transaction FAGL_CO_PLAN to transfer the planned costs from Cost Center Accounting to General Ledger Accounting. In the new model, this happens automatically, as we will see in the next step.

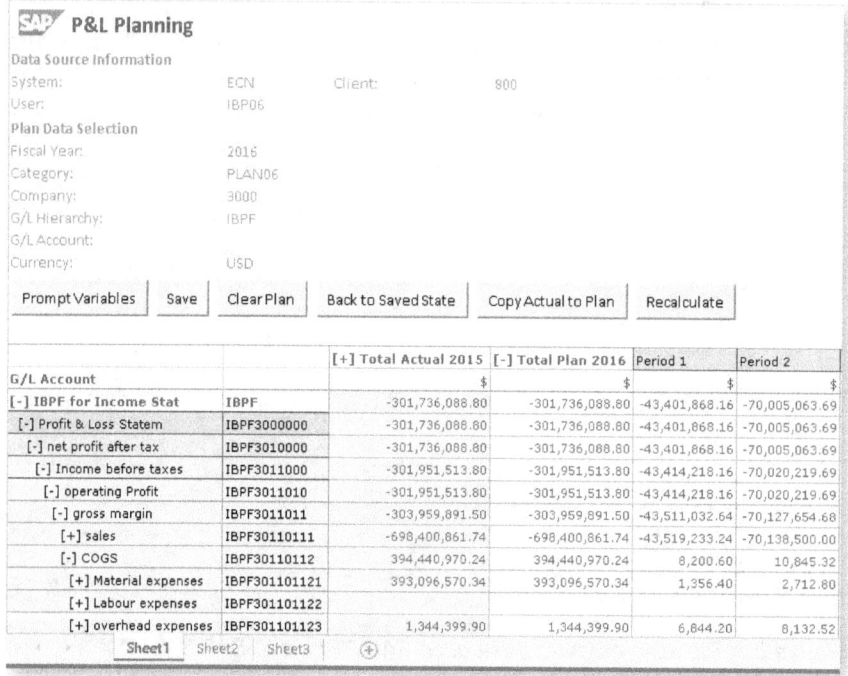

Figure 5.4: P&L planning

Figure 5.5 shows a sample application for cost center planning in SAP BPC for SAP S/4HANA. As we enter expenses by cost center, these are automatically aggregated to give a view by account and so on. Again, if you are not ready to make the move to the new planning solution, you can follow the instructions in SAP Note 2142447 (*https://launchpad.support.sap.com/#/notes/0002142447*) to reactivate transactions KP06 and KP07. Bear in mind that the classic transactions are integrated by transferring data between the totals records and that you also have to reactivate the general ledger planning transactions to have a complete picture.

SAP is gradually adding functions for performing simulative allocations on this data but the full functionality of activity price calculation is not yet available. For this reason, SAP also offers a retraction function so that you can push the data from your planning cubes back into the old totals tables in order to run transactions such as planned allocations and planned activity price calculation in the ERP environment.

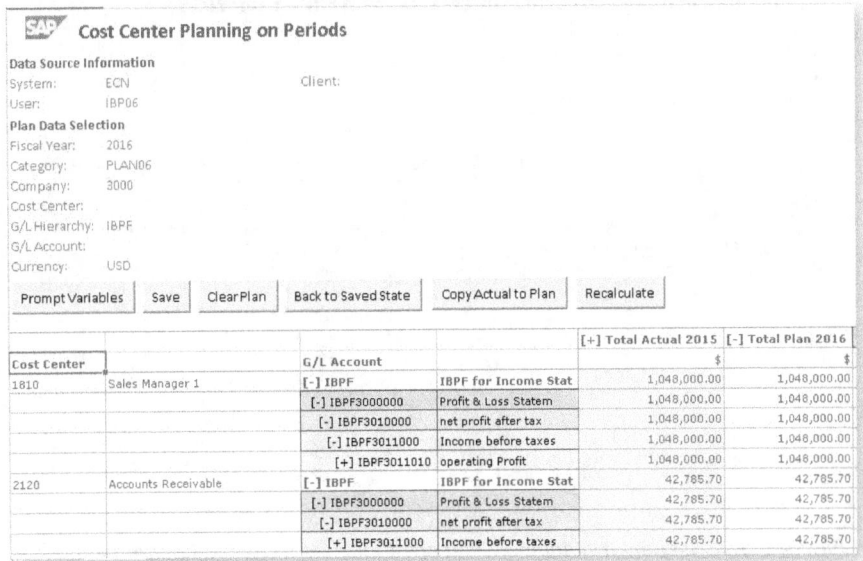

Figure 5.5: Cost center planning

The same basic idea applies to order and project planning. You can either use the new planning functions listed in Figure 5.2 or you can use SAP Note 2148356 (*https://launchpad.support.sap.com/#/notes/ 0002148356*) to reactivate transactions KPF6 and KPF7 for order planning and SAP Note 2135362 (*https://launchpad.support.sap.com/#/notes/ 0002135632*) to reactivate transactions CJR2 and CJR3 for project planning. You will want to use these planning transactions if you continue to use your planning data to provide a basis for setting budget ceilings or as part of the investment planning process.

In all three cases, SAP also offers functions for *retracting* data from SAP BPC to the classic totals tables to allow you to work with a combination of the two planning solutions. Figure 4.6 shows a sample cost center planning function with the option to retract from IBP (the former name for SAP BPC for SAP S/4HANA Finance) to ERP and to extract from SAP S/4HANA to IBP. You might want to move data the other way if you have planned depreciation in Asset Accounting or headcount-related costs in SAP HCM planning or calculate scheduled activity quantities in Sales and Operations Planning.

IBP for Finance - Cost Center Integration with ERP - Year: 2015

System: ECN / User IBP06

Controlling Area: Calendar year, 4 spec. periods

Cost Center: 3353

Copy from IBP   Category: PLAN06

Copy to ERP   Version: 1

| Prompt Variables | Copy IBP to ERP | Copy ERP to IBP | Save Data |

Deb/Cred Ind CO	Cost Center	G/L Account	Posting period	Amount IBP $	Amount ERP	Quantity IBP	Quantity ERP
D	3353	CAUS/415000	1	2,944.00			
			12	3,207.00			
			Result	6,151.00			
		CAUS/430100	1	10,186.00			
			12	9,981.00			
			Result	20,167.00			
		CAUS/430200	1	3,295.00			
			12	2,351.00			
			Result	5,646.00			
		CAUS/430300	1	7,621.00			
			12	6,755.00			

Figure 5.6 : Cost center planning with copy functions for extraction/retraction between SAP BPC and SAP S/4HANA

Figure 5.7 shows a similar planning application for planning market segments. Again, the figures in this planning application roll up into the totals shown in Figure 5.4. In this simple example, we are planning revenues by Customer Group. Because the operating concern is created at the customer's site and columns for the relevant characteristics are created in the universal journal, you may need to extend the BW model to include further characteristics. We will explain how to do this in Section 5.4. What is important here is how quickly you can arrive at a rough plan. Because you have the complete detail of ACDOCA at your disposal for reference data, you can easily pull together a highly granular starting point for your plan by simply copying the actual data from the universal journal and then manipulating the results using further planning functions.

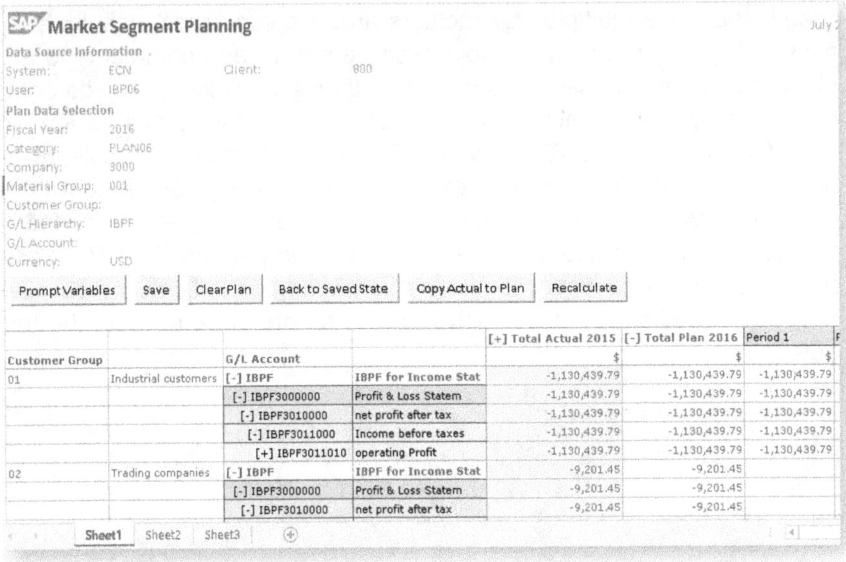

Figure 5.7: Market segment planning

As we look at the many different planning applications in Figure 5.2, it is important to understand that these are designed for a specific person within the planning process: a cost center manager, a project manager, a sales manager, and so on, who has responsibility for specific entities that must be planned. In this context, it becomes important to also orchestrate the planning process as a whole. Figure 5.8 shows a *business process flow* in SAP BPC that monitors the planning of various cost centers.

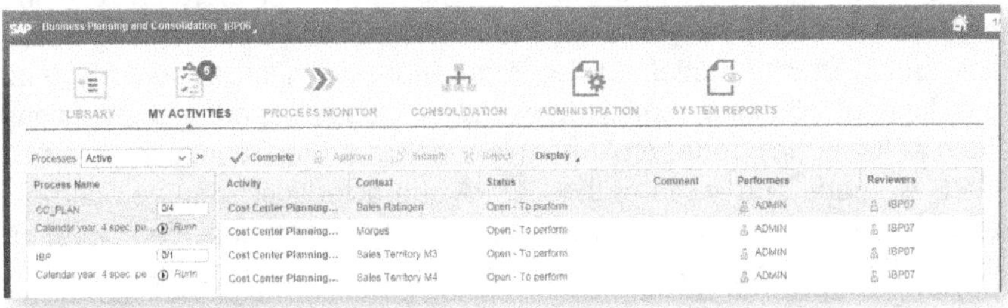

Figure 5.8: Business process monitor in SAP BPC

Clearly, because multiple stakeholders are involved in the planning process, it is also important to allow each person to add comments to explain their planning assumptions to the other stakeholders. To add comments to your planning sheets, follow the instructions given in *https://scn.sap.com/docs/DOC-59001*. Figure 5.9 shows a sample planning application that has been extended to include graphics (top right) and a COMMENT column (far right) in which the manager has added a text comment about the figures entered. Note that in the % OF PLAN column, we have also used *conditional formatting* to indicate which plan data is in good shape and which requires further work to meet the targets.

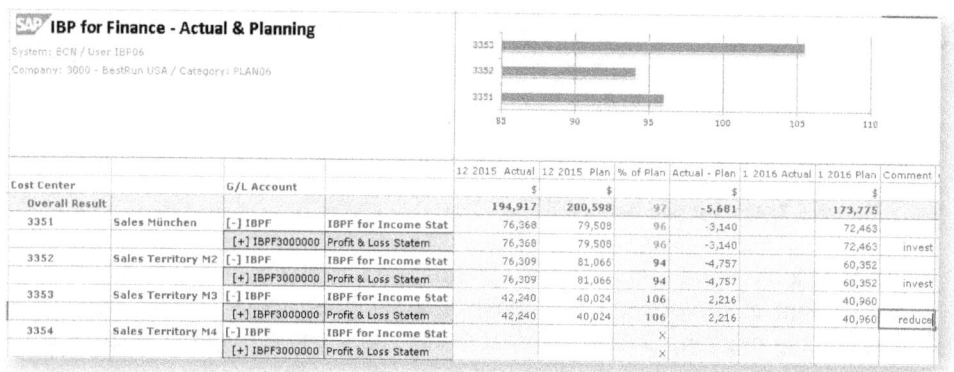

Figure 5.9: Planning with comments

Figure 5.10 provides a summary of the new planning approach, with the old planning transactions on the left and the new integrated planning model on the right. As you think about moving your own planning activities to this kind of model, do not forget that it is much easier to extend this kind of planning model. It already includes reporting dimensions such as company code, profit center, functional area, cost center, order, WBS element, and some of the CO-PA characteristics, and you can extend this model in a way that was only possible with considerable effort in the SAP ERP approach.

The new planning model ensures that you are working with one version of the truth but it puts certain constraints on the process if organizations want to plan costs for a product whose master data is not yet fully available in the system. The new planning model allows you to combine the best of both worlds, planning against your existing cost centers, accounts, and so on, but extending the model to include entities for which master data is not yet available.

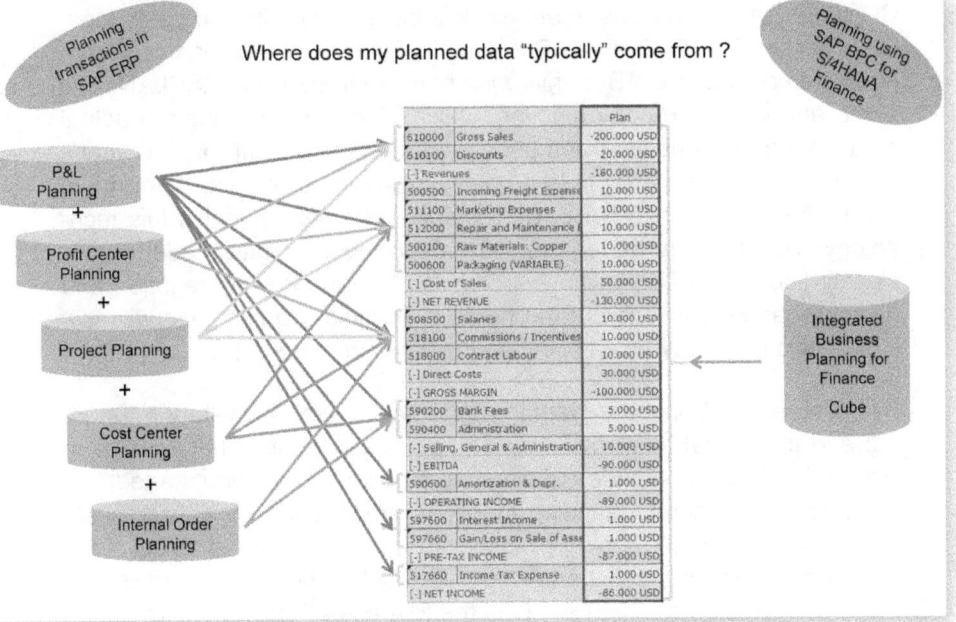

Figure 5.10: Integrated planning approach

Using provisional master data in planning

If you need to extend your planning model to include master data that is not yet available in the system, refer to this SAP Community Network document that walks you through the process of extending the relevant master data: *https://scn.sap.com/docs/DOC-59000*.

5.2 Planning functions

Now that we have explained the basic principles of the new planning model, we will look in more detail at the planning functions that provide the glue to bring the different plans together. Probably the simplest use of a planning function is to aggregate planned data captured by period to the fiscal year or to disaggregate planned data captured by year to the various periods. If you have already worked with *plan distribution* in the CO planning transactions, then you will be familiar with the basic idea. However, in SAP BPC for SAP S/4HANA Finance, these planning functions are created in the BW environment using transaction RSPLAN. The same applies to the *copy function*, which allows you to take the actual data from a previous year and use it as the starting point for next year's plan if you are not performing a strictly zero-based budget. If you have used SAP BW-IP or SAP BW-BPS before, you will recognize this technology. This time, however, we are working with a data model that is closely tied to the underlying ERP model. While basic aggregation and disaggregation functions are the heart of financial planning, we will now look at two more advanced planning functions in more detail.

SAP delivers not only the planning applications we saw listed in Figure 5.2 and the virtual InfoProviders and aggregation levels that we saw in Figure 5.3, but also a series of planning functions to get you started. We have seen the various planning functions embedded in the worksheets we saw in Figure 5.4 (copy) or Figure 5.6 (retract). To get an idea of the full scope, however, call transaction RSPLAN, choose EDIT PLANNING FUNCTIONS and enter /ERP/SFIN* in the PLANNING FUNCTION field. Figure 5.11 shows a selection of the planning functions delivered with SAP BPC for S/4HANA Finance. These include the copy functions and extract functions that we have already discussed, plus delete functions and functions to distribute planned values from years to periods. Of course, even something as simple as a distribution function is different from the old distribution keys in the classic planning layouts because you can use the SAP BW-IP functions to develop much more complex formulas than the *equal distribution* function delivered.

Where the planning functions become truly powerful is in the area of simulations. We will now look at an example delivered originally in edition 1511 and extended in edition 1610.

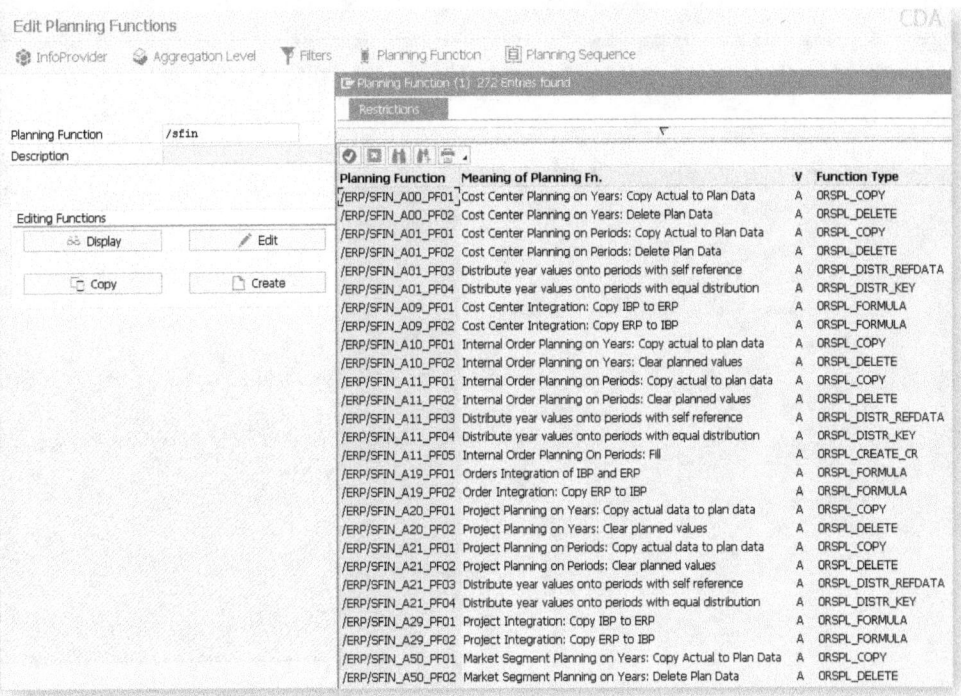

Figure 5.11: Sample planning functions for financial planning (1503 edition)

5.2.1 Cost simulation

We entered the planned primary costs for our cost centers in Figure 5.5 and had them aggregate up to the accounts shown in Figure 5.4. We will now look at a different example (delivered as the Excel workbook /ERP/SFIN_A02_WB01), where we plan primary costs for our cost centers but this time simulate how they are allocated through a network of further cost centers. Figure 5.12 shows a simple planning application for planning the primary costs on three cost centers.

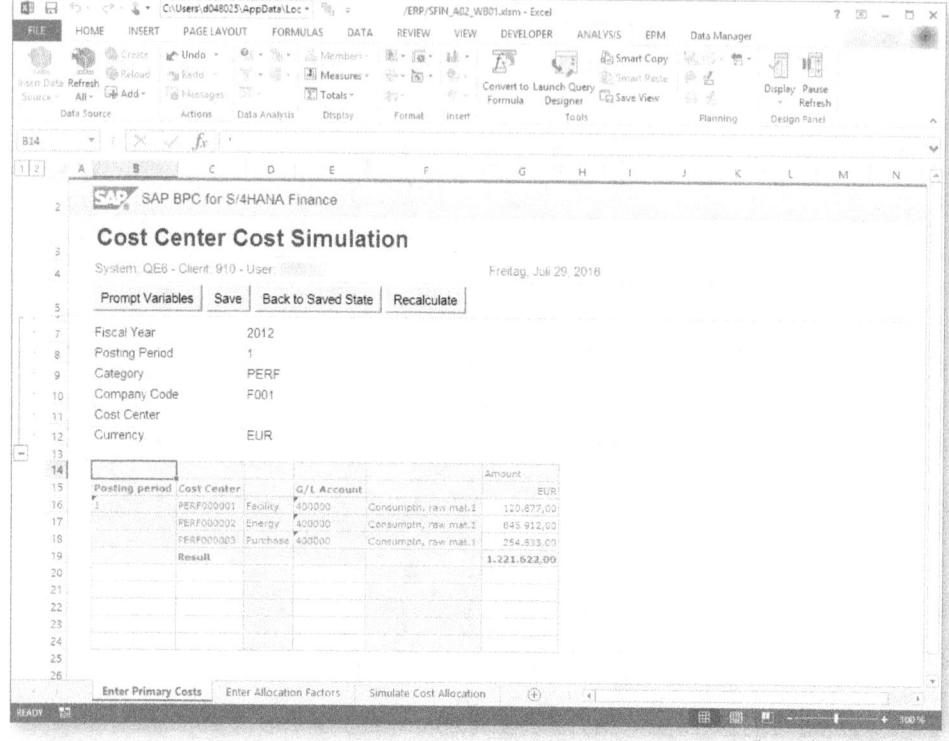

Figure 5.12: Entering primary costs for facilities, energy, and purchasing

The next step in a planning process is to understand and model how these costs flow through the organization. You do this by maintaining the input and output relationships in a network of cost centers using fixed amounts of quantities. Figure 5.13 shows the partner relationships between the sending cost centers (Facility, Energy, and Purchase) and the receiving (or partner) cost centers (Production, Board, Sales, and Research) and from there to the final cost centers (Rockets and Space Ships).

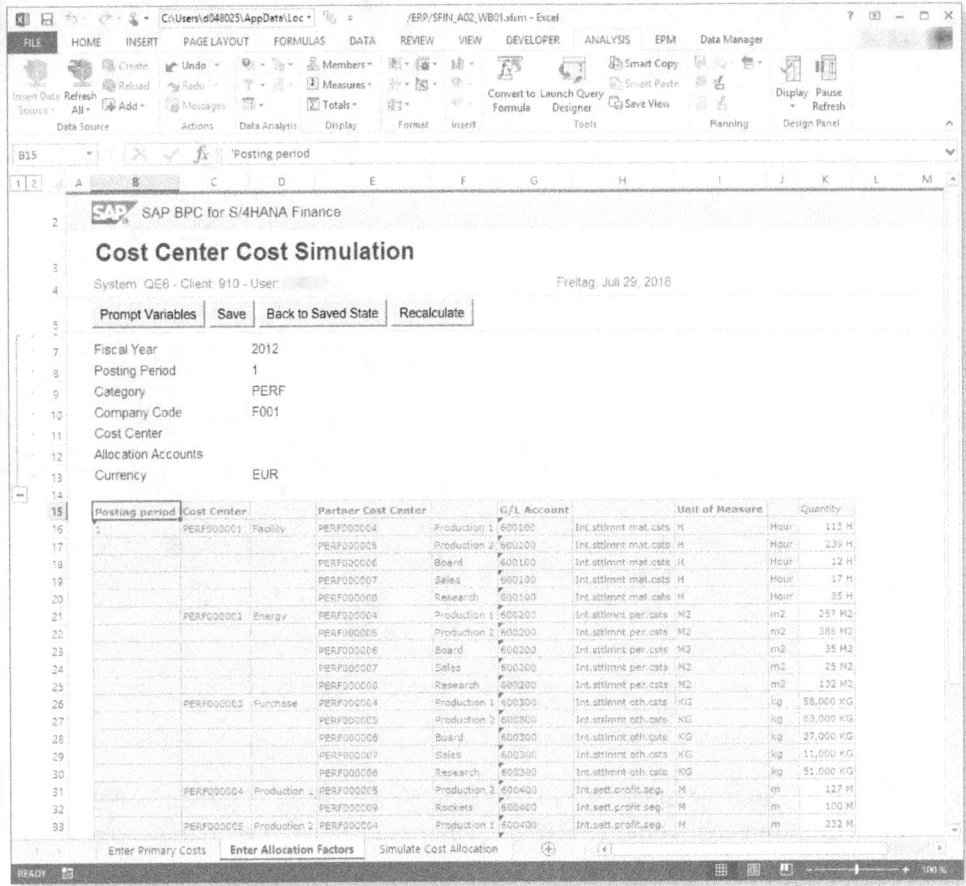

Figure 5.13: Entering allocation factors for cost simulation

Figure 5.13 shows the results of allocating the primary costs entered in Figure 5.12 based on the allocation drivers entered in Figure 5.13.

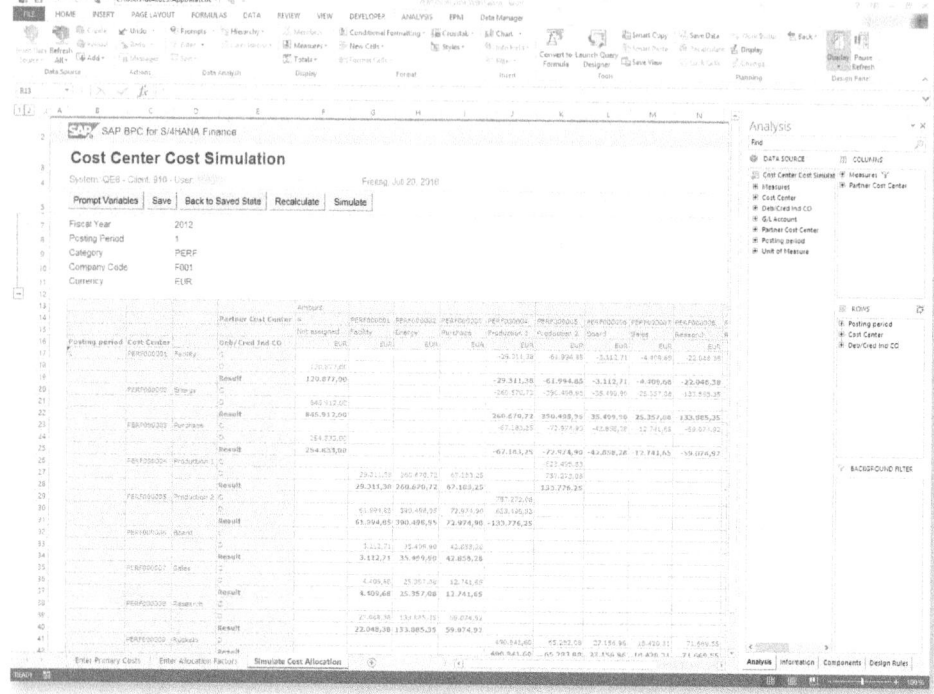

Figure 5.14: Result of cost simulation

Of course, these simulations mainly allow the allocation of general overheads between cost centers. SAP's vision here is also to include simulations that cover product costs.

5.2.2 Balance sheet planning

Balance sheet planning represents a different example, where the balance sheet items are derived via rules from the profit and loss line items. Figure 5.15 provides an example of balance sheet planning by period in which the *Business Rule Framework* (BRF+) is used to establish the rules for deriving the balance sheet items.

Because it is impossible to deliver business content that anticipates firstly the chart of accounts that contain your profit and loss items and secondly how to derive the balance sheet items from here, SAP offers a how-to paper documenting how to use the Business Rules Framework (BRF+) to build your own application:

*http://www.sdn.sap.com/irj/scn/go/portal/prtroot/docs/library/
uuid/907d0087-8e85-3310-8182-f2d61c17c90b?QuickLink=
index&overridelayout=true&60803852011620*

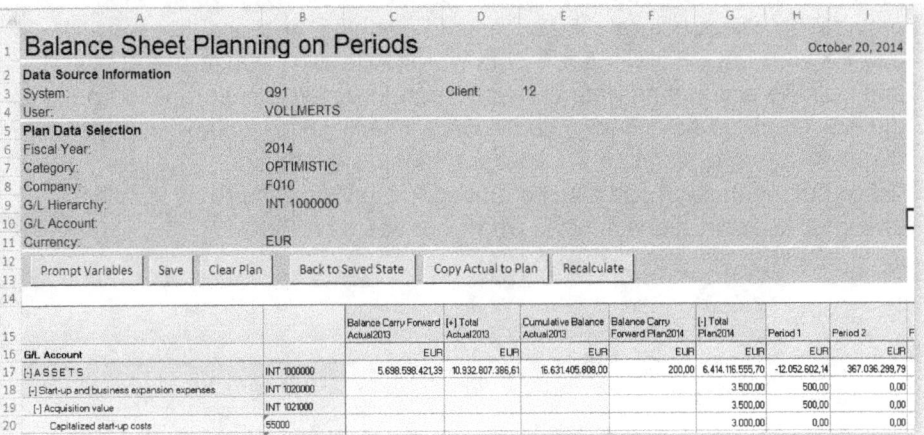

Figure 5.15: Balance sheet planning

5.2.3 Sales planning

SAP S/4HANA 1610 includes the first application for sales planning by quantity (previously, only amounts could be planned for the market segments). This allows you to perform simple quantity multiplied by price calculations as part of your sales plan.

5.3 Implementing SAP BPC for SAP S/4HANA Finance

Compared to the classic CO planning transactions, such as KP06 (Cost Center Planning) and CJR2 (Project Planning), where the planning processor is simply part of the ERP code line, the first thing you have to be aware of is that there is an SAP BW system **within** every S/4HANA system and that you use the cubes in this SAP BW system to store planned data and perform operations on that data. Figure 4.16 provides an overview of the basic architecture that you need to understand before you can implement the different pieces.

The HANA platform includes the universal journal table, the master data tables, configuration data (such as versions), planning data, and a *planning engine* that is optimized for use with SAP HANA. SAP Business Planning and Consolidation 10.1, version for SAP NetWeaver is used to provide the infrastructure—the cubes and planning functions that you will use for your data. This is not a data warehouse. The cubes are **virtual** and pull the accounting data that you need for reference purposes from the universal journal. Finally, you have a user interface. The examples we showed were planning applications running in Microsoft Analysis for Office but the queries can also be embedded in Web Dynpro applications or in mobile applications if this is what your users prefer.

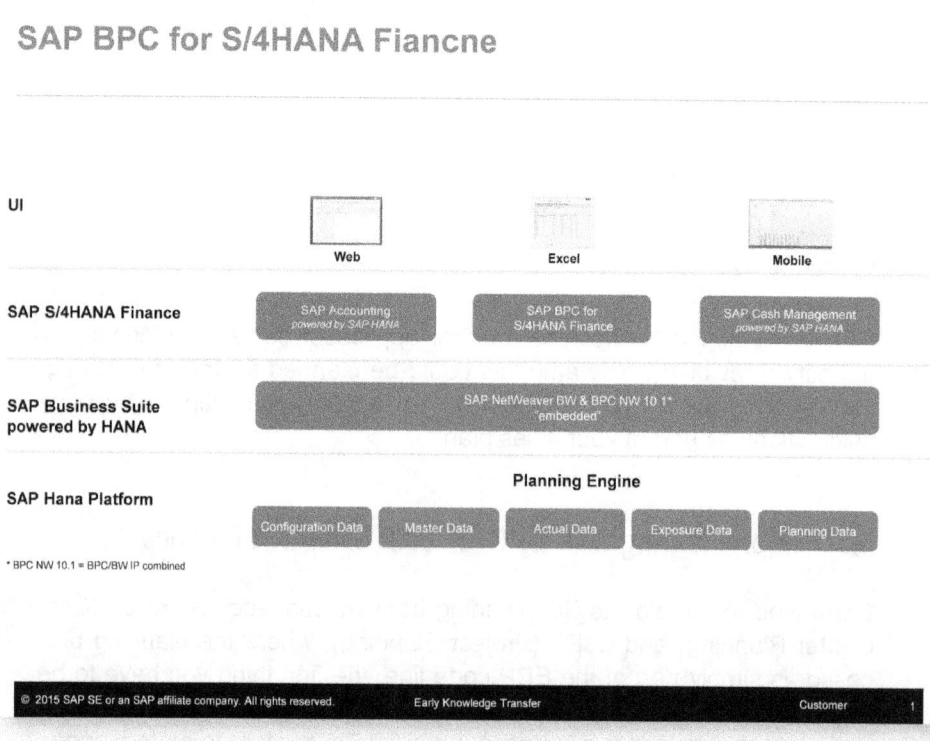

Figure 5.16: Architectural overview of business planning

5.3.1   Excel workbooks for planning

The user interface for business planning is Excel and we use the same *workbooks* as we saw included in the role SAP_SFIN_ACC_PLANNING in Figure 5.2. You can access these within Excel by choosing FILE • ANALYSIS • OPEN WORKBOOK. Then, choose the relevant ERP system, log on using your user authentication, and select the relevant workbooks. Figure 5.17 shows the standard workbooks that SAP delivers for financial planning. If you are familiar with SAP BW as a data warehouse, you will recognize that the workbooks shown below use a different naming convention compared to classic BW content. Workbooks beginning with /ERP/ can be used only in an embedded BW environment. Note that the content includes planning applications for both profit and loss planning and liquidity planning (see Chapter 3).

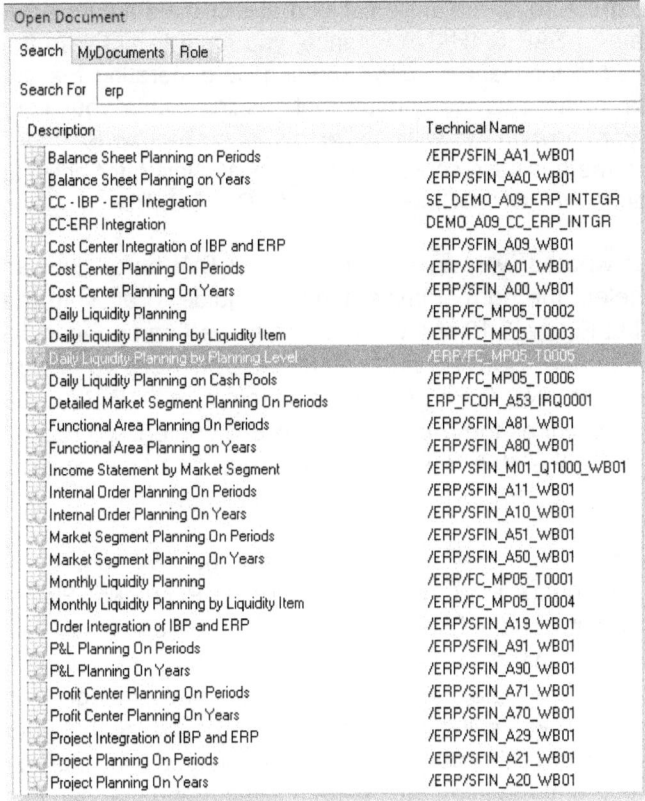

Figure 5.17: Workbooks delivered for financial planning

5.3.2   Activating the BW content for planning

Whereas the table structure for the universal journal is created automatically when you migrate to SAP S/4HANA Finance, you have to **activate** the data structures needed for planning and reporting by generating the appropriate metadata in the data warehouse that resides within your core financial system. From now on, we will refer to this as *embedded SAP BW*. Before you activate the business content, have your administrator activate the business functions FIN_CO_CCMGMT and FIN_CO_CC_PLAN.

If you have never worked with an embedded SAP BW before, it can seem illogical to select the normal implementation guide to activate the SAP BW content but Figure 5.18 shows the steps for setting up Financial Planning in the IMG under CONTROLLING • GENERAL CONTROLLING • PLANNING • SET UP FOR PLANNING. Owing to the architecture of SAP BW, you have to choose one *client* as the client where the BW content will reside. You enter this client in the step BASIC CONFIGURATION FOR OPERATIONAL ANALYTICS.

Once you have chosen the relevant client, activate the BW content by choosing the step ACTIVATE BI BUNDLE CONTENT FOR PLANNING. Figure 5.19 shows the Content Bundle /ERP/SFIN_PLANNING which contains all the BW objects you will need for your planning process. If you cannot find this content bundle in the list, change the business category to Business Functions. If you still cannot find the bundle, check that your administrator has activated the relevant business functions. In this example, you can see that the content has been activated and you can use the logs to check the status of the activation. You can use this BW content directly or take it as a starting point for covering your own planning processes—for example, you might want to extend the market segment information to choose the market segments you report on in CO-PA or build your own planning functions.

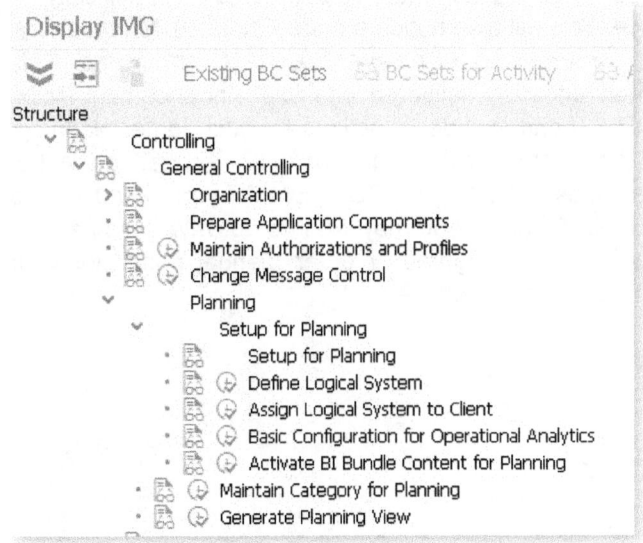

Figure 5.18: IMG steps for setting up financial planning

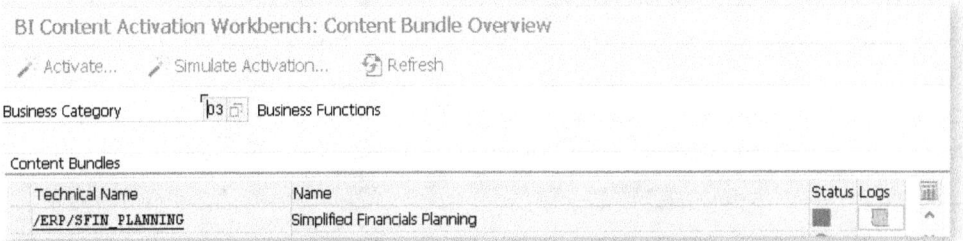

Figure 5.19: Activating the BI content bundle for Simplified Financials Planning

As soon as you have performed this step, you will be able to see the relevant business content for planning by calling up transaction RSA1 in the client you selected in Figure 5.18. If you have worked with SAP BW as a data warehouse before, you will be familiar with the *Modelling Workbench*. The difference is that we are working in an embedded model where the BW infrastructure works directly on top of the accounting tables. As shown in Figure 5.20, you will find all the items we generated with the content bundle under INFOPROVIDER (in the navigation area on the left) and FINANCIALS MANAGEMENT AND CONTROLLING (in the area on the right). Again, note the naming convention that all objects begin with /ERP/SFIN. These are BW objects that have been created specifically for use in Core Finance. You will also notice a node FINANCIAL MANAGEMENT & CONTROLLING • CONTROLLING • OVERHEAD COST CONTROLLING. This business content was originally delivered with SAP Enhancement Package 6 for SAP ERP 6.0 and includes functions for cost center planning, order planning, and project planning. It also uses an embedded BW but updates the totals tables COSP and COSS. Even if you intend to use SAP BPC for S/4HANA Finance, you may want to activate this business content to plan statistical key figures or enter manual prices for your activity rates in a modern user interface.

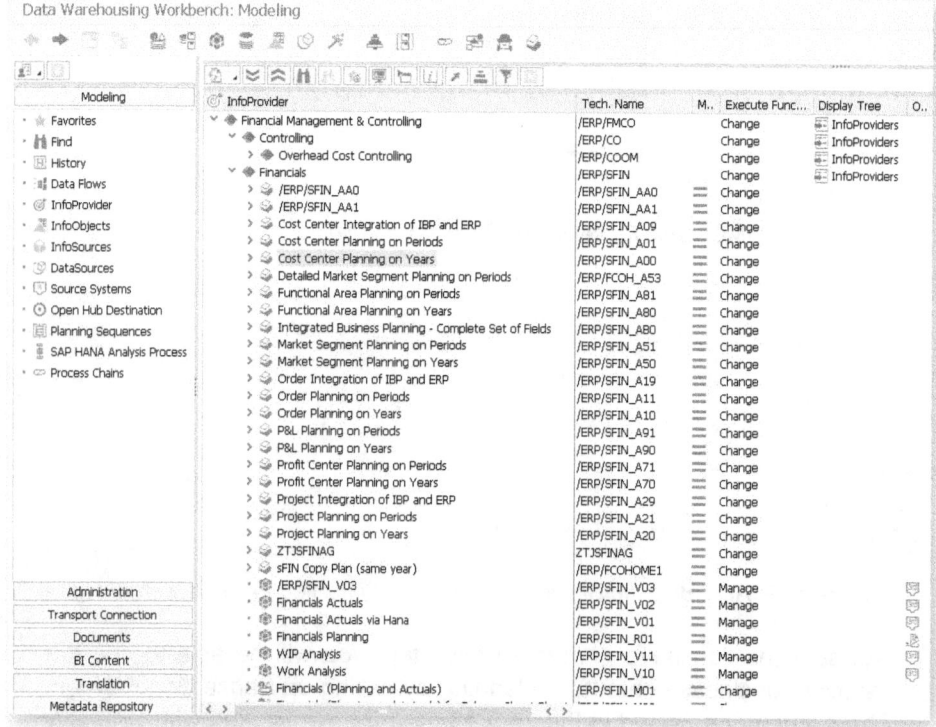

Figure 5.20: BW content for financial planning

We will now look at the generated business content in more detail. Figure 5.21 shows the details of Cost Center Planning, including the *MultiProvider* (/ERP/SFIN_M01) that brings together the actual costs from the universal journal (/ERP/SFIN_V01) and the planning data from the cube store (/ERP/SFIN_R01). Note also the various planning functions, such as distribution across periods, copy, and delete. These will get you started in a project but you will probably add more for your own purposes.

Cost Center Planning on Periods	/ERP/SFIN_A01	Change	
Cost Center Planning Distribution Function Year to Per	/ERP/SFIN_A01_FIL...	Change	InfoProviders
Cost Center Planning on Periods	/ERP/SFIN_A01_FIL...	Change	InfoProviders
Financials (Planning and Actuals)	/ERP/SFIN_M01	Change	InfoProviders
Financials Actuals via Hana	/ERP/SFIN_V01	Manage	InfoProviders
Financials Planning	/ERP/SFIN_R01	Manage	InfoProviders
DSO with comment (Direct Update)	ZCMNTDSO	Manage	InfoProviders
Cost Center Planning on Periods: Copy Actual to Plan D	/ERP/SFIN_A01_PF01	Change	InfoProviders
Cost Center Planning on Periods: Delete Plan Data	/ERP/SFIN_A01_PF02	Change	InfoProviders
Distribute year values onto periods with equal distribut	/ERP/SFIN_A01_PF04	Change	InfoProviders
Distribute year values onto periods with self reference	/ERP/SFIN_A01_PF03	Change	InfoProviders
Cost Center Planning on Years	/ERP/SFIN_A00	Change	
Cost Center Planning on Years	/ERP/SFIN_A00_FIL...	Change	InfoProviders
Financials (Planning and Actuals)	/ERP/SFIN_M01	Change	InfoProviders
Financials Actuals via Hana	/ERP/SFIN_V01	Manage	InfoProviders
Financials Planning	/ERP/SFIN_R01	Manage	InfoProviders
DSO with comment (Direct Update)	ZCMNTDSO	Manage	InfoProviders
Cost Center Planning on Years: Copy Actual to Plan Da	/ERP/SFIN_A00_PF01	Change	InfoProviders
Cost Center Planning on Years: Delete Plan Data	/ERP/SFIN_A00_PF02	Change	InfoProviders

Figure 5.21: Details of cost center planning

Note also the Z objects where comments have been activated for the workbook shown in Figure 5.9.

5.3.3 Additional steps In Core Finance

Now that you have completed the steps for activating the BW content, there are a couple of steps to be completed in Core Finance. All planning applications (and many of the Fiori reports) include the controlling area as a user parameter so it makes sense to set this in your user parameters. To do this, choose SYSTEM • USER PROFILE • OWN DATA and enter the Parameter CAC and your chosen controlling area as shown in Figure 5.22.

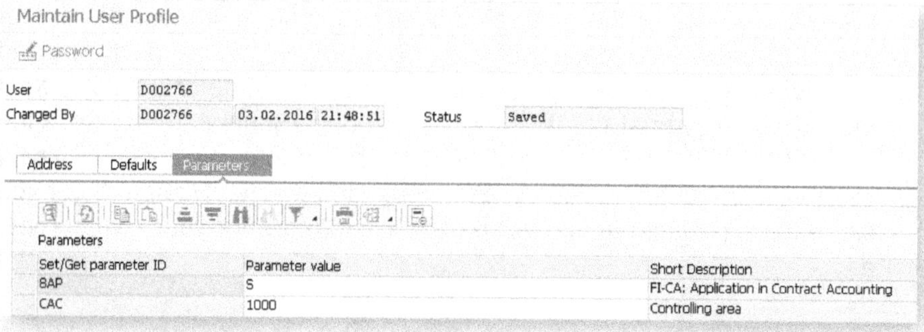

Maintain User Profile

🔒 Password

User	D002766				
Changed By	D002766	03.02.2016 21:48:51	Status	Saved	

Address	Defaults	Parameters

Parameters

Set/Get parameter ID	Parameter value	Short Description
8AP	S	FI-CA: Application in Contract Accounting
CAC	1000	Controlling area

Figure 5.22: User parameter for the controlling area

All plans are created with reference to a category, so refer to the IMG shown in Figure 5.18 and choose MAINTAIN CATEGORY FOR PLANNING. Figure 5.23 shows the plan categories in one of the demo systems. This has the same role as the versions in the classic planning transactions but gives you more than the 999 digits of the old CO version for describing your planning approach. All the selection screens for planning require you to enter this category. There is also a default category ACT01 for the actual costs. We will meet the category again when we look at the new consolidation options in Chapter 7.

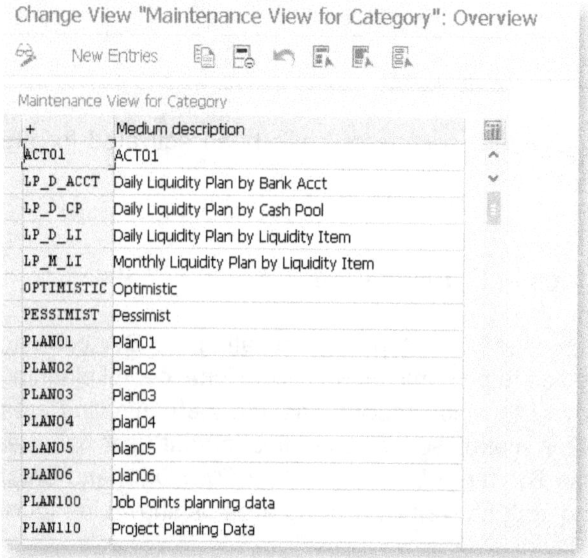

Change View "Maintenance View for Category": Overview

New Entries

Maintenance View for Category

+	Medium description
ACT01	ACT01
LP_D_ACCT	Daily Liquidity Plan by Bank Acct
LP_D_CP	Daily Liquidity Plan by Cash Pool
LP_D_LI	Daily Liquidity Plan by Liquidity Item
LP_M_LI	Monthly Liquidity Plan by Liquidity Item
OPTIMISTIC	Optimistic
PESSIMIST	Pessimist
PLAN01	Plan01
PLAN02	Plan02
PLAN03	Plan03
PLAN04	plan04
PLAN05	plan05
PLAN06	plan06
PLAN100	Job Points planning data
PLAN110	Project Planning Data

Figure 5.23: Sample categories for planning

Finally, if you want to show the accounts in a hierarchical form, you have to make sure that you have used transaction FSE2 to build a financial statement version containing all the relevant accounts for planning, as shown in Figure 5.24.

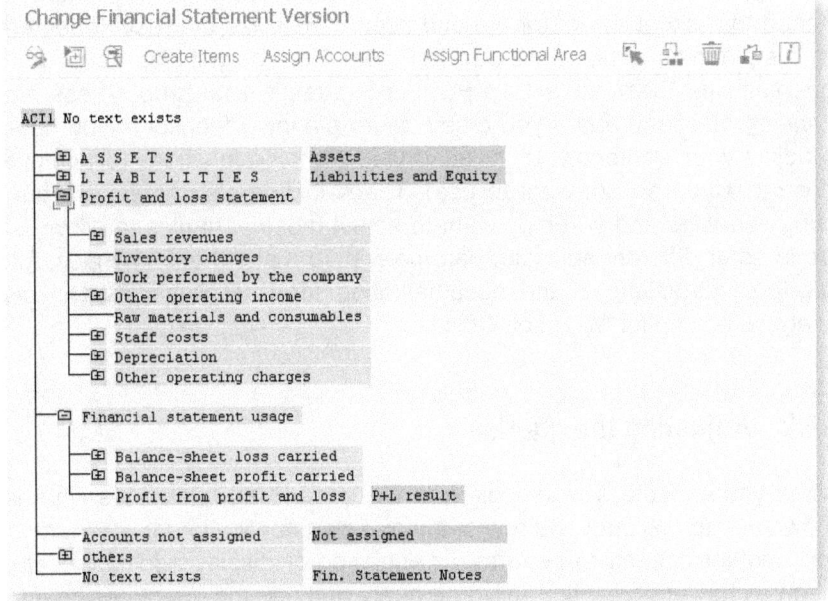

Figure 5.24: Financial statement version

With these steps in place, you can begin testing the planning applications delivered.

5.4   Extending the planning model

We have discussed how to extend the planning model to include provisional master data and additional CO-PA characteristics, but sometimes, additional planning data is required that is not part of the standard model at all, because the standard model only covers the most commonly used financial planning entities. The benefit of using SAP BPC as the data model is that you can build MultiProviders in SAP BW that act as a bridge between the embedded planning model, which is closely tied with the underlying SAP tables, and a cube that you can model according to your requirements.

5.4.1 Adjusting the workbooks

The workbooks for Analysis for Office are essentially spreadsheets that are designed to connect to either an SAP BW or a Finance system. An obvious way to make the workbooks delivered more appealing is to add a chart to make it easier for the end user to visualize the result of entering his planning data, as we saw in Figure 5.9. You will also notice buttons such as COPY ACTUAL TO PLAN in Figures 4.4 and 4.5. These are planning functions and if you create more planning functions, you have to adjust your workbooks to include these planning functions (or remove those that you do not want to use). The selection parameters are built using *variables* and you may want to adjust those variables to allow users to enter different selection parameters. To make these changes, follow the instructions in the documentation for SAP Business Objects Analysis, edition for Microsoft Office.

5.4.2 Adjusting the queries

When you execute a workbook, it is the *query* that determines what is shown in each column and row of the planning application. If you want to add another column to perform a calculation or display additional data, then you have to copy the delivered query and use the query designer to make the required changes. You may also want to change the settings for the hierarchies if you prefer to use a multilevel product hierarchy rather than the single-level material group that we used in our example. In order to make changes to the query, follow the instructions in the documentation for SAP BEx Query Designer.

5.4.3 Adding further planning functions

If you find that you need more than the simple planning functions that are delivered as standard content, you can create your own planning functions using transaction RSPLAN and link them together to form *planning sequences* (for example, you might copy last year's actual data and then apply a percentage change to them as a second planning function). We are reusing functions from the *Planning Application Kit* and you can find details of how to modify the planning functions in the documentation for SAP Planning Modeler.

5.4.4 Adjusting the InfoProviders to include new market segments

If you are only planning by cost center, order, project, profit center, and so on, you may not need to adjust the InfoProviders that we looked at in Figure 5.20 because the underlying data structures are fixed. However, if you use market segment planning, then you will almost certainly want to extend the content delivered to include your own characteristics because the operating concern is generated at the customer's site and most organizations use their own characteristics alongside the standard ones delivered by SAP. During planning, the actual costs are read from the universal journal using the following HANA views:

▶ sap.erp.sfin.fi.gl.FAC_ACDOCA_COM

▶ sap.erp.sfin.fi.gl.FAC_GLACCT_LINE_ITEM_COM

▶ sap.erp.sfin.co.pl.FCO_C_IBP_ACDOCA

If you need to add extra characteristics, then you have to adjust these views to read the additional fields. This means using the HANA studio and selecting the additional fields you need from table ACDOCA. For full details, refer to the instructions in the online help documentation: *http://help.sap.com/saphelp_sfin200/helpdata/en/32/bb0e5401c05518e1000 0000a423f68/content.htm.*

Before you can use these additional fields in planning, you also have to generate the missing InfoObjects by running transaction FCOM _RKEGEN for each of the fields you have added. Figure 4.25 shows the characteristics in a sample operating concern for which InfoObjects exist and are therefore available for reporting and planning (these begin with /ERP), and those which are part of the operating concern but are not yet included in the new planning applications and reports (these begin with /RKE). Once you have selected the required characteristics and generated InfoObjects for them, you have to add them to the relevant InfoProviders and HANA views.

Assigning and Generating InfoObjects

Field Description	Field Name	InfoObject Description	InfoObject	Ge...	Ch...
Product	ARTNR	Material	/ERP/MATERIAL	■	✎
Order reason	AUGRU		/RKE/AUGRU	●	✎
Industry	BRSCH	Industry	/ERP/INDUSTRY	■	✎
Company Code	BUKRS	Company Code	/ERP/COMPCODE	■	✎
Sales district	BZIRK	Sales District	/ERP/SALESDST	■	✎
Cost center	COPA_KOSTL		/RKE/KOSTL	●	✎
CRM Cost Elmnt	CRMCSTY		/RKE/CRMCSTY	●	✎
Marketing Element	CRMELEM	Marketing Element	/RKE/CRMELEM	■	✎
Billing Type	FKART	Billing Type	/RKE/FKART	■	✎
Functional Area	FKBER		/RKE/FKBER	●	✎
Size/dimensions	GROES		/RKE/GROES	●	✎
Business Area	GSBER	Business Area	/ERP/BUSAREA	■	✎
CustomerHier01	HIE01	CustomerHier01	/RKE/HIE01	■	✎
CustomerHier02	HIE02	CustomerHier02	/RKE/HIE02	■	✎
CustomerHier03	HIE03	CustomerHier03	/RKE/HIE03	■	✎
Sales Order	KAUFN	Sales Order	/RKE/KAUFN	■	✎
Customer group	KDGRP	Customer Group	/ERP/CUST_GRP	■	✎
Sales Ord. Item	KDPOS		/RKE/KDPOS	●	✎
Customer	KNDNR	Customer	/ERP/CUSTOMER	■	✎
CO Area	KOKRS	Controlling Area	/ERP/CO_AREA	■	✎
Cost Element	KSTAR	G/L Account	/ERP/GL_ACCT	■	✎
Cost Object	KSTRG		/RKE/KSTRG	●	✎
Customer class.	KUKLA	Customer class.	/RKE/KUKLA	■	✎
Ship-to party	KUNWE	Ship-to party	/RKE/KUNWE	■	✎
Country	LAND1	Country	/ERP/COUNTRY	■	✎
Material Group	MATKL	Material Group	/ERP/MATL_GRP	■	✎
MaterialGroup 1	MVGR1	MaterialGroup 1	/RKE/MVGR1	■	✎
City	ORT01		/RKE/ORT01	●	✎
ProdHier01-1	PAPH1		/RKE/PAPH1	●	✎

Figure 5.25: Generating InfoObjects for the fields in the operating concern

Note that this procedure changes with edition 1610 when transaction FCOM_MET becomes available that allows you to extend the planning and reporting views when fields are added to table ACDOCA or AC-DOCP.

This wraps up how to set up the planning applications in SAP BPC but we will come back to this topic in the SAP Fiori chapter because the same technology is also used in many of the standard reports. Figure 5.26 shows the Fiori launchpad for a financial analyst and all the tiles for plan/actual reports require you to follow the procedure above to activate the appropriate business content for your reports.

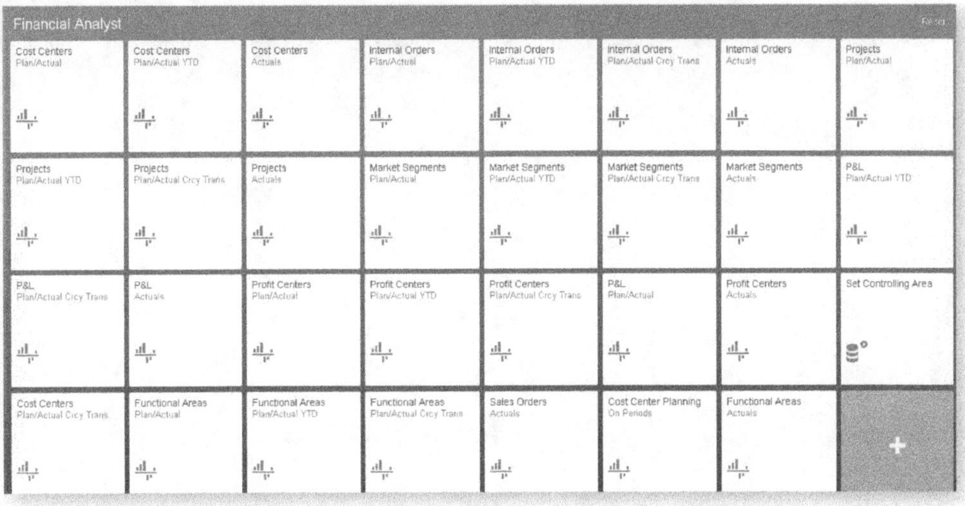

Figure 5.26: SAP Fiori launchpad

6 Migrating to SAP S/4HANA Finance

In Chapter 2, we learnt how the universal journal combines transactional data from Accounting and Controlling. If you are involved in a new SAP implementation, you can skip this chapter because your transactional data will be stored in the new structures from the start. However, if you are coming from an earlier release of SAP ERP, this chapter explains how to bring your existing transactional data, which is currently spread over several tables, into the new data model. We also look at how the migration removes the totals and index tables that we discussed in Chapter 1.

There are several parts to a migration project:

▶ Blueprinting and defining how the new system should behave

▶ Testing on a cloned system (you will generally repeat this around five times until all errors have been identified and fixed)

▶ The migration proper using real data in the live system

▶ The sign-off for the migration from your auditors

It is important to understand that this is **not** simply a technical upgrade but that the topics we discussed in Chapter 2 have a business impact: you will need business users as well as IT people to decide the configuration settings that make sense for your organization, to ensure that the correct master data is in place before you start enriching the existing data with profit centers, functional areas, and so on, and to sign-off on the consistency of the data after the migration.

6.1 Documenting a migration

In Chapter 2, we looked at the key fields for each application in the universal journal. Because the migrated data is subject to the normal **audit** requirements on financial data, it is important to understand how to identify a universal journal entry that has been migrated and to explain what type of line item you are dealing with. Indeed, you should involve your auditors in the project to ensure that your audit requirements are met during the migration. Figure 6.1 shows the migration-specific fields in the universal journal table.

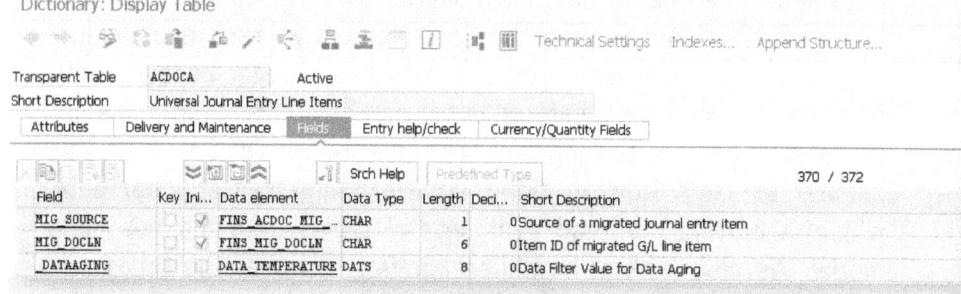

Figure 6.1: Migration-specific fields in the universal journal

The entry in the MIG_SOURCE field is used to show what sort of line item has been migrated (General Ledger Accounting only, Asset Accounting, Controlling, or Material Ledger) and whether the line item is a true line item from one of the applications or one that represents a former entry in the totals table. Finally, line items for reposting/correction document changes made in the course of migration where it was not possible to merge the FI and the CO document for the same business transaction retrospectively. The result will be an FI document that contains the original posting lines and a correction document that contains the CO account assignments with a reference to the original CO document number.

Figure 6.2 shows the keys that identify the original line items that have been migrated and the correction postings entered where the totals do not match the sum of the line items. If there is no entry in the MIG_SOURCE field, it means that the document was not migrated but is a new journal entry (the normal case once operations start after conversion).

Migration Source	Short Descript.
	Not created by migration
F	FI excluding NewGL, potentially including CO, ML, AA
G	FI including NewGL, potentially including CO, ML, AA
C	Controlling only
M	Material Ledger only
A	Asset accounting only
R	Reposting / correction
S	Totals correction for Controlling
T	Totals correction for Material Ledger
U	Totals correction for General Ledger

Figure 6.2: Details of the migration source

There are different types of migration record depending on the data source:

▶ M (Material Ledger only) and A (Asset Accounting only) records represent data from the subledgers that is enriched with the assignment to an account assignment object in Controlling and the reporting dimensions in General Ledger Accounting. These are usually the most granular records.

▶ C (Controlling only) records represent data from Controlling that is enriched by the reporting dimensions in General Ledger Accounting.

▶ F and G (General Ledger Accounting) records represent either data from SAP ERP General Ledger Accounting, which includes the reporting dimensions from FAGLFLEXA, or data from classic General Ledger Accounting that has been enriched to include the relevant reporting dimensions.

Normally, the entries in the totals table are an aggregation of the data in the line item tables (and therefore redundant), meaning that the migration can simply take the data from the totals tables and put it in backup tables (we saw these when we looked at the GLT0 view in Chapter 1) because it can be aggregated on the fly and does not need to be pre-calculated and stored. However, where the sum of the line items is **not** the same as the totals to be migrated, the system creates a separate document for the **difference**. This document effectively makes it clear for an auditor that some of the supporting line items for a totals entry are no longer in the system because they have already been archived.

This correction entry accounts for the fact that old line items might have been archived, leaving only the totals for the early years. The correction entries do not include all the reporting dimensions because they can only access the fields in the original totals records. However, they do ensure that your balance sheet and profit and loss statement for the closed periods meet the audit requirements for such data. Depending on the source of the totals difference, you will find entries for S (Controlling), U (Material Ledger) and V (General Ledger Accounting). There may also be errors in the migration process itself, which are documented with source R (reposting/correction).

Before you start, it is important to understand that the migration process will migrate **every** financial document in the system. It therefore makes sense to archive as much as possible before beginning the migration. Obviously, this will speed up the process because there will be fewer objects to handle, but it also means that you will not be faced with correcting errors in documents from previous migrations, such as those from SAP R/2 to SAP R/3 or SAP ERP or conversions from local currencies to the euro.

We will now walk through the key things that you need to know in order to prepare for a migration.

6.2   Preparation

As you move into the blueprinting stage, it is important to understand what kind of SAP S/4HANA system you are migrating to because the installation and migration steps will be different in each case. Figure 6.3 provides an overview of the paths supported. As you can see from ❶ you can move from the SAP Business Suite to the SAP Simple Finance Add-On and migrate later via ❸ to SAP S/4HANA. Alternatively, you can take the direct route via ❷ from the SAP Business Suite to SAP S/4HANA.

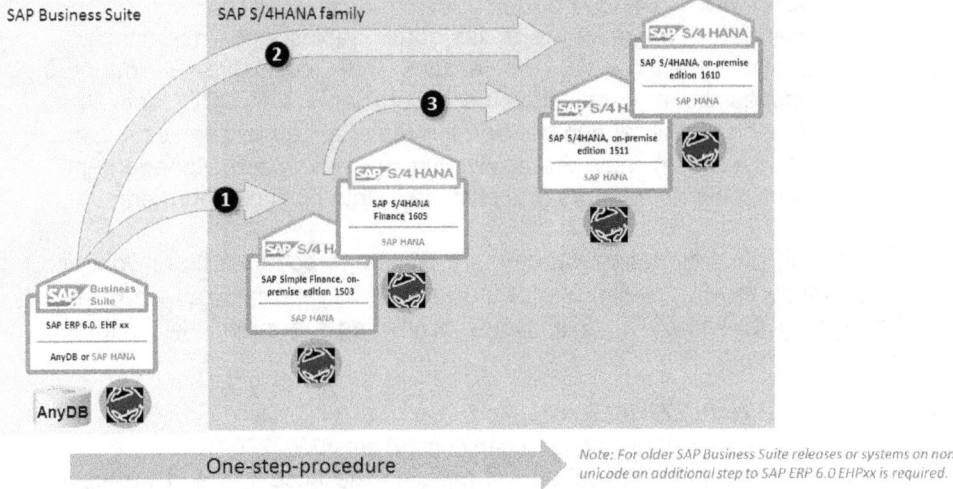

Transition Paths to Move to SAP S/4HANA

Figure 6.3: Transition paths to SAP S/4HANA

In the description that follows, we focus on SAP S/4HANA Finance but try to make any differences clear. Before you start, read the relevant **Administration Guides on the SAP Service Marketplace**, listed here (you will need to provide log-on information to access the SAP Service Marketplace):

▶ SAP Simple Finance Add-On
http://service.sap.com/~sapidb/012002523100001443872016E/SFIN_ADMIN_GUIDE_180.pdf
In this case, the migration removes totals tables and index tables and extends table COEP to link the FI and CO postings and activates new Asset Accounting.

▶ SAP S/4HANA Finance
https://service.sap.com/~sapidb/012002523100013523782015E/SFIN_ADMIN_GUIDE_203.pdf
Here, the migration removes totals tables and index tables, moves the financial transactions into the universal journal, and activates new Asset Accounting and new Cash Management.

- SAP S/4HANA
  *https://uacp.hana.ondemand.com/http.svc/rc/PRODUCTION/
  pdf3be8f85500f17b43e10000000a4450e5/1511%20000/
  en-US/INST_OP1511.pdf*
  Here, the migration removes totals tables and index tables, moves the financial transactions into the universal journal, moves the material movements into table MATDOC, activates the long material number and the Material Ledger (unless it is already active), new Asset Accounting, new Cash Management, and converts vendors and customers into business partners.

Embarking on a migration journey is a challenge because there appear to be many moving parts. One of the easiest ways to find out what has changed is to search for SAP Notes containing the term S4WTL. Some examples are:

- SAP Note 2270419
  (*https://launchpad.support.sap.com/#/notes/0002270419*)
  explains the implications of merging the accounts and the cost element.

- SAP Note 2270404
  (*https://launchpad.support.sap.com/#/notes/0002270404*)
  introduces the new data structures in Controlling and explains their impact.

- SAP Note 2270387
  (*https://launchpad.support.sap.com/#/notes/0002270387*)
  introduces the new data structures in Asset Accounting and explains their impact.

- SAP Note 2352383
  (*https://launchpad.support.sap.com/#/notes/0002352383*)
  introduces the new data structures for the Material Ledger and Actual Costing.

Do your homework before you begin a migration project and make sure that you really understand the impact of the changes that are about to take place.

6.2.1 Readiness checks

Initially, the preparation process does not require you to install any software at all. The idea is to look in the system for anything that might prevent a migration or cause problems during the migration. It is important to keep your eye on the various simplification items in SAP S/4HANA and the following blog is a good place to keep abreast of changes: *http://scn.sap.com/docs/DOC-70833*.

As you work your way through the various simplification items, you need to understand how these will impact your current system. Here are a couple of examples of things to check:

▶ Your own use of index and totals tables:
The *select statements* that pull data for reporting via the compatibility views will work automatically. If you are planning an upgrade, however, you need to look for *write statements* (INSERT, UPDATE, DELETE, MODIFY) on these tables because these will need to be replaced. You also have to check that no custom DDIC views have been created on top of the removed tables. You can find full details about how to handle your totals tables in SAP Note 2135632 (*https://launchpad.support.sap.com/#/notes/0002135632*). If you have added fields to your index tables, refer to SAP Note 2191738 (*https://launchpad.support.sap.com/#/notes/0002191738*) for details of how to handle the extra fields.

▶ Addition of fields to tables COEP and BSEG:
You have to manually extend table ACDOCA to include any fields that your organization has added to COEP or BSEG as described in SAP Note 2160045 (*https://launchpad.support.sap.com/#/notes/0002160045*). If you have added coding block fields to structure CI_COBL, these will be migrated automatically and do not require special treatment.

6.2.2 Deprecated transactions

It is also important to check for transactions that have been removed and to understand your alternatives **before** you begin migration. For example, in Chapter 5, we discussed the need to make a choice between using the new SAP S/4HANA options for planning or continuing to use the classic planning transactions for an interim period. The business rationale was that there was to be a principle of one, so if a transaction has been removed, there will usually be an alternative which will be documented in the relevant *simplification list.*

Again, the list of deprecated transactions is different depending on the SAP S/4HANA system in question:

▶ SAP Simple Finance Add-On for SAP Business Suite powered by SAP HANA and SAP S/4HANA Finance:
Refer to SAP Note 2270335
(*https://launchpad.support.sap.com/#/notes/0002270335*).

▶ SAP S/4HANA:
Refer to the details in the *simplification list* included in the SAP Help:
https://uacp.hana.ondemand.com/http.svc/rc/PRODUCTION/
pdfa4322f56824ae221e10000000a4450e5/1511%20000/
en-US/SIMPL_OP1511.pdf

6.2.3   Data preparation

Essentially, the data preparation steps are the same as for any migration project:

▶ Perform period-end closing activities and reconciliation

▶ Create a data snapshot for comparison after migration

▶ Prepare all business areas, not only finance

However, in addition to the standard closing programs, you should also execute various check reports delivered by SAP:

▶ FINS_MIG_PRECHECK_CUST_SETTNGS
(SAP Note 2129306 (*https://launchpad.support.sap.com/#/notes/*
0002129306) explains how to check your ledger, company code, and controlling area settings)

▶ RACHECK_ACTIVATION_PARVAL
(SAP Note 1968305 (*https://launchpad.support.sap.com/#/notes/*
0001968305) explains how to use new Asset Accounting if you are already using SAP ERP General Ledger Accounting)

▶ RASFIN_MIGR_PRECHECK
(SAP Note 1939592 (*https://launchpad.support.sap.com/#/notes/0001939592*) explains how to use this report and which solutions are not compatible with new Asset Accounting)

▶ Follow the instructions in SAP Note 2176077 (*https://launchpad.support.sap.com/#/notes/0002176077*) to check your ability to use the solution in general.

6.3 Installation

To install SAP S/4HANA as we discussed in Chapter 2, the following parts are compulsory:

▶ SAP HANA database:
This is the primary database for storing all data. The architectural changes are only possible if an in-memory database is used.

▶ SAP NetWeaver kernel:
The SAP NetWeaver kernel provides certain functions that are required, such as CDS views to provide a virtual view of the universal journal from the viewpoint of the removed tables.

▶ SAP Simple Finance Add-On for SAP Business Suite powered by SAP HANA
This add-on replaces the existing coding for the Finance modules.

In Chapter 8, we will learn about the following optional parts:

▶ SAP Fiori:
Used to provide the user interfaces we saw in Chapter 1

▶ SAP Gateway:
Used to handle communication between the SAP system and the mobile devices that the SAP Fiori user interfaces run on

▶ SAP Smart Business:
Used as a framework for reporting the key figures we saw in Chapter 1

Checklist for SAP installation

 Because more and more information is added on the basis of each SAP S/4 Finance project, use the Excel checklist in SAP Note 2157996 (*https://launchpad. support.sap.com/#/notes/0002157996*) to inform the project teams of the main concerns prior to installation.

Once you have installed the relevant software, you can find the relevant **Migration/Conversion Guides** for each release listed here:

▶ SAP Simple Finance Add-On for SAP Business Suite powered by SAP HANA
http://help.sap.com/saphelp_sfin100/helpdata/en/87/ 2f6152b82bf35fe10000000a423f68/frameset.htm

▶ SAP S/4HANA Finance
http://help.sap.com/saphelp_sfin200/helpdata/en/87/ 2f6152b82bf35fe10000000a423f68/frameset.htm

▶ SAP S/4HANA
https://uacp.hana.ondemand.com/http.svc/rc/PRODUCTION/ pdfe68bfa55e988410ee10000000a441470/1511%20000/ en-US/CONV_OP1511.pdf

6.4 Customizing

Once you have installed the latest software updates, you have access to the IMG shown in Figure 6.4. This is a change from the *Migration Cockpit* used to migrate to the new G/L. You do not have to wait until the end of a fiscal year—you can perform the steps listed in the IMG at any time.

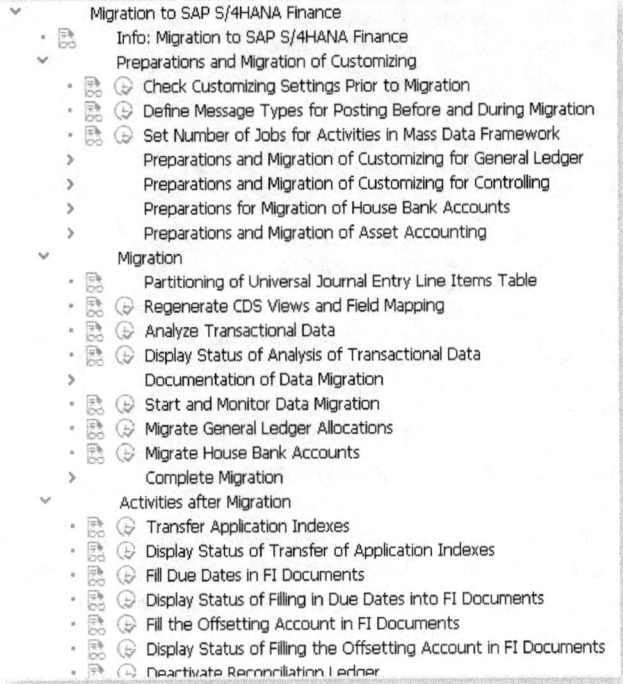

Figure 6.4: Implementation Guide for the migration process (1605 edition)

We will now walk you through the critical Customizing settings that you need to configure prior to a migration.

6.4.1 General Ledger Accounting

If you refer back to Figure 5.2, you will notice that there are two potential sources for general ledger data—SAP ERP General Ledger Accounting (new G/L) and classic General Ledger Accounting. Bear in mind that a conversion to the universal journal is not the same as a new G/L migration: a conversion to the universal journal converts **every** document in the system, while a new G/L migration takes place on a key date.

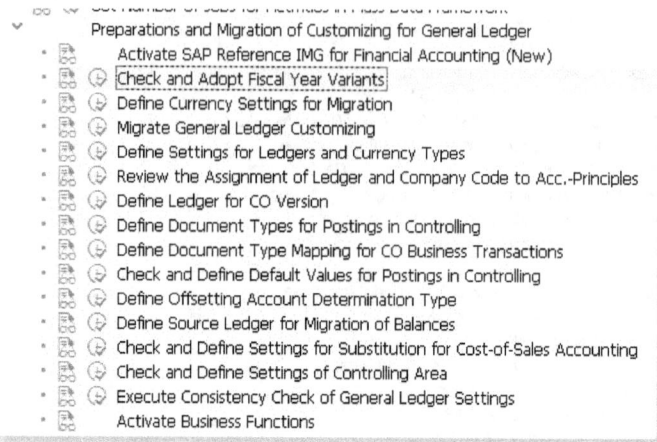

Figure 6.5: Customizing settings for General Ledger Accounting

1. All financial applications must use the same *fiscal year variant* because every application has to have the same periods. Therefore, you have to make sure that every company code has the same fiscal year variant as the controlling area.

2. Because you are merging documents from Accounting and Controlling during the migration, you may be taking currencies such as the controlling area currency that was previously only available in Controlling and moving it to the universal journal.

3. Make sure that the settings for your ledgers are correct. If you are coming from SAP ERP General Ledger Accounting, the system migrates your existing settings. However, if you are using classic General Ledger Accounting, you have to create at least one ledger.

4. We discussed the ledger and currency settings in Chapter 2, Section 2.2.4. You have to decide whether you have use cases that require you to implement an extension ledger. With effect from edition 1602, you have the option to set additional currencies (up to eight new currencies in addition to the local currency and group currency). Therefore, draw up a list of the relevant currency settings for each of your ledgers along with the exchange rate types.

5. Prior to the migration all controlling data is stored with reference to a *version* rather than a ledger, so at the very least, you have to assign version 0 to the relevant ledger. If you are also using group valuation or profit center valuation, you have to map the versions you currently

use for this valuation to the appropriate ledger.

Note that at the time of writing, there is still a restriction on the use of the business function FIN_CO_COGM (parallel cost of goods manufactured), so watch out for release notes confirming that this limitation has been lifted.

6. Going forward you will effectively be performing reposting transactions in the general ledger. Therefore, you may wish to define additional document types to identify the journal entries for each of the Controlling business transactions. A new document type CO is delivered as a default but you may want to add others with the appropriate number ranges and authorizations. You then link these with the appropriate Controlling business transaction (such as RKU1 for reposting).

7. How you migrate your balances in the general ledger will depend on whether you have used SAP ERP General Ledger Accounting since your initial implementation or migrated to it. A migration to the universal journal migrates all the totals, both those in GLT0 (classic) and those in FAGLFLEXT (new).

8. If you are using cost of sales accounting, you have to make sure that the settings for filling your functional areas are correct.

9. Because some of the code needed within SAP S/4HANA was contained within business functions in previous releases, your administrator has to activate the following business functions prior to migration:

   ▶ EA-FIN (Financials Extension)

   ▶ FIN_GL_CI_1 (Enhancements to the new G/L)

   ▶ FIN_GL_CI_2 (Enhancements to the new G/L)

   ▶ FIN_GL_CI_3 (Enhancements to the new G/L)

In addition to the configuration settings, it makes sense to check your master data because the profit centers, functional areas, and so on in your Controlling master data determine how the documents are enriched during the migration.

If you are coming from SAP ERP General Ledger Accounting (new G/L), then you may already be using different ledgers for each of your accounting principles and *document splitting* to fill the segments and profit centers for balance sheet reporting. This information will be included in the migration and you will be able to carry on as before. If you are coming from classic General Ledger Accounting, then your system does not have these features yet. At the time of writing (fall 2016), the migration process is being extended to support the addition of a **new ledger** during the migration project and the correct document assignments. You will not be able to add document splitting for historic documents until a future release.

6.4.2 Controlling and Profitability Analysis

The Controlling settings for the migration are essentially concerned with Profitability Analysis, as shown in Figure 6.6.

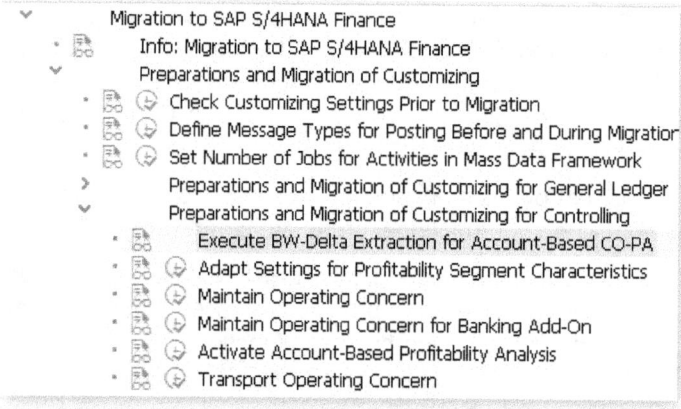

Figure 6.6: Customizing settings for Controlling

As discussed in Chapter 2, the universal journal contains columns for each of the characteristics in the operating concern. If you are already using account-based Profitability Analysis, the only thing you need to know is that **all characteristics** in the operating concern are available to you (there is no longer a transaction to reduce account-based Profitability Analysis to a subset of the characteristics in costing-based Profitability Analysis). If you are already using costing-based Profitability Analysis, provided that you flag the operating concern as relevant for account-based Profitability Analysis, the migration adds columns for each of the characteristics in your operating concern to the universal journal.

Note, however, that account-based Profitability Analysis will only be updated **going forward**. The historic data in the transactional tables for costing-based Profitability Analysis (tables CE1) will **not** be migrated to the universal journal. Therefore, following migration, you will see pre-existing revenue line items in the granularity of the general ledger (company code, profit center, and so on) rather than with an assignment to products, customers, and so on. If you are new to Profitability Analysis, then clearly you need to prepare a list of the characteristics that you want to report on and document where they come from (invoice, settlement, and so on) and what extra derivations you will be performing to enrich this data (such as deriving a product hierarchy from the product sold or setting up real time derivation to derive CO-PA characteristics from the cost center, order, or WBS element as we saw in Chapter 2).

6.4.3 Asset Accounting

As discussed in Chapter 2, new Asset Accounting is no longer an optional business function (FIN_AA_PARALLEL_VAL) as it was in SAP Enhancement Package 7 for SAP ERP 6.0, where it worked in combination with SAP ERP General Ledger Accounting—it is **compulsory** in SAP S/4HANA Finance. Figure 6.7 shows the Customizing settings for Asset Accounting.

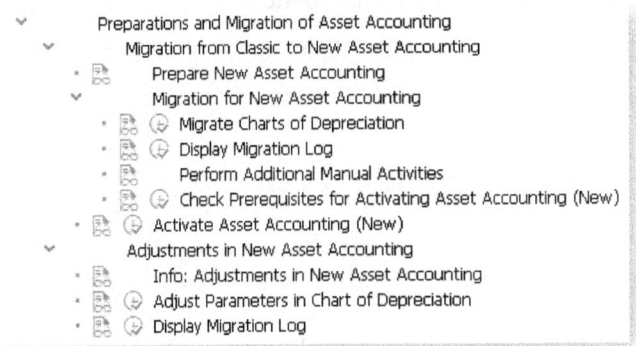

Figure 6.7: Customizing settings for Asset Accounting

As you go into the blueprinting phase, make sure that you have a clear understanding of the new posting logic in Asset Accounting.

- ▶ Start by listing your existing *charts of depreciation* and understanding how they map to the various accounting principles you are using (if you use more than one) and how these are represented as ledgers.

- ▶ Decide for which accounting principles you are able to post in real time and how this update to the general ledger will work.

- ▶ Determine which charts of depreciation (if any) only need to post periodically.

6.5 Migration steps

One of the first technical steps in the migration is that the former totals tables that we looked at in Chapter 1 are converted into SAP Core Data Service (CDS) views. As we discussed in Chapter 2, **before** you run this step you need to understand which of your function modules currently update these tables (read statements do not matter) and which interfaces call these tables from outside the system (including ALE scenarios). Do not forget to also check for tools such as SLT which read these tables at database level rather than by function module.

The basic steps of the migration are essentially similar in each release:

- ▶ Merge cost elements into the chart of accounts
- ▶ Enrich data (add profit centers, functional areas, and so on)
- ▶ Migrate line items into the universal journal
- ▶ Migrate balances
- ▶ Migrate house bank depreciation values

In the early editions, each step is a separate task in the IMG, while from edition 1605, all of the steps are included in one migration task monitor (START AND MONITOR DATA MIGRATION) in Figure 6.8.

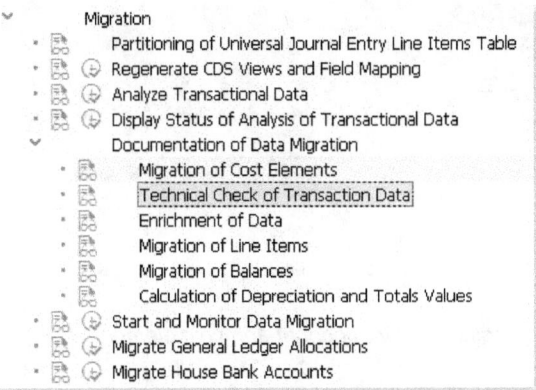

Figure 6.8: Migration IMG (edition 1605)

Note that because the steps of the migration are so critical, the recommendation is to perform test migrations on a **copy** of the existing system in order to identify issues before moving into the migration proper. Generally, the work with a cloned system is iterative until you have identified and solved all barriers to the conversion.

6.5.1 Migrating cost elements

As we saw in Chapter 2, during the migration the system creates new G/L accounts for all secondary cost elements and adjusts the account type and updates the cost element category for all primary cost elements. Before you start, you should check that you do not have any rogue primary cost elements without an associated G/L account. You should also check that the secondary cost elements are correct before you generate G/L accounts during the migration. If you have not already used transaction OKB9 to enter default account assignments, the system creates default account assignments based on the cost centers and orders entered in your existing cost elements. Figure 5.9 shows the result of migrating the secondary cost elements in one of the SAP demo systems (which is why the number of migrated cost elements is fairly small). You can see details of the items processed by double-clicking on the relevant line. You will find equivalent check reports for each of the steps in the migration.

Display Status of G/L Account and Cost Element Merge

Client	Run ID	Proc. Step ID	Proc. Status	Unfinished	Finished	Warn. Msg	Error Msg
> ●○○ 000 SAP AG			Waiting	1	0		
> ●○○ 066 early Watch			Waiting	1	0		
> ●○○ 600 Solution Manager - Targe			Waiting	1	0		
> ●○○ 777 Working Capital Analytic			Waiting	1	0		
˅ ▒ 800 IDES-ALE: Central FI Sys			Finished	0	168		
˅ ▒ First Run			Finished	0	168		
˅ ▒ Migrate Secondary Cost Elements to Chart of Accounts	GCM_1		Finished	0	168		
· OO▪ Finished	GCM_1		Finished	0	168	0	0

Figure 6.9: Status report for merging the G/L account and cost elements (1503 edition)

6.5.2   Enriching actual data

In Chapter 2, we talked about how the relevant reporting dimensions are written to the universal journal. Wherever possible, the migration process fills these fields as if the relevant data had always been there—this is what SAP means by the idea of enriching actual data. Therefore, going into a migration, you might have been running Profit Center Accounting as a separate ledger but the migration will need to assign profit centers to the relevant line items in the universal journal by reading the appropriate assignments in the cost centers, orders, WBS elements, and so on. In Chapter 2, we looked at how the CO object is "unpacked" to fill fields ACCAS and ACCASTY (shown in Figure 2.14) along with the relevant fields for the cost center, order, WBS element, and so on. For historical data, the migration process unpacks the object number and updates the account assignment type and the account assignment. Technically, a cost center that was stored as object number KS10000000001000, for example, fills the fields ACCOUNT ASSIGNMENT TYPE (ACCASTY)=KS, CONTROLLING AREA (KOKRS) = 1000, and COST CENTER (KOSTL) = 1000 during the migration and it is the new fields that are displayed using the Fiori reports.

6.5.3   Migrating line items

With the migration of the line items from the various transactional tables, the idea of the universal journal becomes **reality**. The system brings together, into a **single journal entry**, the line items that represent a single business transaction but were separated in the example of an asset posting into an Asset Accounting document, a Controlling document and a General Ledger Accounting document or in the example of a goods movement into a Material Ledger document, a Controlling document and a General Ledger Accounting document. It is not just a question of merging data from different storage points but also of bringing all the data relating to one business transaction to the same granularity—for example, a posting for ten assets might impact four cost centers and only two G/L accounts. The result will be ten asset line items that also include the relevant cost centers and account and offsetting account. Refer back to the migration source shown in Figures 5.1 and 5.2 to see how to recognize the source of each migrated document. Clearly, this is the most challenging step in the migration. Figure 6.10 gives you an impression of the migrated tables in a small demo system.

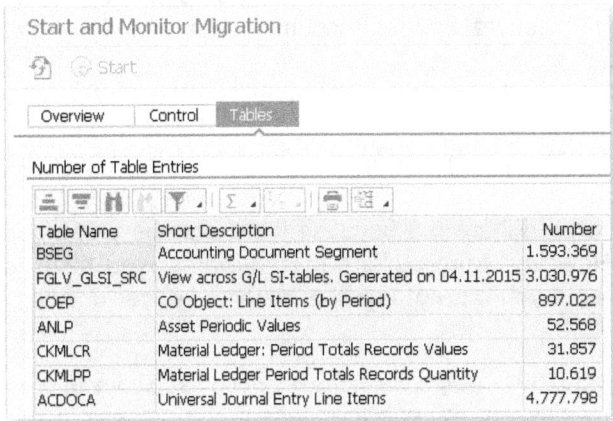

Figure 6.10: Table entries handled during a migration

6.5.4 Migrating balances

Executing the MIGRATION OF BALANCES step in the IMG ensures that where line items had been archived such that the sum of the line items does not match the associated entry in the totals table, a *correction posting* is created. These entries will only contain a handful of reporting dimensions because the totals tables do not contain many fields and the system cannot invent information when the supporting line item has been removed. Again, refer back to Figure 5.2 to understand how to later recognize such migrated totals. This step is necessary to ensure that the financial documents can be audited. It also ensures that processes such as results analysis and settlement, which consider the life time of an individual order or project rather than a specific accounting period, will find all the data that they need for further processing.

Another shift in the new data model is that the balance carryforward values can no longer be stored in the totals tables. The migration creates a new document to represent the balance carryforward.

6.5.5 Migrating depreciation values

In terms of project planning, you do not have to wait until SAP S/4HANA to activate new Asset Accounting; you can switch it on earlier if you are already using SAP ERP General Ledger Accounting with the ledger solution.

6.5.6 Migrating the Material Ledger

This step is not shown in Figure 6.8 because it will only be performed from edition 1511. However, from edition 1511 onwards, you have to perform this step even if you did not use the Material Ledger or Actual Costing in the past.

- ▶ SAP Note 2332591 (*https://launchpad.support.sap.com/#/notes/ 0002332591*) walks you through the steps in the process in edition 1511.

- ▶ SAP Note 2352383 (*https://launchpad.support.sap.com/#/notes/ 0002352383*) walks you through the steps in the process in edition 1610.

6.5.7 Partitioning the universal journal table

Partitioning is a key element of the HANA story in that data is divided into *hot data* that is readily accessible and *cold data* that is not kept in memory. This means that during migration, the system sorts the data into the correct category and sets the flag for data aging shown in Figure 5.1.

6.5.8   SAP Core Data Service (CDS) views

CDS views with the same name as the old tables are created during the migration for the index tables and totals tables that we discussed in Chapter 1. The data that is no longer required is moved to back-up tables—if you refer back to Figure 1.2, you will see that the field names for Table GLT0 now end in _BCK. Similar views are created for all the totals tables and index tables that we discussed in Chapter 1, Section 1.3.1.

CDS views are also created for all the transactional tables made redundant by the move to the universal journal. To understand this, let us think about what happens to the controlling line item table COEP. During migration, the system creates an equivalent view V_COEP for table COEP and redirects all select statements to V_COEP instead of COEP. When a program calls the old table COEP, V_COEP is used to aggregate the data in the relevant journal entries from the universal journal.

6.6   Activities after migration

If you refer back to the steps shown in Figure 6.4, you will see that there are a number of steps to be performed once the migration has completed.

These include the following:

- ▶ Moving deleted index tables into cold store partitions
- ▶ Filling out due dates in FI documents
- ▶ Filling clearing accounts
- ▶ Deactivating the reconciliation ledger because it is no longer needed

7 Deploying Central Finance

If you have a system landscape that comprises multiple ERP systems, Central Finance can provide an alternative to migrating each of the separate systems to SAP S/4HANA Finance. Any SAP S/4HANA Finance system can be deployed as a Central Finance system provided you set up the appropriate connections between the central system and the sending systems. The advantage of this approach is that you can experiment with the new finance structures without making significant changes to your existing system landscape.

The idea behind Central Finance is that it provides a *central reporting layer* which collects accounting information from each of the sending systems. It can therefore provide the base layer for your consolidation, planning, and much of your management reporting. You can also implement the cash and treasury functions to work on the same system instance. Of course, the use of Central Finance and a data warehouse are not mutually exclusive: you can extract data from the universal journal to SAP BW using the SAP S/4HANA Finance extractor (DataSource: 0FI_ACDOCA_10) which includes all relevant fields for reporting from the universal journal.

Central Finance is available from SAP S/4HANA Finance 1503. You can access the documentation via *http://help.sap.com/saphelp_sfin200/ helpdata/en/48/57c0540cf5ef05e10000000a4450e5/frameset.htm* and follow frequently asked questions in SAP Note 2184567 (*https://launchpad. support.sap.com/#/notes/0002184567*).

7.1.1 Replication approach

As you post each accounting document in the local system, this triggers the creation of a **new** financial document in the central system that links back to the original document in the sending system. The document in the Central Finance system is effectively a **shadow** of the original financial document.

This might sound like the sort of thing that has been going on in data warehouses for years, but the difference is that this approach is **document-based**. Every document runs through the same master data checks and validations as a normal journal entry that is processed by the accounting interface and carries with it a link back to the sending system.

In order to allow these checks and validations, you have to create master data in the Central Finance system for all the organizational units (controlling areas, companies, company codes, plants, and so on) and all the master data (cost centers, profit centers, materials, customers, vendors, and so on) for which you will be transferring transactional data.

The easiest way to understand this is to look at an example. Figure 7.1 shows a sample journal entry for DOCUMENT NUMBER 100000000 in COMPANY CODE 3000 and FISCAL YEAR 2016. The document looks like a normal journal entry except that if you navigate to the DOCUMENT HEADER, you can see that it was originally created as DOCUMENT NUMBER 100037384 in COMPANY CODE 3000 and FISCAL YEAR 2016 in the sender system (ECN_00_000). The document has not been cloned but *reposted* in the central system, while keeping that all-important audit link back to the local system.

The idea that the document is reposted might make you fear that system reconciliation could become a major headache, but if you call up the DOCUMENT RELATIONSHIP BROWSER as shown in Figure 7.2, you will see a different example of a journal entry in which the ACCOUNTING DOCUMENT in the central system is 1400000058 in FISCAL YEAR 2016 and the original ACCOUNTING DOCUMENT in the local system is 4900000057 in FISCAL YEAR 2016. The system uses the links we saw in Figure 7.1 not just to link the source document and its shadow document in the central system but also to display the material document, delivery document, sales order, and so on associated with the original document. This involves making a *remote function call* to the local system to call up all pertinent documents that explain the accounting document in the central system. Auditors and managers reporting from the central system have access to exactly the same information as users looking at the accounting document in the local system. SAP delivers standard RFCs to make such calls to SAP ERP systems. If the sending system is a non-SAP system, then a *user exit* can be implemented to pass parameters and call the document details in the sending systems.

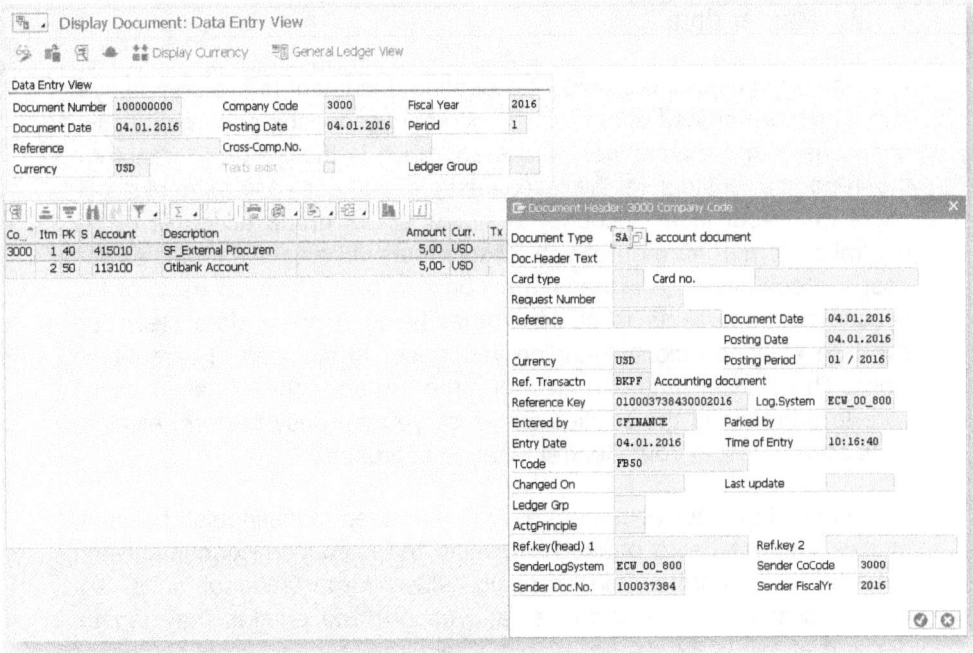

Figure 7.1: Journal entry in Central Finance

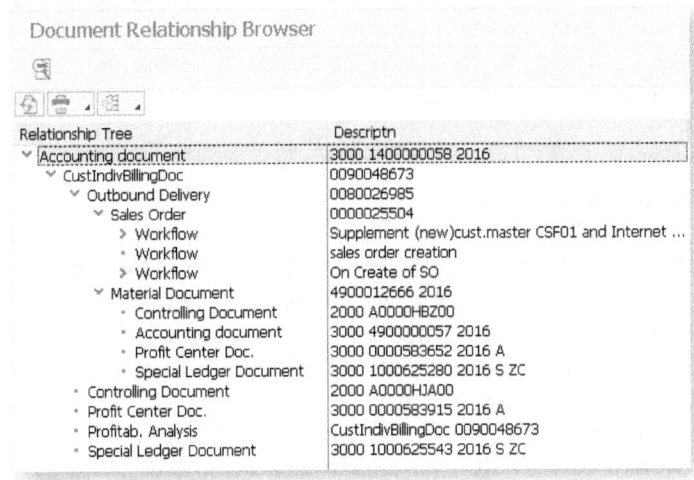

Figure 7.2: Document Relationship Browser showing the audit trail to original documents in the sender system

7.1.2 Master data

In these examples, the shadow accounting document in the central system was more or less a **copy** of the original accounting document. However, one of the advantages of this approach is that you can transform the reporting entities in the accounting document—for example, you might map your local accounts to a new set of group accounts in the central system or harmonize your cost centers via *mapping tables* as you post the document. This transformation can take place as each of the accounting documents is posted rather being a major data cleansing exercise at period close, bringing you closer to the idea of a real-time close. This master data can also form the basis for consolidation, so be sure to understand the entities for which you currently perform eliminations as you design your Central Finance approach.

As you build up your document design, you need to distinguish between entities that are being **passed on** within the accounting document and potentially transformed via mapping tables (organizational units, accounts, cost centers, customers, and so on) and entities that can be **derived** afresh in the central system if required (such as profit centers or CO-PA characteristics). It is also possible to transfer orders and projects and it is important to decide whether you want a 1:1 relationship between the local and central orders or whether you want to post multiple local production orders to a single internal order or product cost collector in the central system. But before we look at the business details, let us first look at the high-level system landscape.

7.2 System landscape

Figure 7.3 shows a high-level architecture of the Central Finance approach. In Figure 7.1 and Figure 7.2, we looked at a journal entry that was created in the Central Finance instance as a **shadow** of an accounting document created in a local instance of SAP ERP. The sending system can be on any version of SAP ERP, and therefore, many customers are actually leaving these systems on fairly old versions of the software. The sending system can also be the latest version of SAP S/4HANA, however. The sender systems do not even need to be SAP systems at all, and plenty of projects are underway to bring accounting data from non-SAP ERP systems into the Central Finance instance. Stay abreast of changes by following SAP Note 2148893 (*https://launchpad.support. sap.com/#/notes/0002148893*).

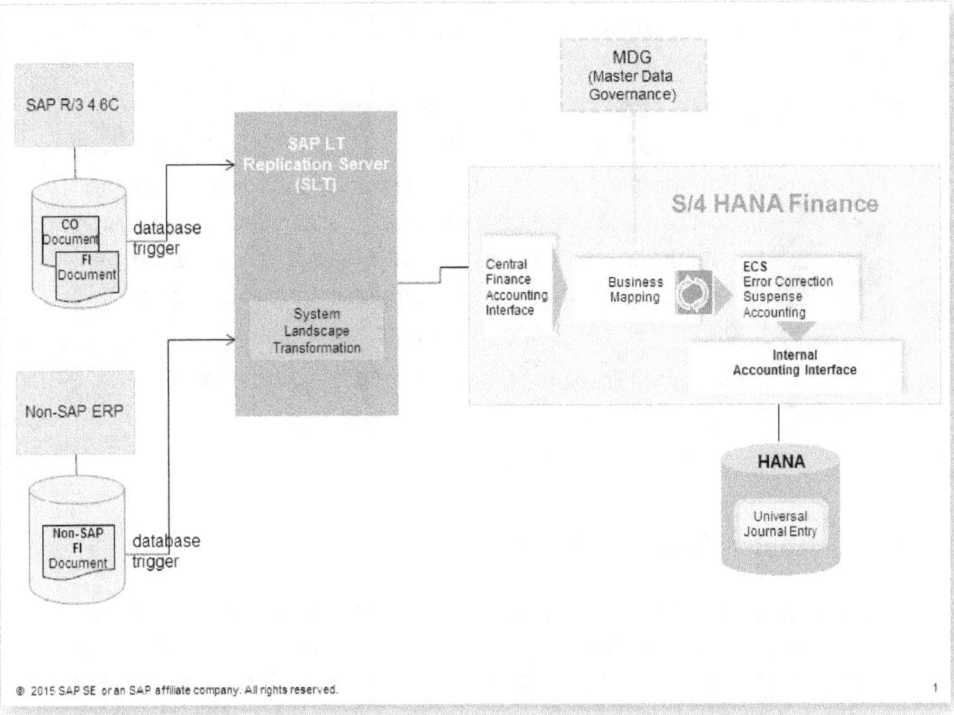

Figure 7.3: Central Finance architecture

7.2.1   SAP Landscape Transformation

As we can see in Figure 7.3, the system connections are made via SAP Landscape Transformation (SAP LT)—the middle box in the diagram. SLT works on the database level, so while you can connect and read tables from SAP systems, it is relatively easy to connect non-SAP systems to your Central Finance instance because only the database of the non-SAP system needs to be accessed, rather than the application. This means that you do not need to make modifications to the application server of the sender system. You can install the SLT software as a separate system on top of any of the source systems or the Central Finance system. To make the connections you have to make sure that the add-on

DMIS 2011_1_700 or higher is installed on both the source and the target systems (Support Package [SP] 08 is recommended) and that you have implemented SAP Note 2124481 (SLT SP 08, Correction 3) (*https://launchpad.support.sap.com/#/notes/0002124481*) on these systems.

Administration Guide

 For more details on the system landscape and setting up the necessary connections, you can refer to the Administration Guide for Central Finance available on the SAP Service Marketplace, provided that you have a logon for the SAP Service Marketplace:

https://service.sap.com/~sapidb/012002523100007722892015E/ SFIN_CF_INST_GUIDE.PDF

7.2.2 Master data governance

Because clean master data is a key element of the Central Finance approach, it is also a good idea to consider *master data governance* as part of the project. This does not mean that all the associated systems have to have consistent master data (this is very rarely the case). However, note the Central Finance Accounting Interface in Figure 7.3: this allows you to harmonize master data between systems by setting up mapping tables or, if you use SAP Master Data Governance for distributing master data, then you can reuse the entries in the SAP Master Data Governance tool. What happens then is that as the document is prepared and checked for posting in the central system, the local reporting dimensions can be switched in accordance with the mapping tables. You can also run additional derivation steps (for example, if you want to fill the profit center) and make substitutions before the document is passed to the accounting interface.

As well as mapping master data, you also have to consider what happens when the master data is not available in the central system. This might happen if you are sending a cost center that does not yet exist in the central system. If this is the case, the documents containing that cost center are parked in a *message list* for subsequent correction.

To get an idea of all the implementation steps associated with Central Finance, take a look at Figure 7.4, which shows the Implementation Guide for Central Finance which is available in all SAP S/4HANA Finance systems. This means that you can also run Central Finance in a hybrid mode, where the SAP S/4HANA Finance system is the system of record for some of the journal entries but not for others, allowing you to bring data from newly acquired companies into the SAP instance quickly and efficiently.

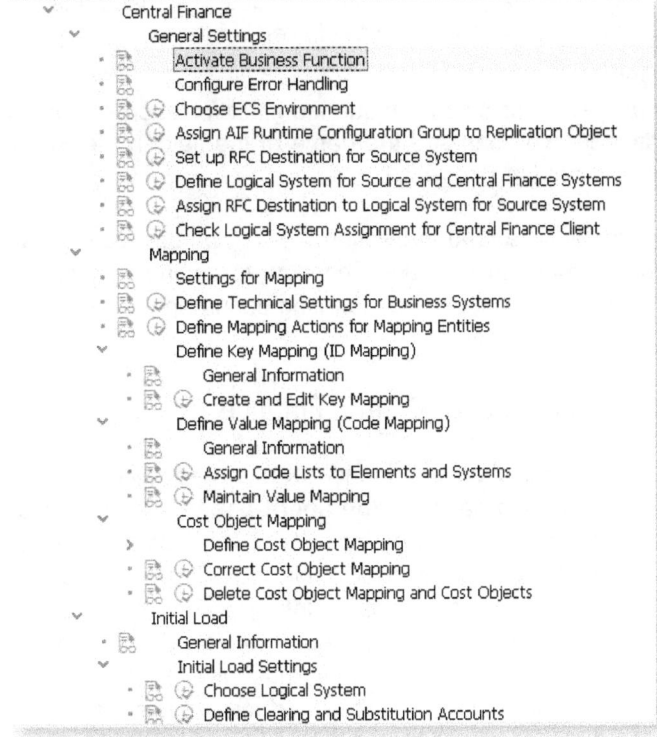

Figure 7.4: Implementation Guide for Central Finance

Start in the GENERAL SETTINGS section by having your administrator activate the business function FINS_CFIN (Central Finance). The use of this business function has license implications so make sure that the appropriate licensing arrangements are in place.

In SAP S/4 HANA Finance 1503, Error Correction and Suspense Accounting was used to handle any journal entries arriving with master data for which no equivalent was available in Central Finance. In subsequent editions, SAP Application Interface Framework is used to handle errors.

You also need to work with your system administrators to set up your system landscape. You need:

▶ RFC destinations for each sender system:
We used an RFC (remote function call) to recreate the audit trail for the accounting documents shown in Figure 7.2. You also use RFCs during the initial data load and to create the mappings between the master data in each of the linked systems.

▶ Logical systems:
The *logical system* acts as a unique identifier for each system in your landscape. You can see the name of the field in the SENDERLOGSYSTEM field in Figure 7.1.

We will look at the initial data load in Section 7.3, but before we do that, we will explain the accounting interface and how to set up the master data you need before you can post an accounting document.

7.2.3   Accounting interface for Central Finance

The key difference between Central Finance and a data warehouse is that the Central Finance approach is **document-based** and all documents are posted via the accounting interface. If the connected system is an SAP system, then you effectively read table ACCIT where the raw data for a document is stored before the accounting document is created via the accounting interface in the local system. The reason you do this rather than transferring the complete accounting document **after** posting is that all the **detail** is still available in the interface. As we discussed earlier, if the invoice contains so many items that it hits the 999 line item limit in BSEG, the local system is set up to **summarize** the material column to reduce the number of line items in order to allow posting. If you pick up the entry in ACCIT, then you can transfer all the posting line items from the invoice to the central system. The invoice contains sales conditions that are used in costing-based CO-PA but these do not appear in the accounting document because posting line items are only created for those conditions that are mapped to G/L accounts and the other line items are rejected. If you use SAP ERP General Ledger Accounting, you effectively send the entry view and document splitting is performed in the central system.

Figure 7.5 shows the new transfer structure for the accounting documents. We have called up the new development package FIN_ CFIN_INTEGRATION and the header table CFIN_ACCID that will act as the trigger for the transfer of the relevant accounting documents. Note that the tables listed on the left do not just include the accounting document itself but also the profitability segments that will be needed for a posting to CO-PA, a cost component split if you are valuing your cost of goods sold with the standard costs from a cost estimate, withholding tax, clearing information, and so on. Assuming that your local systems are not yet on SAP S/4HANA, you also need to set up a database trigger to read the CO documents from table COBK (if the local system is already on SAP S/4HANA Finance, then secondary costs will be part of the universal journal). If you plan to do order controlling or cost object controlling, you need to set up a database trigger to read new order master records from table AUFK. Note that these tables contain the **transactional data**. All related master data has to be in place **before** you start to trigger postings for the transactional data because the postings are validated against this master data.

SAP Landscape Transformation uses the database trigger to identify the existence of a record to be transferred to Central Finance. This is a largely technical step. The business logic takes place in the interface, where the accounting document is subjected to exactly the same checks as if it were being posted directly as a result of a business transaction in the central system. This means that checks are performed to check that all the organizational data exists (controlling area, company code, and so on) along with the accounts, the account assignment (cost center, order, project, and so on) and any other data needed for the posting (such as the tax settings or an activity type). Setting up this master data can require significant data cleansing but it means that the quality of the data in your Central Finance instance is likely to be better than the quality in a typical data warehouse.

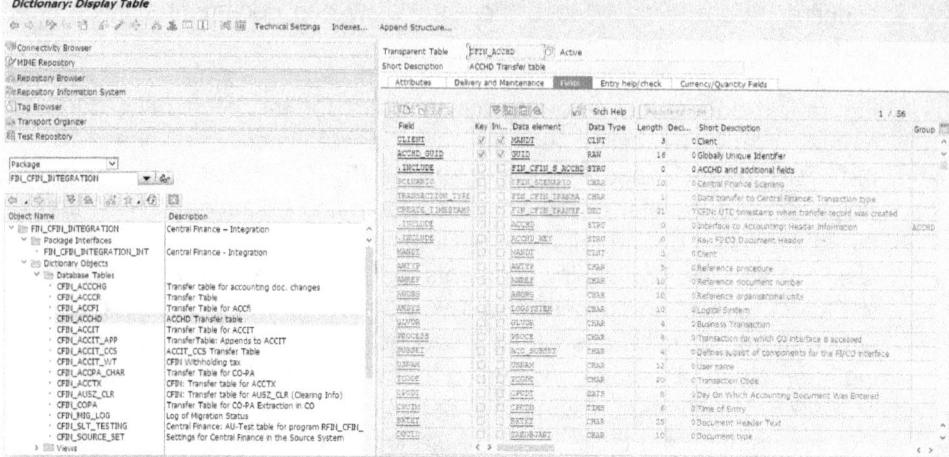

Figure 7.5: Transfer structure for accounting documents

Now that we have explained the basic idea of the Central Finance interface, we will look at the mapping options for the master data, assuming
that you do not want a 1:1 relationship between each item of master
data.

7.2.4 Value mapping for organizational data

If you refer back to the transfer structure shown in Figure 7.5, then the
easiest way to create a document is simply to post a copy of that document in the central system as we did in Figure 7.1. Doing this means that
you miss a huge opportunity to **harmonize** a heterogeneous finance
landscape. It makes sense to start with a list of all the parameters that
you want to transfer to Central Finance and to use this to understand the
relationships between the local system and the central system. In terms
of global parameters that require a value mapping, this list might include:

► Participating Countries:
 You have to create master data for the countries and make sure
 that you prepare a list of any country-specific reporting requirements and decide whether in future these will be met in the local
 or in the central system.

► Participating Companies:
The companies are the basis for consolidation so instead of considering the companies in isolation, think about the relationships between these trading partners and specifically, how you are going to perform intercompany reconciliation centrally and how you will handle the sequence of implementation for any intercompany relationships.

► Participating Company Codes:
As you define the settings for the company code, it becomes clear that you are dealing not simply with a reporting layer but rather you are defining key settings for the chart of accounts and the fiscal year variant. You do this using the same IMG steps as you would for a company code for which the Central Finance instance is the system of record.

► Number of Ledgers:
You need a ledger for each accounting principle and must make sure that you take account of the new currency options that we discussed in Chapter 3.

► Controlling Area:
This setting controls the fiscal year variant, the chart of accounts (do not forget the secondary cost elements), and the group currency. It also controls which components are active and thus which account assignments are updated (cost center, order, project, and so on).

► Operating Concern:
This setting controls the CO-PA dimensions that you use centrally. This may be a subset of all the dimensions you have in the local systems and should be harmonized so that the reporting dimensions are consistent across the world.

These global parameters are usually handled using *value mapping* in Central Finance. This approach is also used for Customizing settings that are usually set up at the start of a project and then remain stable, such as the dunning areas and payment terms for a customer. You can define these in the IMG (see Figure 7.4) under MAPPING • DEFINE MDG MAPPING. Figure 7.6 gives you an idea of the number of entities that can be covered in Central Finance.

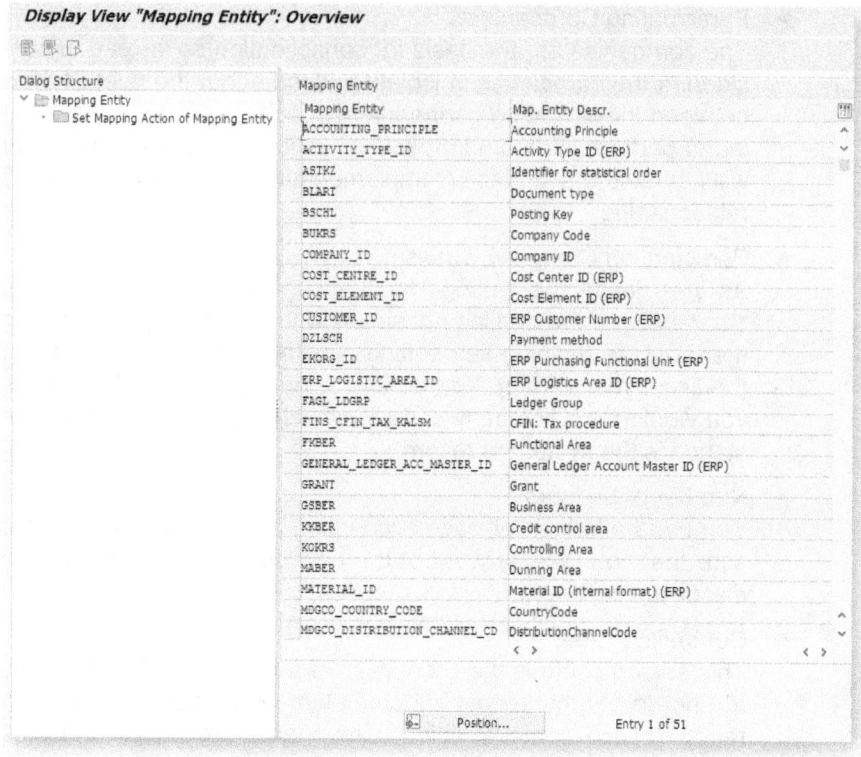

Figure 7.6: Mapping entities for global parameters and master data in Central Finance

7.2.5 Key mapping for master data

By contrast, the master data is usually handled via *key mapping*. The case for Central Finance often goes hand in hand with a case for better master data governance, so this topic needs to be handled properly. Again, you will probably want to draw up a list that includes:

▶ G/L accounts:
  Start with the trial balance for each relevant country and then include the secondary cost elements (unless the sending system is an SAP S/4HANA Finance system). Then decide if you want a 1:1 transfer or if you need to set up mapping tables to bring your entries into a single chart of accounts.

- Profit centers and segments:
  You do not have to run Profit Center Accounting in the local systems—you can also derive the profit centers afresh in the central system provided you set up the relevant master data (cost centers, materials, orders, and so on) needed for the derivation. Note that the profit center is only transferred in the document if the sending system uses SAP ERP General Ledger Accounting. If you run Profit Center Accounting as a dedicated ledger locally, you should be aware that these documents are not currently transferred and all profit center derivations will take place in the central system. Any correction or reclassification postings that you perform in ledger 8A will not be transferred.

- Cost centers:
  This is probably the most critical item of master data after the account because it is used to derive so many of the other reporting dimensions, including profit centers, functional areas, and so on.

- Material master records:
  Of course, you do not need every single view in the material master record, but you do need all the assignments for reporting, including the assignment to a profit center, product hierarchy, material group, and so on. There is also a strong chance that the material master codes will not be harmonized across systems and that you will need to perform mapping here.

- Customers/vendors:
  Again, you are not interested in all the master data for the customers and vendors but those items that you need for intercompany reconciliation and to derive CO-PA characteristics for reporting.

Once you have your list of master data, you need to decide where you can define a 1:1 transfer from the sending system and where you need to perform key mapping as shown in Figure 7.7. Here, you see a simple mapping of the customers from the local system (ECW_800) to the central system (ECNCLNT800). You should create key mappings for all those entities that are added on a regular basis, such as vendors, customers, materials, and G/L accounts. The most common mapping type is a *pair mapping*, in which account A in the local system maps to account B in Central Finance. To prepare this pair mapping, use the Web Dynpro application MDG_BS_WD_ID_MATCH_SERVICE. Where you need a more complicated mapping, consider using the BAdI BADI_FINS_CFIN_ MAPPING_RULE to implement the required logic.

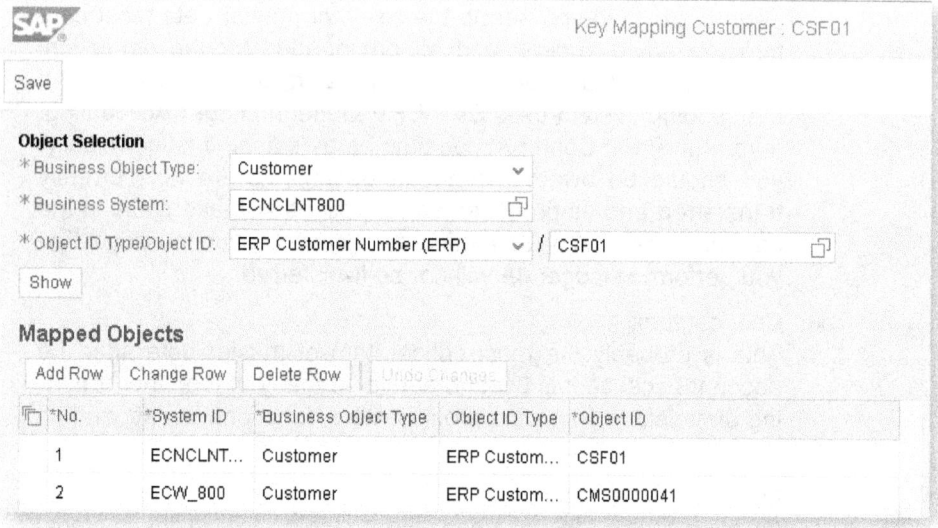

Figure 7.7: Key mapping for customers in a Central Finance instance

Because Central Finance uses the universal journal, make sure that you consider the CO-PA characteristics in your master data lists and understand how the derivations work and where you want to perform a validation to ensure that the relevant master data exists. In your local system, the CO-PA characteristics for the various dimensions are stored in table CE4 and are always read in combination with the transactional table (CE1 for costing-based Profitability Analysis and COEP for account-based Profitability Analysis). In Chapter 2, we saw that the universal journal includes a column for each characteristic in your operating concern. The decision as to which characteristics to use for reporting becomes more critical in Central Finance because many organizations have built operating concerns that are specific to individual countries or lines of business and struggle to consolidate the different reporting entities. The challenge is to understand how the standard fields have been used in terms of naming conventions and so on and to understand how company-specific characteristics are derived. Do not forget that the limit of 50 characteristics for an operating concern still applies because table CE4 continues to be updated.

As you think about transferring the characteristics, refer back to Figure 7.5 and note the transfer structure CFIN_ACCPA_CHAR, which is used to transfer CO-PA characteristics between systems. Although you can potentially transfer all the relevant characteristics from the local system, the technical name for the combination of characteristics, field PAOB-JNR, will be different in each system because you are creating a new document by reposting. There are three ways of transferring characteristics from the local system:

▶ The characteristic values are the **same** in both systems (this is often the case for organizational units such as plants and company codes)

▶ The characteristic values require **mapping** between systems (this might be the case if you are harmonizing codes for the material master in the central system)

▶ The characteristic value either should not be transferred from the local system or does not exist in the local system and is to be **derived afresh** in the central system (this might be the case if you are assigning products to new product hierarchies in the central system)

7.2.6 Mapping cost objects for transactional objects

Before you can post costs by order or project, you have to make sure that the master data for these cost objects is available in the central system. This need not be a problem for long-living internal orders that behave much like cost centers, but many orders are extremely dynamic and we often find production orders, process orders, and maintenance orders that are created and closed on the same day. Clearly, creating the master data for such orders before you start is not practical because it would involve the creation of new orders on a daily basis. Instead, Central Finance allows you to set up product cost collectors to collect the costs of the many production orders or keep a 1:1 relationship between cost objects if you prefer. The various options are delivered as *scenarios*. The key point here is that the master data for the orders and product cost collectors is considered **transactional data** in terms of Central Finance and transfer is triggered by a new entry in table AUFK.

Figure 7.8 gives an overview of the scenarios delivered for mapping cost objects between the local and the central systems. Note the CARDINALITY column, which determines whether there is an N:1 relationship between the orders in the local system, as we see for Scenario SAP001, where N production orders map to one product cost collector, or Scenario SAP004, where N maintenance orders map to one central maintenance order, or a 1:1 relationship as we see for Scenario SAP002, where product cost collectors already exist locally and are transferred 1:1, or in Scenario SAP003, where internal orders are transferred 1:1. There is also an additional scenario that maps maintenance or production orders to internal orders in the central system.

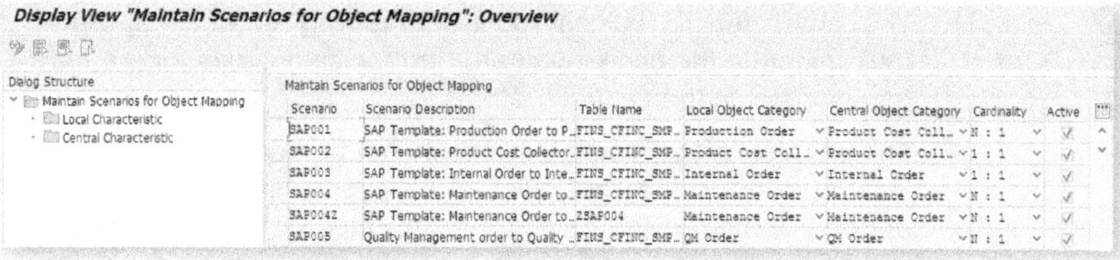
Display View "Maintain Scenarios for Object Mapping": Overview

Dialog Structure
Maintain Scenarios for Object Mapping
Local Characteristic
Central Characteristic

Maintain Scenarios for Object Mapping

Scenario	Scenario Description	Table Name	Local Object Category	Central Object Category	Cardinality	Active
SAP001	SAP Template: Production Order to P...	FINS_CFINC_SMP...	Production Order	Product Cost Coll...	N : 1	✓
SAP002	SAP Template: Product Cost Collector...	FINS_CFINC_SMP...	Product Cost Coll...	Product Cost Coll...	1 : 1	✓
SAP003	SAP Template: Internal Order to Inte...	FINS_CFINC_SMP...	Internal Order	Internal Order	1 : 1	✓
SAP004	SAP Template: Maintenance Order to...	FINS_CFINC_SMP...	Maintenance Order	Maintenance Order	N : 1	✓
SAP004Z	SAP Template: Maintenance Order to...	ZSAP004	Maintenance Order	Maintenance Order	N : 1	✓
SAP005	Quality Management order to Quality ...	FINS_CFINC_SMP...	QM Order	QM Order	N : 1	✓

Figure 7.8: Scenarios for object mapping in Central Finance (1503 edition)

If you want to check the link between the local cost objects and the cost objects in the central system, refer to the entries in table FINS_CFINT_ASGNT. This will show you the relationships between the many local production orders (object category PROD_ORD) and the single product cost collector (object category PCC).

At the time of writing, a similar mapping is planned for projects, work breakdown structure elements, and the objects associated with the projects (networks, network activities, and so on).

7.2.7 Error handling using the SAP Application Interface Framework

Once you have thought your way through the global parameters and master data settings, it makes sense to think about how the system should react if key master data is missing when you transfer a document. The SAP Application Interface Framework (AIF) handles any transactional records arriving with an account, a cost center, and so on for which appropriate master data does not yet exist in the central system. These documents will not be posted as accounting documents but stored for post-processing.

Figure 7.9 shows an overview of the three types of interface that are monitored for Central Finance:

▶ Accounting Documents

▶ Controlling Documents

▶ Cost Objects

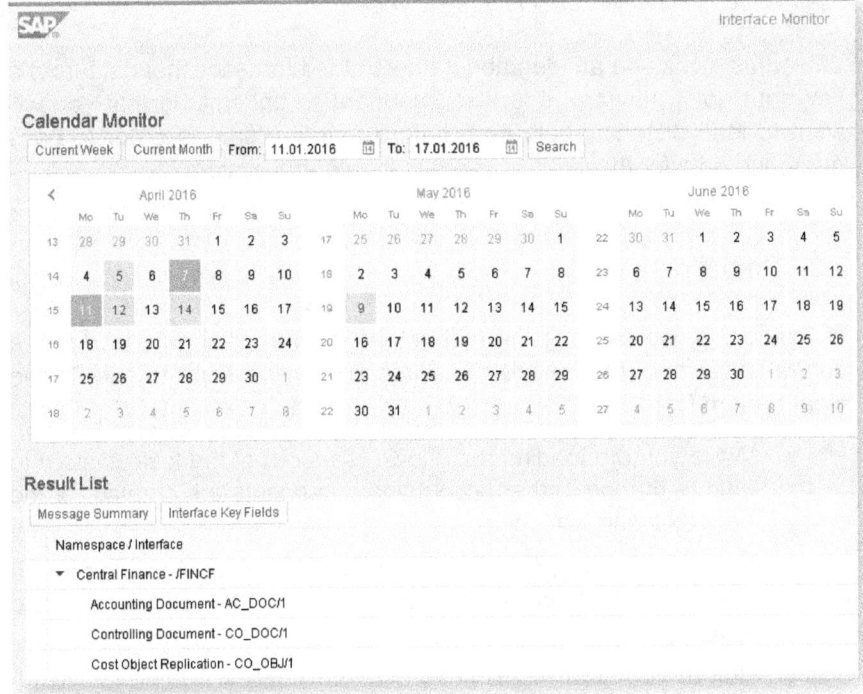

Figure 7.9: Interface Monitor

Figure 7.10 shows a list of errors in the accounting documents. You can navigate to details of the error by selecting an item and then reprocess the item once the underlying problem (such as missing master data) has been fixed.

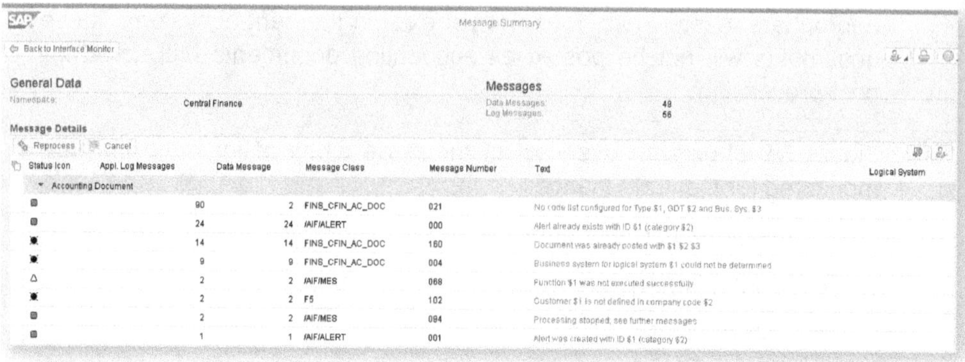

Figure 7.10: Summary of error messages in SAP AIF

While this gives you an idea about how to load transactional data from a key date going forward, it is also important to understand that you will want to load historical data from before that key date in order to have reference data for the last two years in the central system.

7.3 Initial data load

In Figure 7.4, we can see the main steps for the initial data load in the central system, but there are of course key precautions to take in the local system first.

▶ While you are loading data, lock users out of the local system to ensure that no further accounting documents are created for the periods being loaded.

▶ Ensure that period close is complete in Asset Accounting and prepare the balance carryforwards for all currencies and subledgers.

▶ Before you start, there are a series of check reports to ensure that the data being transferred is clean, so make sure that you reconcile Financial Accounting with Materials Management and with Accounts Payable and Accounts Receivable and check that the index entries are clean.

You are now ready to define the settings shown in the INITIAL LOAD SETTINGS area of the IMG (see Figure 7.4). Start by entering the logical system from which you will select data for the initial load. Then, define clearing and substitution accounts for each company code that will be used to create offsetting entries during the data load. Once the data load is complete, the balance on these accounts should be zero.

You can execute the initial data load steps from the IMG. In many cases, you will find a simulation step before each load step so that you can check that the mappings are correct before you start to load data in bulk. In the case of the Financial Accounting documents, it makes sense to simulate and load data company code by company code. You should also distinguish between the time periods for which you need full line item details (usually two years) and the prior periods where balance information is sufficient. You maintain this information in table VCFIN_ SOURCE_SET.

With the initial data load complete, you are now ready to create your first journal entries to Central Finance. At this point, you should set the initial data load status to complete because the procedure for loading real-time data is different.

7.4   Real-time consolidation

When we think about real-time finance as a goal of SAP S/4HANA, the group close process is often the furthest from this target because headquarters often has to wait several days for each subsidiary to submit its data, then perform various cleansing and validation activities before it finally begins the actual consolidation and can deliver figures for the group as a whole. The introduction of the real-time consolidation functions with SAP S/4HANA 1610 changes all this. If, instead of the data from the subsidiaries arriving several days after the close it is available in near real time and has already been transformed and cleansed according to the corporate guidelines, the only step that remains is to perform a group close with the elimination of intercompany profits in Central Finance.

The architecture is similar to the architecture we discussed for planning in Chapter 4.

 ▶ The user interface and consolidation rules are delivered in SAP Business Planning and Consolidation (BPC) and this is offered as an embedded model rather than the traditional data warehouse approach. Of course, for those subsidiaries not sending journal entries to Central Finance, you can continue to use SAP BPC in the classic mode to load data.

▶ The link between the consolidation model in SAP BPC and the universal journal containing the raw data for the consolidation is provided by a virtual InfoProvider which transforms the fields in table ACDOCA into InfoObjects in BW that can then be processed by SAP BPC. Just as we saw in the planning chapter, this is a virtual call and no data is replicated.

▶ The elimination entries are prepared in SAP BPC and stored not in the universal journal but in a new consolidation table, AC-DOCC, which was designed explicitly for this purpose to be similar to ACDOCA but also to include consolidation-specific fields.

We will now look at each of the layers in more detail.

7.4.1 SAP Business Planning and Consolidation

SAP BPC was originally designed to be a system-agnostic consolidation solution and later adjusted to run on SAP BW. Figure 7.11 shows the four main elements of a consolidation. These are the same whether you are consolidating on a data warehouse or using the virtual model.

▶ The CONSOLIDATION MONITOR is used to execute and monitor the consolidation steps.

▶ The OWNERSHIP MANAGER is used to create and manage the ownership hierarchies.

▶ The CONTROLS MONITOR is used to perform the validations on the data to be consolidated.

▶ In JOURNALS you create the elimination entries and enter the correction items to document your consolidation.

To understand how consolidation works, we need to select ADMINISTRA-TION (top right) and then explore the modelling options. Figure 7.12 shows the three models in SAP BPC: CONSOLIDATION, OWNERSHIP, and EXCHANGE RATES. If you are familiar with the classic SAP BPC approach, you will notice immediately that the models begin with /ERP/ and are designed specifically for use in combination with the universal journal in

SAP S/4HANA, an approach we have already seen in the planning chapter.

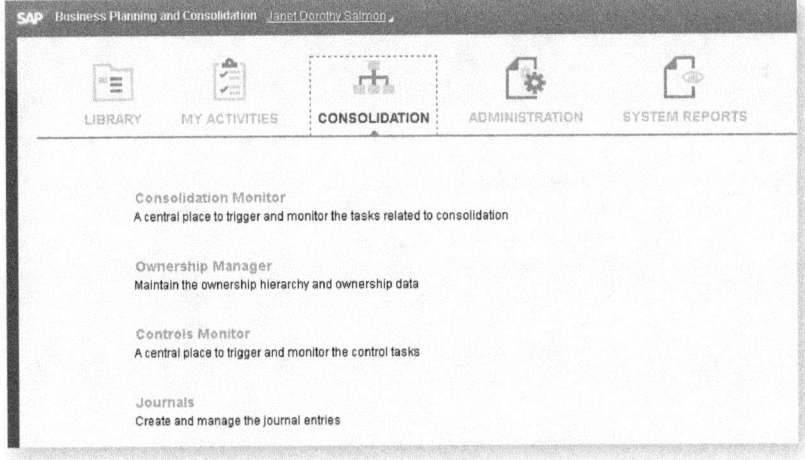

Figure 7.11: Consolidation Monitor in SAP BPC

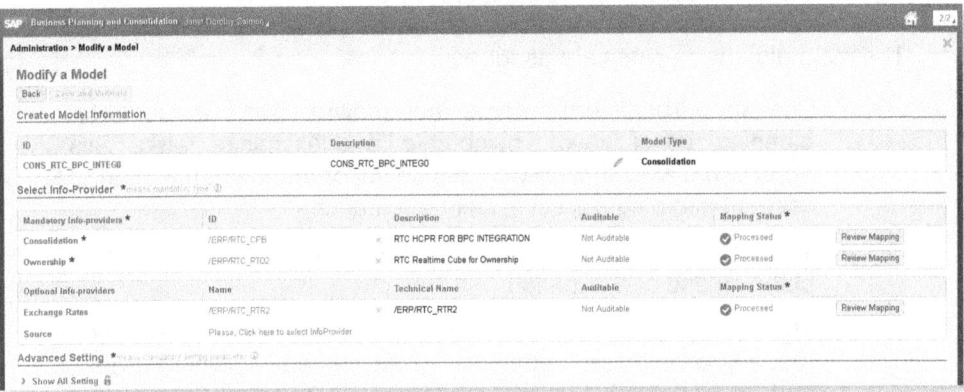

Figure 7.12: Consolidation models in SAP BPC

If we select the CONSOLIDATION model in Figure 7.12, we can access the DIMENSIONS shown in Figure 7.13. These represent the heart of the consolidation model.

Administration

Dimensions

Edit Members   Edit Hierarchies   View Structure   AC_BTN_CREATE_LOCAL   Delete   Process

ID	Description	Visibility	Status
/ERP/EPRCTR	RTC Entity Profit Center	Central	Processed
/ERP/ESBOM	RTC Entity Segment	Central	Processed
/ERP/FLOW	RTC Flow	Central	Processed
/ERP/FLOW1	RTC Flow1	Central	Processed
/ERP/GROUP	/ERP/GROUP	Central	Processed
/ERP/IBUGIARE	RTC InterCompany Business Area	Central	Processed
/ERP/ICOMP	RTC InterCompany Company	Central	Processed
/ERP/ICOSTCTR	RTC InterCompany Cost Center	Central	Processed
/ERP/IPPCTR	RTC InterCompany Profit Center	Central	Processed
/ERP/ISEGM	RTC InterCompany Segment	Central	Processed
/ERP/LEDGER	Ledger	Central	Processed
/ERP/RTCMODEL	RTC Consolidation Model	Central	Processed
OCLIENT	Client	Central	Processed
OCURRENCY	Currency	Central	Processed
OFISCPER	Fiscal year/period	Central	Processed
OFISCPER3	Posting period	Central	Processed

Figure 7.13: Consolidation dimensions in SAP BPC

The main dimension types are as follows:

▶ The ACCOUNT dimension type (not shown) covers accounts for planning, consolidation, ownership, and exchange rates. This approach makes it clear why it is so important to get the chart of account mapping correct in Central Finance.

▶ The CATEGORY dimension type (not shown) covers categories for planning and consolidation.

▶ The ENTITY covers the entities to be included in consolidation (usually companies, segments, profit centers, business areas, and cost centers). Figure 7.13 shows RTC ENTITY PROFIT CENTER and RTC ENTITY SEGMENT (others not shown). Again, as you draw up your list of entities for Central Finance, it is important to understand which entities are part of your consolidation model and how you currently handle flows between these entities.

▶ The GROUP covers the scope of the consolidation. Note also the dimension RTC CONSOLIDATION MODEL in Figure 7.13. You can perform multiple consolidations for different purposes (legal and management).

▶ The INTERCOMPANY dimension covers the flows between the entities (usually companies, segments, profit centers, business areas, and cost centers). Figure 7.13 shows RTC INTERCOMPANY BUSINESS AREA, RTC INTERCOMPANY COMPANY, RTC INTERCOMPANY COST CENTER, RTC INTERCOMPANY PROFIT CENTER, and RTC INTERCOMPANY SEGMENT.

▶ The FLOW dimension is used to manage the flows on balance sheet accounts such as cash and assets.

▶ The CURRENCY dimension is used to manage the exchange rates used in consolidation.

▶ The TIME dimension is used in all consolidation, reporting, and planning applications.

7.4.2 Embedded BW

In an embedded consolidation model, instead of loading data to a data warehouse, you can access it via a view, just as we saw in Chapter 4. Figure 7.14 shows the virtual InfoProvider that connects the dimensions we saw in Figure 7.13 and the business rules on the handling of these entities in consolidation with the fields in the universal journal. To access this model, select transaction RSA1 (Administrator Workbench), choose InfoArea RTC and InfoProvider /ERP/RTC_V01. Again, you see the GROUP, CATEGORY, FLOW, and CURRENCY together with the various entities and intercompany flows that we saw in Figure 7.13. Note also the field AUDIT, which is needed to explain the various correction and elimination postings that arise during consolidation.

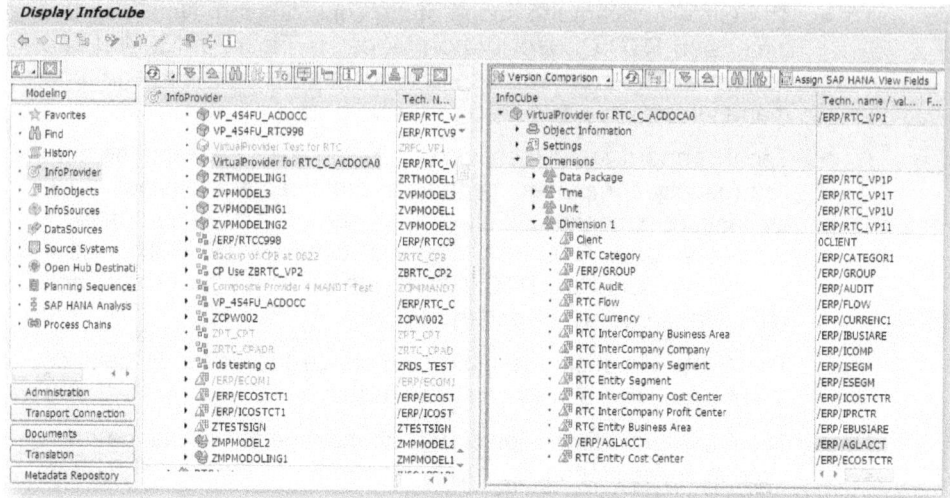

Figure 7.14: Virtual InfoProvider for RTC in SAP S/4HANA

7.4.3 Storing consolidation results in SAP S/4HANA

We met table ACDOCA for the journal entries in Chapter 2 and table ACDOCP for planning in Chapter 5. The third table in this series is AC-DOCC, which is used to store the consolidation entries in SAP S/4HANA. Figure 7.15 shows the new table which has the Consolidation Model in SAP BPC as one of its key fields. Note here that many of the field names begin with RTC_ to provide the link to SAP BPC, whereas some are direct links to table ACDOCA (RCOMP (company), KTOPL (group chart of accounts), and RACCT (group account number).

The real-time consolidation functions are new so it makes sense to stay up to date by referring to SAP Note 2205112 (*https://launchpad.support. sap.com/#/notes/0002205112*). Nonetheless, the consolidation functions provide an important justification for many Central Finance implementations.

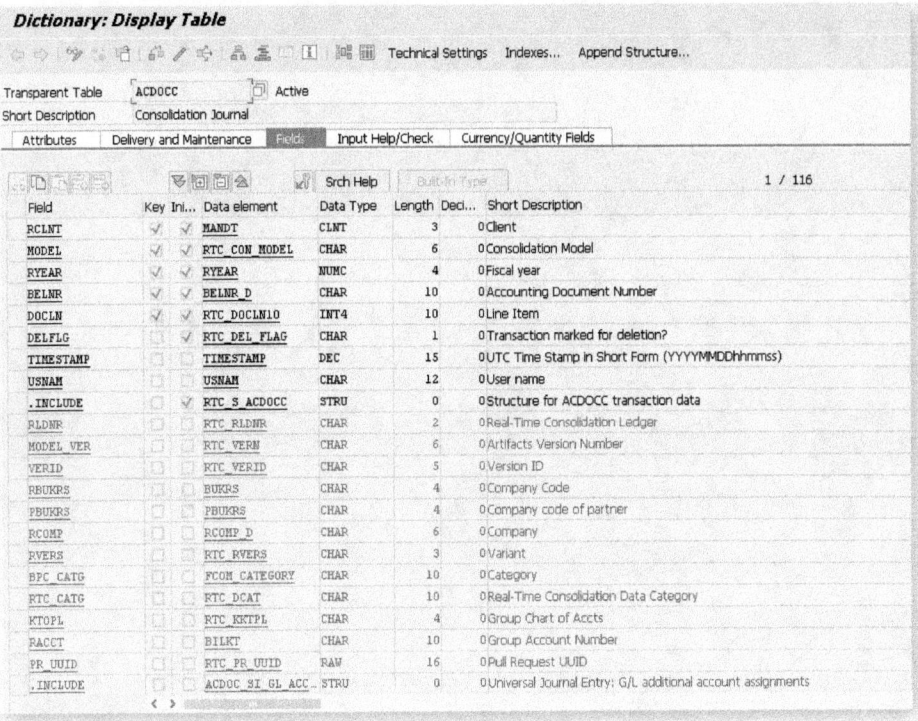

Figure 7.15: Consolidation table ACDOCC

8 SAP Fiori

In Chapter 1 we introduced the SAP Fiori applications as the new face of Finance for the end user. In this chapter, we explain how to set up the roles and business catalogs to provide your users with access to the Fiori applications. Because SAP Fiori is not actually one UI technology but several, we explain how to set up the different types of Fiori applications.

SAP Fiori is SAP's new approach to user interface design and aims to ensure that all applications are:

▶ *Role-based*: that is, designed with a specific user in mind

▶ *Responsive*: that is, the application responds to the device on which it is being run, regardless of whether this is the desktop, a tablet, or a mobile device

▶ *Simple*: the design paradigm here is 1-1-3 (1 user, 1 use case, 3 screens)

▶ *Coherent*: in other words, the applications all speak the same language

▶ *Instant value*: in other words, there is a low barrier to adoption

To check whether your devices are compatible with SAP Fiori and which Internet browsers are supported, refer to SAP Note 1935915 (*https://launchpad.support.sap.com/#/notes/0001935915*). Within the SAP Fiori umbrella there are three types of applications:

▶ *Analytical applications*, such as Overdue Receivables (Chapter 1) or Cash Position and Bank Risk (Chapter 3)

▶ *Transactional applications*, such as My Spend, the Master Data Applications, and Journal Entries

▶ *Search models* and *fact sheets*

In this chapter, we will walk you through the various types of Fiori app used in Finance. To access the complete catalog of Fiori apps, see: *https://fioriappslibrary.hana.ondemand.com/sap/fix/externalViewer/*

8.1 Roles and business catalogs

To access any of the above applications, the user has to be assigned to a *role*. The roles structure the Fiori applications from a business perspective and user research is conducted to understand the typical tasks of each role and the context in which they work (shared service center, corporate headquarters, and so on). This is known in Fiori as the persona description. Examples of base roles (BR) in Finance include:

- ▶ Accounts Receivable Accountant (SAP_BR_AR_ACCOUNTANT)
- ▶ Accounts Receivable Manager (SAP_BR_AR_MANAGER)
- ▶ Accounts Payable Accountant (SAP_BR_AP_ACCOUNTANT)
- ▶ Accounts Payable Manager (SAP_BR_AP_MANAGER)
- ▶ General Ledger Accountant (SAP_BR_GL_ACCOUNTANT)
- ▶ Cash Manager (SAP_BR_CASH_MANAGER)
- ▶ Controller (SAP_BR_CONTROLLER)

These roles are associated with *business catalogs* (BC) which contain the tiles that are used to access the Fiori applications that we saw in Chapters 1 and 3. One role might be assigned to several business catalogs, as we see in the following examples:

- ▶ Accounts Receivable Accountant (SAP_SFIN_BC_AR_OPERATIONS, SAP_SFIN_BC_AR_DISPUTE_RES, SAP_SFIN_BC_REC_CLERK)
- ▶ Accounts Receivable Manager (SAP_SFIN_BC_AR_ANALYTICS)
- ▶ Accounts Payable Accountant (SAP_SFIN_BC_AP_OPERATIONS, SAP_SFIN_BC_APAR_OPER. SAP_SFIN_BC_AP_CHECK_PROC)
- ▶ Accounts Payable Manager (SAP_SFIN_BC_AP_ANALYTICS)
- ▶ General Ledger Accountant (SAP_SFIN_BC_GL_MASTER_DATA, SAP_SFIN_BC_GL_DOC_PROC. SAP_SFIN_BC_GL_GEN_REPORTING)

▶ Cash Manager (SAP_SFIN_BC_CM_MANAGER)

▶ Controller
(SAP_SFIN_BC_CO_REP_CCA,
SAP_SFIN_BC_CO_REP_COS,
SAP_SFIN_BC_CO_REP_OPA, SAP_SFIN_BC_CO_MD_CCA,
SAP_SFIN_BC_CO_MD_PCA)

Figure 8.1 shows a sample tile catalog for ACCOUNTS RECEIVABLE – OP-ERATIONAL PROCESSING which is part of the Accounts Receivable Ac-countant role. Note the difference between these apps and those in the Accounts Receivable Manager role in that they show an icon rather than a color-coded KPI. This is the first difference between an *analytical app*, which calculates the trend for the KPI and shows the result so that you do not even need to go into the application if the trend is green, and a *transactional app*, which assumes that you are going to take action, by for example, processing receivables or collections.

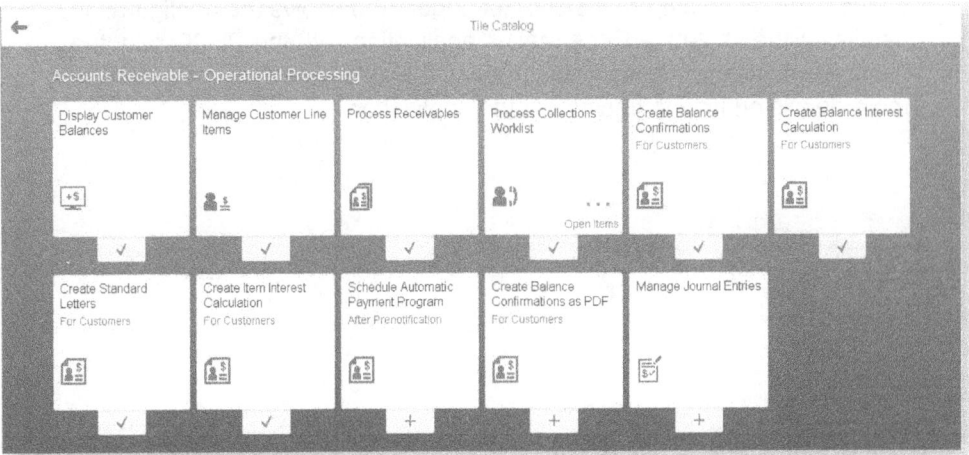

Figure 8.1: Tile catalog for operational processing in Accounts Receivable

A user can only execute the applications in these catalogs if he also has authorization for the individual applications in SAP S/4HANA. Figure 8.2 shows the role for the OVERDUE PAYABLES application. This application uses an *ODataService* in SAP Gateway as the connection between the user interface in SAP Fiori and the data in SAP S/4HANA. In turn, the ODataService uses a CDS view to select the relevant data from SAP

S/4HANA. The role for the OVERDUE RECEIVABLES application that we looked at in Chapter 1 has to be created manually.

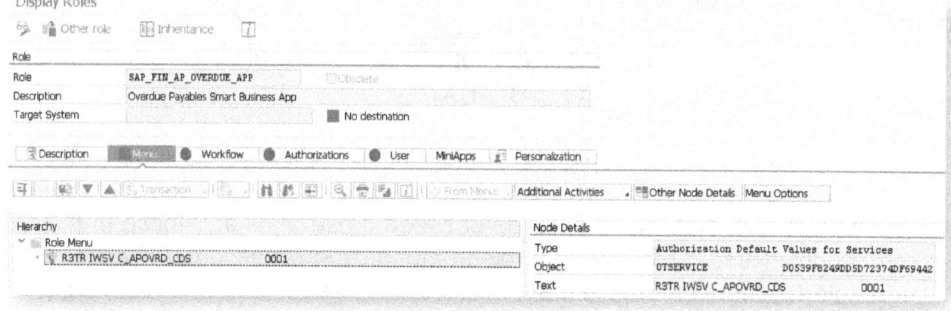

Figure 8.2: Role for Overdue Payables application

The best way to find out about the link between the role, the business catalog, and the ODataServices is to use the Fiori library that we referenced at the beginning of the chapter. Figure 8.3 shows the configuration details for the OVERDUE RECEIVABLES application with the PFCG role, the business catalog, and the oDataService. From here, you can access more details on how to implement the application.

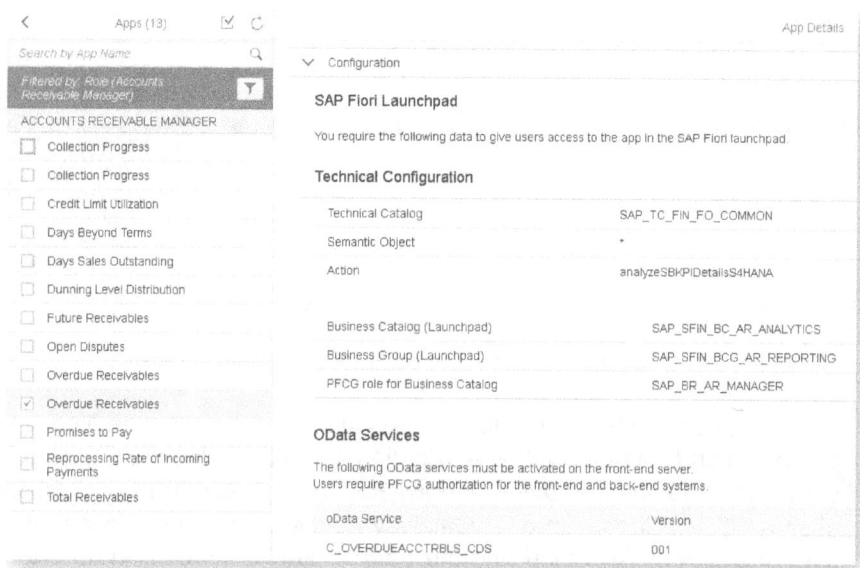

Figure 8.3: Role, business catalog and ODataService for Overdue Receivables

8.2   Implementing SAP Smart Business

In Chapter 1, we looked at the SAP Smart Business application for Overdue Receivables and in Chapter 3, we looked at the SAP Smart Business applications for Cash Management. The best way to find out how to implement these apps is also in the Fiori library. Figure 8.4 shows the front-end and back-end components for the OVERDUE RECEIVABLES app.

▶ The back-end components are essentially the latest versions of the S/4HANA software layers with the coding for the existing transactions and the all-important access to the data in the SAP S/4HANA tables.

▶ The front-end components are where the user interface itself resides. They make the connection to the backend that contains the data to be shown via SAP Gateway.

Obviously, to run an SAP Fiori application, it is critical to have both components in place. You can install SAP Fiori on your own hardware or you can also consider the option of using SAP Fiori as a service which ensures that the new Fiori UI layer is deployed on the SAP HANA cloud (HCP) and is connected to your on-premise systems. While the decision about where your SAP Fiori will be deployed is best left to IT, it is critical to understand the difference between the various front-end and back-end layers. In the context of SAP Smart Business, this knowledge is important because the SAP S/4HANA Finance 1503 and 1605 apps use a different view technology to the SAP S/4HANA 1511 and 1610 apps.

Figure 8.4: Front-end and back-end components for the Overdue Receivables app (1511 edition)

Figure 8.4 shows the 1511 back-end edition and the SAP Fiori for SAP S/4HANA 1511 front-end. If you now compare the front-end and back-end components for the same application in the 1605 edition in Figure 8.5, you will see that this application uses an additional software component HCO_HBA_R_SFIN700 300. This is the technical term for the HANA studio. If you are considering a migration from the 1503 edition to the 1511 edition, make sure that your favorite apps will continue to be available. SAP is working to re-implement all the delivered apps as CDS views rather than HANA views, but unfortunately not all are complete at the time of writing.

Figure 8.5: Front-end and back-end components for the Overdue Receivables app (1605 edition)

Whichever back-end environment you work with, you need to distinguish in the front end between the SAP Smart Business *runtime*, which controls what you see in the overview tile and the configuration drill-downs, and the SAP Smart Business *design time*, which is used to define the KPI, the filters, and thresholds (the evaluation) and the visualization in the app. One of the advantages of using SAP Smart Business is that every KPI has a coherent look, making it easy for a user in a shared service center to move from Accounts Receivable to Accounts Payable and from there to the Cash KPIs.

8.3   Responsive Fiori apps

Figure 8.6 shows the launchpad for the G/L Accountant role (SAP_BR_ GL_ACCOUNTANT) which allows you to access financial reporting apps such as DISPLAY FINANCIAL STATEMENT and TRIAL BALANCE. It also provides access to master data applications, including accounts, profit centers, cost centers, internal orders, and activity types. As you work through the Fiori Apps Library for these applications, it is important to understand that some of the apps (DISPLAY FINANCIAL STATEMENT, DISPLAY G/L ACCOUNT BALANCES, DISPLAY G/L ACCOUNT LINE ITEMS, POST GENERAL JOURNAL ENTRIES) are built in SAPUI5 and are genuinely responsive. Others, such as the TRIAL BALANCE and all the master data apps, are built in Web Dynpro and have different restrictions.

G/L Accountant							
Display Financial Statement	Trial Balance Comparison	Display G/L Account Balances	Display G/L Account Line Items	Post General Journal Entries	Manage Journal Entries	Analyze Financial Statement	Trial Balance
Cash Position Details	Cash Flow Detailed Analysis	Manage G/L Account Master Data	Display Chart of Accounts	Open Posting Periods	Manage Profit Center Master Data	Manage Activity Type Master Data	Manage Internal Order Master Data
Manage Depreciation Runs	Manage Cost Center Groups	Manage Activity Type Master Data	Manage Internal Order Master Data	Manage Internal Order Groups	Manage Activity Type Group	Journal Entry Analyzer	Trial Balance Analysis AO workbook

Figure 8.6: SAP Fiori launchpad for a G/L Accountant

We will start by looking at some of the SAPUI5 apps. Figure 8.7 shows the FINANCIAL STATEMENT app. If you compare this app with the classic reporting transactions, you will notice immediately that the selection parameters are part of the application. You no longer have to return to the selection screen to change reporting periods or company codes, making the application immediately more intuitive. You can, of course, navigate through the various nodes of the chart of accounts but you can also enter an account name or part of one in the SEARCH field and have the application search for the relevant account names. This immediately makes it easier to bring new users who are not familiar with your chart of accounts up to speed in their daily work.

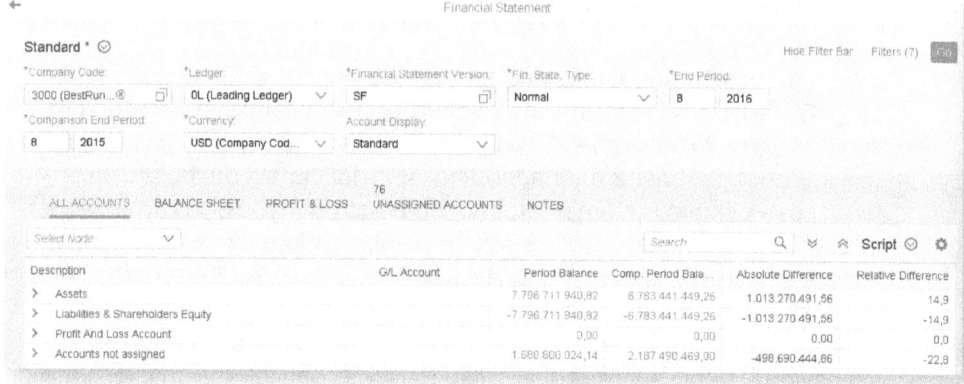

Figure 8.7: Financial Statement app

If we look at the configuration settings for the Financial Statement app in the Fiori library, we can see that this app is a SAPUI5 app with the technical name FIN_FINSTATEMENT.

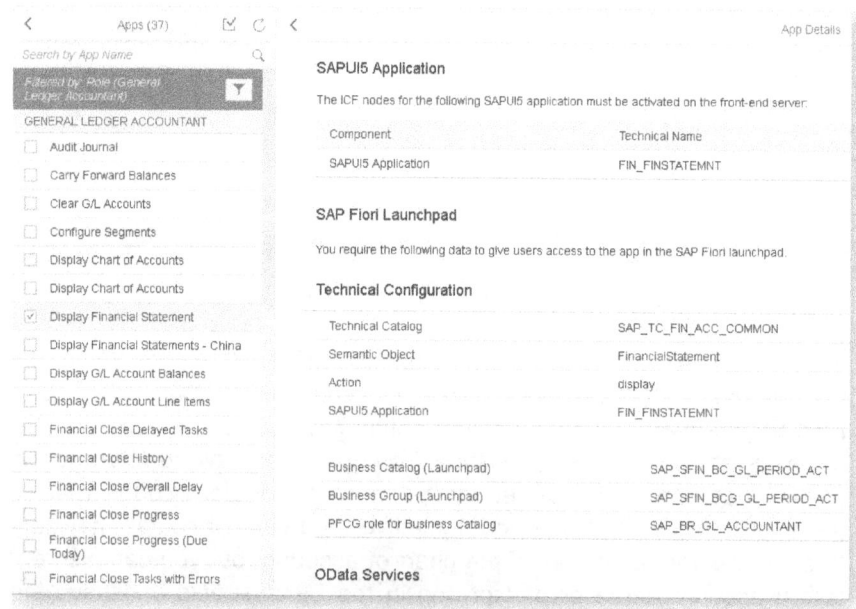

Figure 8.8: Library entry for Display Financial Statement

If you compare Figure 8.7 and Figure 8.9, you will immediately see similarities in the way the search works and the look of the results list.

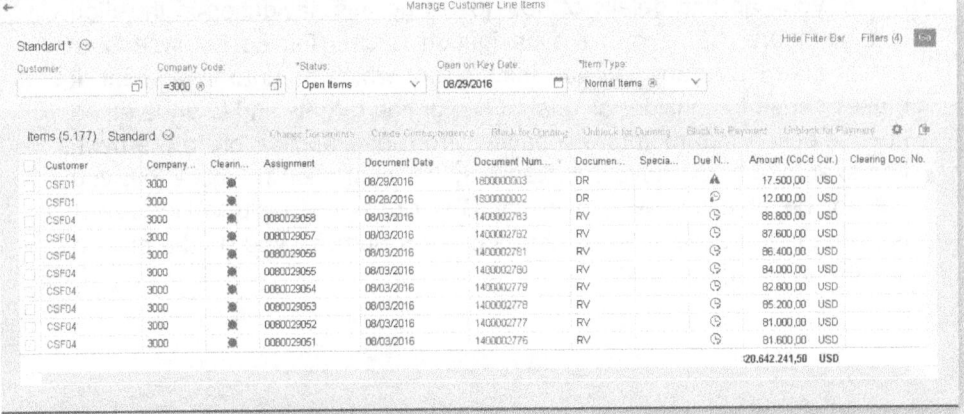

Figure 8.9: Manage Customer Line Items app

Another key aspect of such applications is the ability to navigate to other applications. Figure 8.10 shows a list of the other applications that you can navigate to from the MANAGE CUSTOMER LINE ITEMS app.

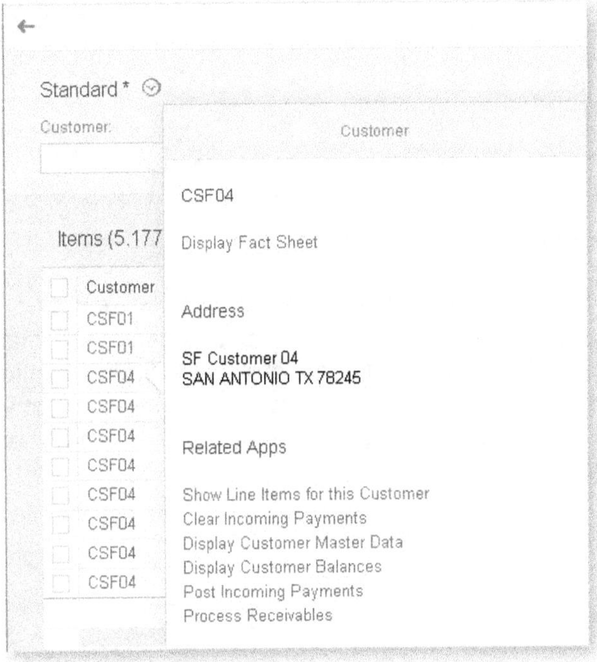

Figure 8.10: Navigation targets associated with customer CSF04

Again, you can find details of how to set up this navigation in the Fiori library. Figure 8.11 shows the navigation targets for the MANAGE CUS-TOMER LINE ITEMS app. As you think about which apps to implement, it makes sense to consider all related navigation targets and to understand how selection parameters are passed from one application to the next. For example, if you have selected only the customer in Figure 8.9, you will not be able to navigate to the CUSTOMER ACCOUNTING DOCUMENT app; but if you have selected the document number, you will be able to see the associated fact sheet.

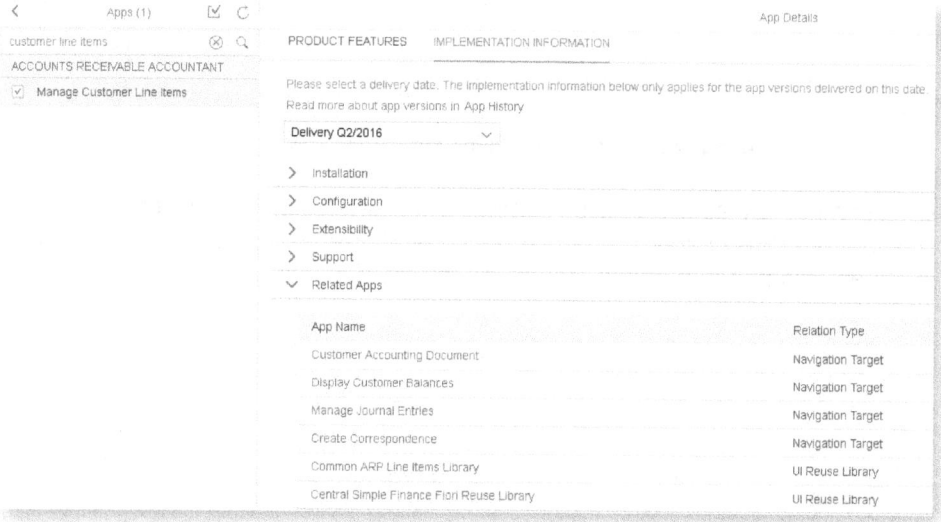

Figure 8.11: Related apps for Manage Customer Line Items

Of course, there are posting apps as well as reporting apps. From MAN-AGE JOURNAL ENTRIES (see Figure 8.11), you can post a general journal entry, as shown in Figure 7.12. This is first and foremost a posting app to capture general journal entries and also allows you to upload attach-ments to document why you are making a journal entry at all and what the rationale for the posting is.

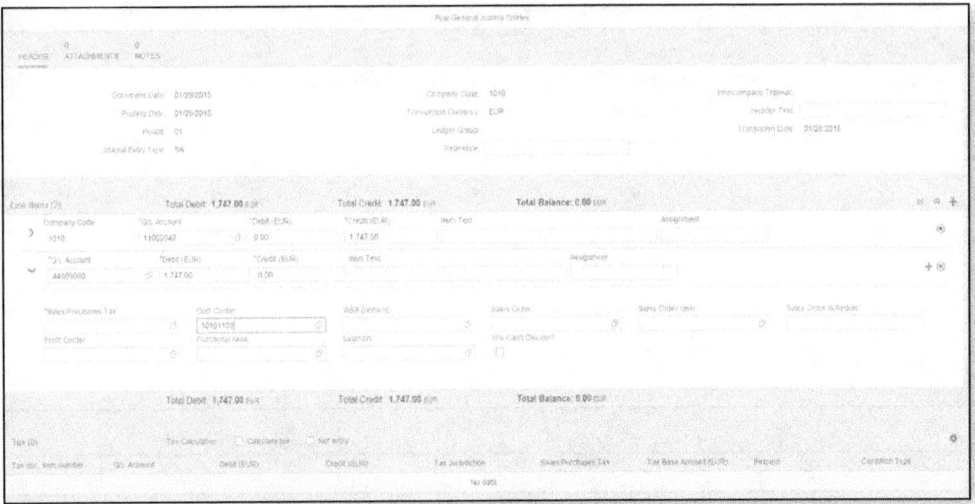

Figure 8.12: Fiori app for Post General Journal Entry

8.4 Fiori apps for plan/actual reporting and the trial balance

We used the trial balance as our reporting example for most of Chapter 2 and ended Chapter 5 with an image of the plan/actual reports for the Financial Analyst. These differ from the apps in Section 8.3 in that they are not SAPUI5 apps but *Web Dynpro applications*. In Figure 8.13, we can see from the library entry that the trial balance is the Web Dynpro application FIS_FPM_OVP_TRIAL1 and the same technology is used for all the plan/actual reports that we showed at the end of Chapter 4.

To use the plan/actual reports, you have to follow the instructions on activating the BW content bundle in Chapter 4. While the planning applications worked with workbooks for Analysis for Office, the reports are simply queries that have been embedded in Web Dynpro applications. Again, you can use the same approach as we discussed for planning to change the queries and the MultiProviders to include fields from your own operating concern in these reports.

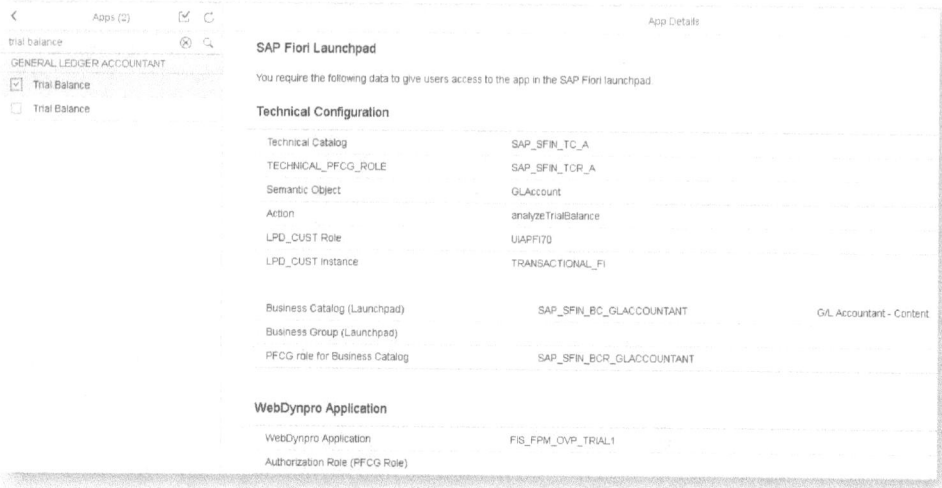

Figure 8.13: Library entry for Trial Balance

From a technical perspective, the trial balance and the plan/actual reports are queries and therefore, you can also use SAP Business Objects Microsoft Excel as an Excel front-end for the same report. Figure 8.14 shows the trial balance as a spreadsheet rather than the Web Dynpro applications we showed throughout Chapter 2. You can perform all the drill-downs we showed in Chapter 2 using a DISPLAY panel in Analysis Office.

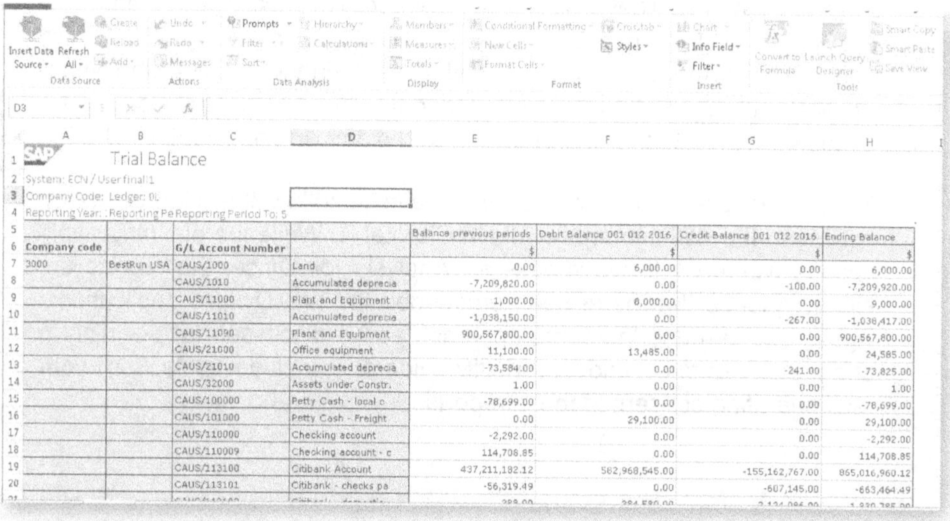

Figure 8.14: Trial Balance in SAP Business Objects Analysis for Office

8.5　Fiori apps for master data maintenance

Instead of displaying the G/L account that we looked at in Figure 2.5 using a classic user interface, we can choose the MANAGE G/L ACCOUNT MASTER DATA app from the launchpad shown in Figure 8.6 and display the same account using a Fiori app as shown in Figure 8.15.

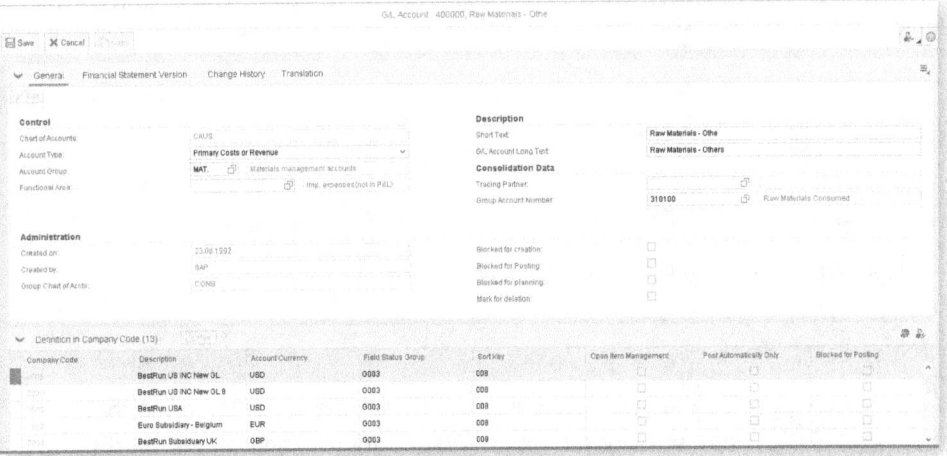

Figure 8.15: Fiori app for G/L account maintenance

Similar apps are available for the maintenance of profit centers and profit center groups, cost centers and cost center groups, internal orders and internal order groups, activity types and activity type groups, and statistical key figures. Figure 8.16 shows the MAINTAIN COST CENTER app.

While the default fields are the same whether you use the classic GUI or the new application, you can potentially configure the new application to show only those fields that are relevant for your organization. This is particularly useful for internal orders, where of the two hundred fields offered, most organizations use only a handful.

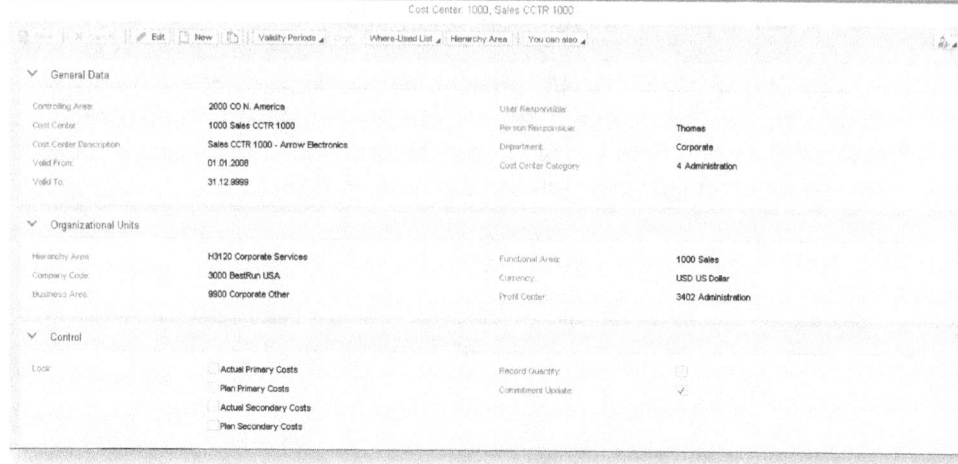

Figure 8.16: Fiori app for cost center maintenance

Configuring Web Dynpro applications

To understand how to work with the reporting apps that are embedded within Web Dynpro applications or the master data apps, refer to the instructions in the following guide: *https://service.sap.com/~sapidp/012002523100012043332015E.pdf*

8.6   Fiori apps for My Spend

Probably the best known example of a Fiori app in Finance is MY SPEND, which is designed specifically for the casual user, the manager on the go, who needs a quick update on his budget situation. Figure 8.17 shows the MY SPEND tile in the Fiori launchpad. Note that like the SAP Smart Business KPIs, you can immediately see the total spend for the manager's cost centers.

As we drill down in Figure 8.18, we can see the relative spending for each of the departments for which the manager is responsible. Each department is compared against the plan for that cost center to determine whether the area should be red, yellow, or green.

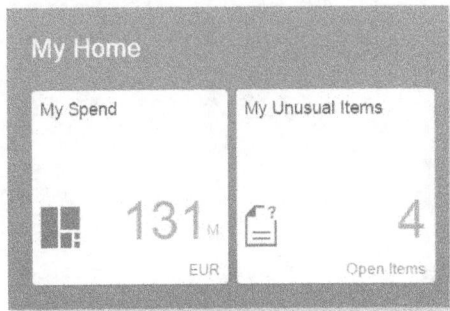

Figure 8.17: My Spend tile in Fiori launchpad

Figure 8.18: Relative spending in each department

By clicking on one of the blocks, the user arrives at the view shown in Figure 8.19, which shows the individual spend categories and ultimately the line items for each item. Note also that the app shows the sum of actual and committed spending.

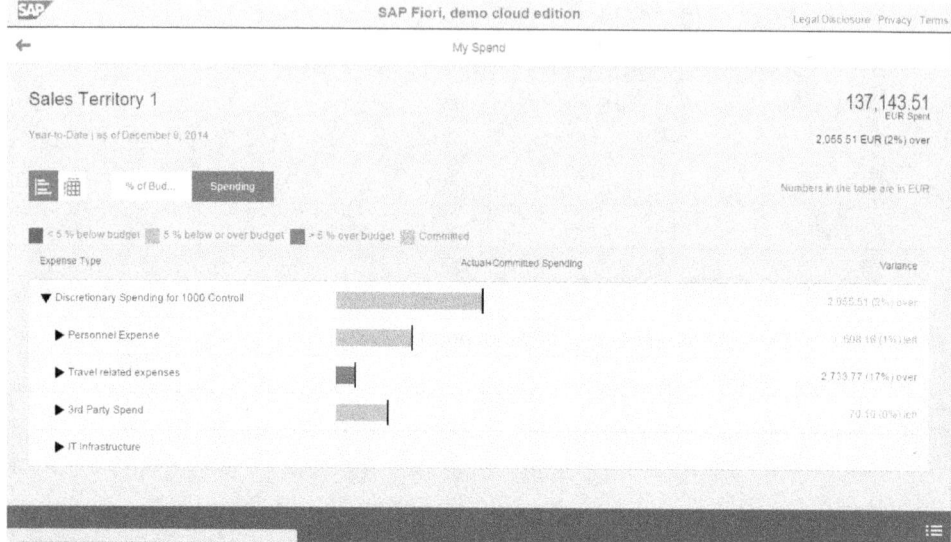

Figure 8.19: Details of spending

While this app might be too simple for the expert controller, it can be a perfect way of getting managers to take ownership of their budgets and monitor spending regularly and to ensure buy-in to the SAP S/4HANA project. It is also an excellent way of gradually weaning managers away from their spreadsheets and the static reporting we talked about in Chapter 1.

8.7   Search models and fact sheets

In a similar vein, if you are trying to persuade reluctant users to use SAP S/4HANA, the fact sheets can be a great place to start because they feel like an Internet search. Every Fiori launchpad has a search icon, as shown in Figure 8.20. Clicking on this icon opens up a search box where you can search either for all objects containing 4230 (for the example below) or for specific objects (assets, cost centers, and so on).

Figure 8.20: Search box in Fiori launchpad

Figure 8.21 shows the result of the search. We can see accounting documents, fixed assets, and so on.

Figure 8.21: Result of the search for objects containing 4230

Clicking on one of these items takes you into a fact sheet like the cost center fact sheet shown in Figure 8.22. Of course, this is not the only way to access a fact sheet: we could have accessed the fact sheet for a customer accounting document via the navigation in Figure 8.10.

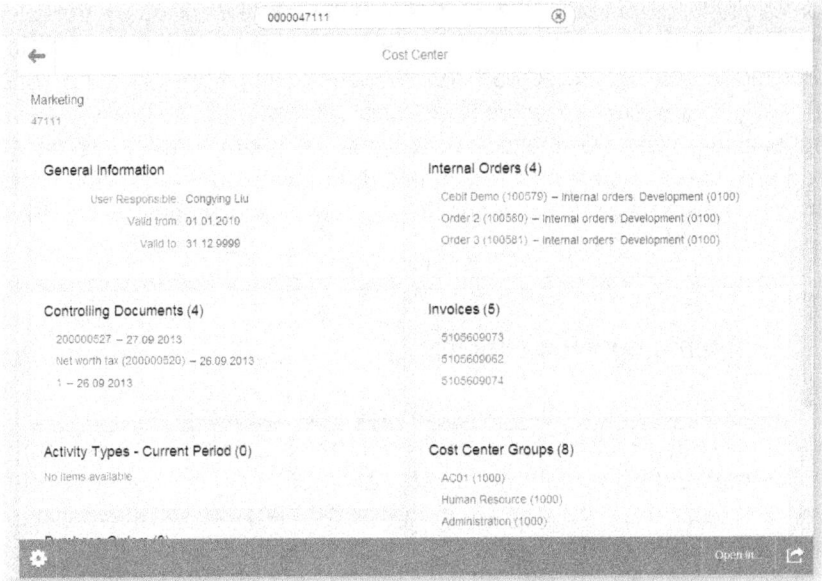

Figure 8.22: Cost center fact sheet

In this example, we see the GENERAL INFORMATION which we might have expected to find in transaction KS03 (display cost center) but also the result of multiple searches to identify further documents that include this cost center and further master data assignments. Applications such as these take some of the mystery out of using SAP S/4HANA because they are so much more like the Internet searches we all use in our private life.

8.8   Digitizing the finance function

As you work through the list of Fiori apps, you need a strategy as to which apps to approach in what sequence. Perhaps you might try to tempt new users online by offering apps such as MY SPEND or some of the key figure apps in SAP Smart Business. Alternatively, you might focus on a particular role where there is a high coverage, such as those in Accounts Receivable, Accounts Payable, or Cash. It is not generally a good idea to go directly from a transaction to a Fiori app. Of course, the POST GENERAL JOURNAL ENTRIES app that we looked at in Figure 7.12 is the natural follow-up to transaction FB50 and there is a link between the old master data transactions and the new apps, but the point is to think through the work performed in the various finance departments and how you can help users in these departments work more efficiently. A transaction list alone does not tell you the whole story and it can be just as interesting to look at the spreadsheets documenting who has done what and why to understand what is actually happening in a key business process. Digitizing the finance function can be a simple matter of bringing these spreadsheets online: you might, for example, transform a list of closing tasks and who is responsible for what into entries in the SAP Financial Closing Cockpit.

8.8.1   Intercompany reconciliation

The process of intercompany reconciliation is another good example in this context. Everybody documents open items between affiliated companies before they go into the consolidation process, but the INTERCOMPANY RECONCILIATION app shown in Figure 8.23 lets you have the system match what intercompany open items it can and then offer a list of those that it was unable to match and which therefore require clarification. You can automatically generate e-mail notifications where differences become apparent. Note below that for many entries, a status and notes have already been created. We can see how an organization can gradually bring tasks which were previously handled in various spreadsheets online. Anybody calling up this app can see how far clarification has proceeded on the first items in the list and can easily take over.

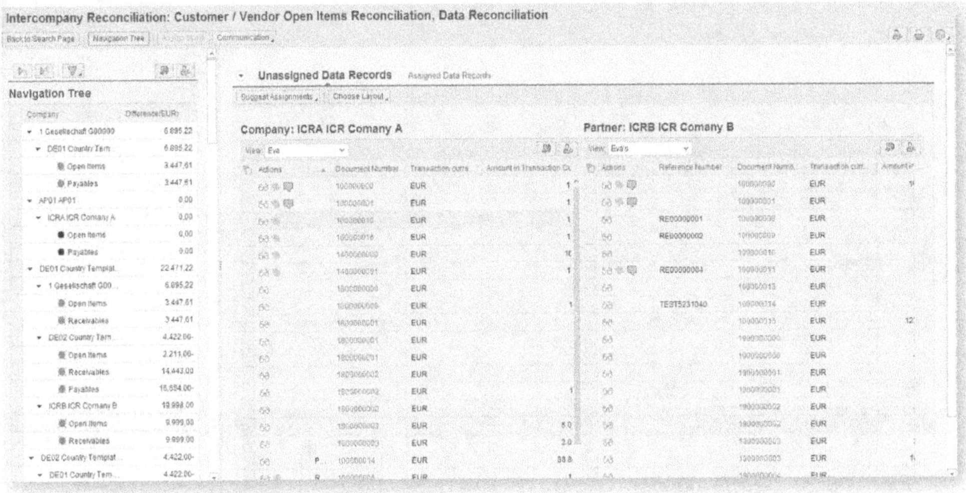

Figure 8.23: Intercompany reconciliation

8.8.2 GR/IR monitor

If you have worked in finance, you will be familiar with the business problem that the invoice receipt does not always match the goods receipt. Sometimes this is because we are simply waiting for one document or the other, and sometimes it is because the values in the two documents are different. In either case, the classic approach is to open a spreadsheet and start documenting why the two do not match before ultimately writing off the difference if the issues cannot be clarified satisfactorily.

Figure 8.24 shows an application built to handle exactly this problem. The system reads the relevant data in procurement and makes a proposal for the difference (in this case, the system has identified that there is no invoice receipt for the selected purchase order). In the past, every shared service center had its own version of a spreadsheet to handle these differences, but now the application matches what it can and a rules framework makes proposals. Finally, a worker in the shared service center can document the situation to explain why there is a difference and whether there is an expectation that the missing invoice receipt will follow at some point.

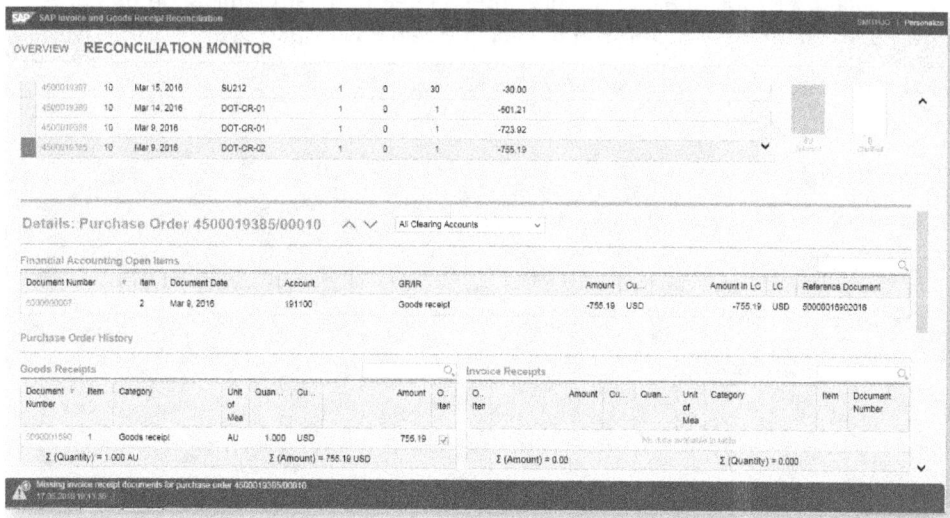

Figure 8.24: GR/IR monitor

9 Outlook

Probably the most common question during presentations on SAP S/4HANA is about what comes next. As the business world evolves and changes, so do the requirements of a finance system. Finance departments are being asked to do more with less and this is changing the type of software systems that they use. Most organizations now use cloud software in some form or other and this brings its own changes.

9.1 On-premise and cloud editions

Most of the screenshots in this book were captured from a demo system running not *on premise* (the deployment option with which most of us are currently familiar) but in the *cloud*, in this case, the SAP HANA Enterprise Cloud. It is becoming increasingly common for organizations to run their migration testing for S/4HANA Finance on a cloned version of their operational system or to implement Central Finance on an SAP HANA Enterprise Cloud rather than installing a new system for the purpose. What this means is that the systems run in a secure data center, such as the one in St Leon Rot in Germany, rather than on site at the customer's premises.

This changes the dynamics of a software investment for a CIO—instead of a significant **capital investment** in hardware, software, and consulting services to make the system available to the users, the investment is in **operational expenses** where an organization pays a monthly fee for the use of the software services in the cloud. This shift in approach has been compared to the early industrial age where organizations ran their own power plants as long as there was no reliable power grid and gradually shifted to using power companies to supply the power. The new power companies in turn benefited from economies of scale that allowed them to offer power more cheaply and efficiently. Essentially, the cloud gives organizations the option to be more flexible because they are not constrained by their own IT resources. It also allows them to scale where their own growth outstrips the performance of their IT systems.

Running SAP S/4HANA Finance in a data center that is not your own is one option, referred to as the *managed cloud*, but SAP has also begun to offer versions of the software designed specifically for the *private cloud*. This shift in approach is reflected in the product names, so you will notice that all software editions have a new notation that denotes the year of release (1503 released in March 2015, 1511 in November 2015, and so on) and either OP for on premise or CE for the cloud edition, the idea being that all cloud customers have the latest version of the software rather than waiting months or even years to implement the next wave of enhancements.

Innovations are being shipped first in the cloud edition and then made available on premise. One example of this is the SAP S/4HANA Professional Services Cloud. The package uses S/4HANA Finance as its core, so it contains the universal journal, new Asset Accounting, new Cash Management, and so on, but it offers features that are designed for a specific industry, namely professional services. The focus is on creating a customer project, recording consulting time, procurement, and travel expenses against that project, billing for the services rendered, and checking the profitability of the project. While there are already consulting houses running SAP ERP, what is interesting is the specific features that have been added to make the package attractive to the industry in question.

> ### S/4HANA cloud edition
>
>  To access the Feature Scope Description for the SAP S/4HANA cloud edition, refer to the following document:
>
> *https://cp.hana.ondemand.com/dps/d/preview/*
> *pdf5eb7d4d30467d917131b698a509e3/1503%20000/*
> *en-US/FSD_PC1506.pdf*

9.2   SAP S/4HANA Professional Services Cloud

While many of the finance and logistics features described in the document above could be used in any industry, a few are specific to the professional service industry. Service providers are typically concerned about the effectiveness of every consultant, which has led to plenty of workarounds in the past because the employee was not generally recorded in the financial applications. For the cloud edition, the universal journal has been extended to include the field PERSONNEL NUMBER and the HANA views and reports extended to include this field using the same techniques we described in Chapter 5. The financial transactions associated with that employee (time recording, procurement, travel, billing, and so on) now update the universal journal with the personnel number of the employee recording his work.

Professional service companies do not typically calculate an activity price by dividing the cost center expenses by the number of hours delivered; instead, they set rates dependent on the seniority of the consultant, the country out of which he is operating, and so on. The manual activity rates that we are all used to maintaining using transaction KP26 have been replaced by sales conditions which allow organizations to define their activity rates depending on a number of factors.

Service companies also typically have plenty of work in process, in the form of work that has been performed but not yet billed to the customer. Now, event-based revenue recognition immediately creates a revenue journal entry as the time recording is posted. New functions are also available for intercompany projects.

These functions were originally offered in the S/4HANA cloud edition but are not offered as part of the on-premise edition from 1610 for use not just by pure professional service companies but also by manufacturers who have an additional service business or by engineer-to-order companies who have contractors working to put the final machine together at the customer's site.

9.3 SAP S/4HANA as the digital core

Of course, it is not just SAP S/4HANA Finance in the cloud that concerns us, but also the connectivity between other cloud products and SAP S/4HANA. Gradually, SAP S/4HANA is evolving to become the *digital core* to which many cloud systems connect, including Success Factors, Ariba, Concur, Fieldglass, and so on. Figure 9.1 shows the vision of how the various *business networks* will connect to SAP S/4HANA. Similarly, the *Internet of Things* completely changes the amount of data being collected about a business process: instead of a single backflush and confirmation at the end of the production line, we have sensors all along the line. In theory, this will allow much more accurate views of work in process than were previously possible but such data volumes change our understanding of a financial document and what must be stored and audited dramatically. Most financial users barely consider *social networks* in their professional lives but in future, applications such as sentiment analysis will start to enter their working sphere and we will see many controllers becoming data scientists as they look for patterns in the data. Some of these innovations are possible today. Others will evolve over the next several years.

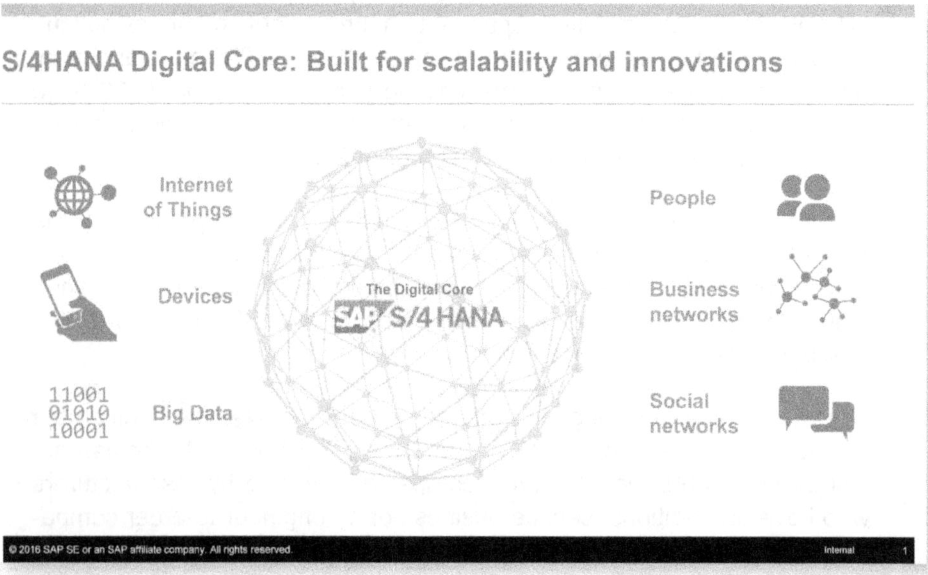

Figure 9.1: SAP S/4HANA as the digital core

ESPRESSO TUTORIALS

You have finished the book.

A   About the Authors

Janet Salmon is currently Chief Product Owner for Management Accounting at SAP SE in Walldorf and has accompanied many developments in the Controlling components of SAP ERP and SAP S/4HANA.

Janet joined SAP AG as a translator in 1992, having gained a degree in Modern and Medieval Languages from Downing College, Cambridge and a post-graduate qualification in Interpreting and Translating from the University of Bath.

Janet became a technical writer for the Product Costing area in 1993 and a product manager in 1996. In 1998, she received an award from the Society of Technical Communication for her paper *Functions in Detail: Product Cost Controlling*. She is an advisor and regular contributor to SAP Financials Expert (*http://www.financialsexpertonline.com*) and regularly presents at Financials conferences.

Claus Wild began his professional career as an in-house SAP consultant in an international corporate group. For almost two decades, he was a project manager for the topics of payment transactions and cash management and also developed the technical conceptual design and integration of FinTech solutions in SAP payment transactions. He also holds courses for SAP in the field of electronic payment transactions.

At the beginning of 2017, Claus Wild will be moving to Stellwerk Consulting GmbH as a senior consultant and expert for SAP payment transactions.

Claus Wild's previous publications include the books SEPA und SAP [SEPA and SAP, currently available in German only] and Neuerungen im Kontoauszug in SAP® ERP [New Features in the Bank Statement in SAP® ERP, currently available in German only], both of which are published by Espresso Tutorials.

B   Index

C Disclaimer

This publication contains references to the products of SAP SE.

SAP, R/3, SAP NetWeaver, Duet, PartnerEdge, ByDesign, SAP Busi-nessObjects Explorer, StreamWork, and other SAP products and ser-vices mentioned herein as well as their respective logos are trademarks or registered trademarks of SAP SE in Germany and other countries.

Business Objects and the Business Objects logo, BusinessObjects, Crystal Reports, Crystal Decisions, Web Intelligence, Xcelsius, and other Business Objects products and services mentioned herein as well as their respective logos are trademarks or registered trademarks of Busi-ness Objects Software Ltd. Business Objects is an SAP company.

Sybase and Adaptive Server, iAnywhere, Sybase 365, SQL Anywhere, and other Sybase products and services mentioned herein as well as their respective logos are trademarks or registered trademarks of Sybase, Inc. Sybase is an SAP company.

SAP SE is neither the author nor the publisher of this publication and is not responsible for its content. SAP Group shall not be liable for errors or omissions with respect to the materials. The only warranties for SAP Group products and services are those that are set forth in the express warranty statements accompanying such products and services, if any. Nothing herein should be construed as constituting an additional warr-anty.

More Espresso Tutorials Books

Bert Vanstechelman:

The SAP® HANA Deployment Guide

- ▶ SAP HANA sizing, capacity planning guidelines, and data tiering
- ▶ Deployment options and data provisioning scenarios
- ▶ Backup and recovery options and procedures
- ▶ Software and hardware virtualization in SAP HANA

http://5171.espresso-tutorials.com

Dominique Alfermann, Stefan Hartmann, Benedikt Engel:

SAP® HANA Advanced Modeling

- ▶ Data modeling guidelines and common test approaches
- ▶ Modular solutions to complex requirements
- ▶ Information view performance optimization
- ▶ Best practices and recommendations

http://5110.espresso-tutorials.com